Personalities

Personalities

Master Clinicians Confront the Treatment of Borderline Personality Disorders

Edited by

Gerben Hellinga,
Bert van Luyn,

and

Henk-Jan Dalewijk

JASON ARONSON INC.
Northvale, New Jersey
London

This book was set in 11 pt. Fairfield Light by Alpha Graphics of Pittsfield, NH
and printed and bound by Book-mart Press, Inc. of North Bergen, NJ.

Library of Congress Cataloging-in-Publication Data

Personalities : master clinicians confront the treatment of borderline personality
    disorders / edited by Gerben Hellinga, Bert van Luyn, Henk-Jan Dalewijk
      p. cm.
    Includes bibliographical references (p.) and index.
    ISBN 0-7657-0294-0
    1. Borderline personality disorder—Treatment. 2. Psychotherapists—
Interviews. I. Hellinga, Gerben. II. Luyn, Bert van. III. Dalewijk, Henk-
Jan.
    RC569.5.B67 M37 2001
    616.85'85206—dc21   0041617

Printed in the United States of America on acid-free paper. For information and
catalog write to Jason Aronson Inc., 230 Livingston Street, Northvale, NJ 07647-
1726, or visit our website: www.aronson.com

Contents

Introduction: How This Book Came About

A series of monthly workshops, begun in the early nineties and called Psychiatry in Progress, were held at Zon & Schild, a major psychiatric hospital in Amersfoort, the Netherlands. They were attended by professionals from many countries, especially the United States, and turned out to be a great success.

After a few years of experimentation and at the suggestion of Otto Kernberg, we began to concentrate on speakers from the field of psychotherapy who were specializing in the treatment of severe personality disorders. During the past five years, we have had the pleasure of having as our guests some of the best-known theoreticians, clinicians, and authors on this subject.

As Salman Akhtar pointed out to us, the workshops placed us in a unique position. For a few days each, we had as our guests individuals who are prominent in many areas of the field. It was Akhtar's suggestion that we might interview them all, putting the same questions to each of them, and then using their answers for discussion. He also suggested that we ask them to imagine themselves in certain standardized or typical situations, and to then evaluate the differences and similarities in their reactions. Wouldn't this enable us to provide, through more than a single point of view, a contemporary picture of the way their originators regard the various approaches to the treatment of severe personality disorders, and the way these approaches relate to one another?

This book, therefore, has been written as a consequence of Salman Akhtar's suggestions. It contains fourteen interviews with some of the generals on the battlefield against personality disorders, not only giving an idea of their fundamental approach, but also an impression of the individuals' personal motives and development. You will find it fascinating to read what some of our subjects experienced during their professional training. It is fun to learn how *Lorna Smith Benjamin* got the time to work on her ideas. The dialogues, transcribed verbatim and presented with only minimal changes, give an impression of *Otto Kernberg's* direct, precise way of speaking and of the enormous density of the information he is providing, of *Salman Akhtar's* quicksilver associations, and of *Arthur Freeman's* openness about his own limitations.

We have also made a point of choosing authors, clinicians, and theoreticians who represent all the major approaches to the work of psychotherapy. Naturally, there are psychoanalysts of several major schools. There is, of course, *Otto Kernberg,* and some of the people who largely follow his approach, such as *Michael Stone* and *John Clarkin.* There is *Gerald Adler,* whose approach has been largely influenced by Heinz Kohut, and also others like *Glen Gabbard, Salman Akhtar,* and *James Masterson.*

Although someone with a personality disorder can in many cases be understood very well from a psychoanalytic basis, treating these people in a psychoanalytically oriented way is often a different matter. Many patients with severe personality disorders do not have the staying power, the tolerance of frustration, or the capacity for self-reflection that are needed for the uncovering process that occurs in psychoanalytic treatment. For them, supportive techniques and methods are necessary, although a psychoanalytic theory may be there in the background, as is the case with *Lawrence Rockland's* approach.

And because there still remained a frustratingly large percentage of patients who could not or would not benefit from psychoanalytically oriented treatment, there was a demand for different techniques, and quite a few have been developed in the last decade. Most of these are cognitive-behavioral in nature, such as the treatment approaches of *Marsha Linehan, Arthur Freeman,* and *Jeffrey Young,* or interpersonal, as in *Lorna Smith Benjamin*'s Structural Analysis of Social Behavior (SASB) model. Compared to the psychoanalytic model, the frames of reference described here focus less on unconscious conflicts, and much more on the here-and-now techniques for changing behavior, cognitions, and feelings.

We have decided not to leave psychiatry out of this book. The enormous advances made in our knowledge of the biochemistry of the brain have led to the development of a psychopharmacology that may, in the case of some patients, ameliorate the most disturbing behavior patterns. Our increasing knowledge of the inherited pattern of our many major personality traits confronts us with the necessity to teach patients to live with their limitations instead of trying to change them.

In the United States, the country where most of the work on personality disorders is being done, managed care has expanded considerably. There is an increasing demand for proof of the effectiveness of what is being done, and that the treatments should be as brief as possible. This situation has led to a more pragmatic attitude. Many therapists will not stick to just one method anymore, although they recognize that if one merely switches from one approach to another on the basis of what happens during therapy, there is always the danger of going along with resistance or the acting-out behavior of the patient. *John Livesley* and *Robert Cloninger,* for example, are attempting to develop frameworks that may be of use in "tailoring the treatment to the patient."

The fourteen names italicized above highlight only the individuals we have interviewed for this book. Of course there are many others, but we believe that this selection gives a valuable overall impression of the numerous ways one can go about treating people with severe personality problems.

1

Gerald Adler

Biography

As an overprotected only child of parents who were in their late thirties when he was born, Gerald Adler grew up in an environment that was likely to lead him to an encounter with psychoanalysis at a relatively young age. The burgeoning analytic movement after World War II happened to coincide with his beginning college and experiencing its inevitable accompanying anxieties. His first analytic experience thus occurred at age 19 and ultimately pointed him toward medical school, psychiatry, and psychoanalytic training.

Both the Jewish middle class neighborhood in the Bronx, New York, where he was raised, and Adler's family valued education and familial loyalty. Thus, he felt the pull of conflict between joining his father and his brothers in a small wholesale business in Manhattan, or ultimately disappointing his loving though authoritarian father by finding his own way. His early interests in music began with listening to the Saturday Metropolitan Opera broadcasts with his father, and included studying the piano. There was never the possibility that he had the talent to be a musician, but the fantasies and wishes were there. Adler became the music critic of his Columbia University (then Columbia College) newspaper, and received the encouragement of members of the music department to pursue a masters degree in musicology and a career in writing about music, perhaps including musical management. However, he realized that his real desire was to be a performing musician, something he knew to be an impossibility. Thus, after graduation from college and a firm decision not to go into the family business or pursue his musical interests professionally, Adler went back to college for an additional two years of premedical courses.

Adler's clinical work, especially his experiences with borderline and narcissistic patients, led to a series of papers on the theoretical and clinical issues involved in their treatment.

During his early years, his affiliation with the Boston Psychoanalytic Society and Institute became a major pleasure and commitment for him. He enjoyed the teaching and administrative opportunities provided. The four years he spent as president-elect and president were particularly challenging and enjoyable, especially at a time when psychoanalysis was in a defensive and beleaguered position in relation to biological psychiatry. During his recent presidency, Adler helped define an important aspect of the organization's mission as a commitment to work collaboratively with its broad community in programs including working with abused and neglected children and inner-city schools, and with therapists working with gay and lesbian patients, as well as programs involving film, theater, music, and art. Currently, he is president of the Boston Psychoanalytic Alliance, whose tasks include the development of these and other collaborative ventures.

Adler has had two marriages, and has four children—two from his first marriage, a son and a daughter, and two stepdaughters who came as part of the happy package with Corinne, whom he met twenty years ago. Their four grandchildren are another pleasure, as are bicycling and hiking trips to Europe and different parts of the United States, and their shared love of music. As he looks at the course of his life, he is pleased that he could move from an overprotected childhood, where he was not allowed to join the Boy Scouts because he might be hit by a car during a hike across the George Washington Bridge, to a fuller, more active, happier life, both professionally and personally, than he might ever have anticipated.

The Interview

Doctor Adler, we would like to start this interview by asking you to give an outline of the basic tenets of your approach, and of the consequences of these tenets for the psychotherapy of people with severe personality disorders.

Well, I've done a lot of work trying to conceptualize our understanding of aloneness in borderline patients. This started in the seventies, and I did this together with a friend and colleague, Dan Buie. In the middle of intense separation issues, borderline patients begin to feel a certain desperation, a certain emptiness, and a certain kind of panic. What they talk about, when you ask them what they're feeling, is this terror, this sense of annihilation, and that they feel terribly alone. They have a sense that there is no one there for them.

Dan and I have tried to put this into conceptual terms. We first tried to analyze the developmental issues that we felt borderlines tended to regress to, and to understand what they were going through. We started with Piaget's work, and Selma Fraiberg's understanding of Piaget, which made it intelligible. Under the stress of separation, and under the stress that comes up when they are angry, borderline patients have problems in maintaining an evocative memory of the person who is important to them or who they depend on. They have no object constancy. They then regress to what Fraiberg defines as "recognition memory." They lose what is a result of Piaget's Stage six of sensory-motor development, defined as *evocative memory*, and regress to Stage four of sensory-motor development, which is *recognition memory*.

Yet this doesn't quite operationalize it when you work with borderline patients. So then we tried to take what borderline patients tell us themselves and tried to put that into a theoretical framework. We then began to use concepts from object relations theory, like *holding* and *soothing introjects*. By "introject" is meant the felt presence, within a person, of another person who is or was important to him. I have introjects of people who matter to me that I can summon up anytime. Borderline patients lose that capacity under the stress they feel when they face separation and lose contact with these introjects. The concepts are called "holding" and "soothing" because that's the way borderline patients talk. They want to be held, they need skin-to-skin contact, they want to be soothed, they want to be contained. The problem borderline patients have is that they can't depend upon internal resources in the face of separation and all the affects that go with that. We defined that as the core issue.

Now when I worked with borderline patients, I noticed that as they began to get better, the aloneness issues would gradually recede as they internalized what they had to from their interactions within the therapeutic situation, and they began to look more and more like narcissistic personality disorder patients as described in *DSM-IV*, where the inability to maintain their own sense of self-worth without another person being there to bolster it up would become the major issue to work on.

In this outline of my approach I should name two people: Winnicott and Kohut. Because even in those early days it was clear to us that if you treated borderline patients in the usual psychoanalytic mode, which did not include real activity and a relationship with the therapist, they tended to regress, the anger would come out, they would feel misunderstood, abandoned. For them silence often meant criticism, a projection of their own self-criticism onto the therapist. We searched for what the "glue" was that held these people together, in life as well as in therapy, and what was necessary to make the work in therapy possible. Now Winnicott talked about *the holding environment* and *good-enough mothering*, and Kohut talked about *the selfobject* and *selfobject transferences*.

Winnicott's ideas are so well known that they need no further discussion here, but I would like to talk a little more about Kohut because his work is not as well known in psychologist circles as it should be. First, about selfobjects. A selfobject is a person out there who performs certain needed functions for the person, and while these functions are being performed, that other person is often experienced as part of the self. Kohut also described the kind of transferences that narcissistic personality disorders, and other people too, form when they have certain needs. He called them "mirroring" and "idealizing" selfobject transferences. To me the important thing was this realization that all people need selfobjects, all people are in a way incomplete. Of course more mature people use their selfobjects in a more reciprocal way, while narcissistic personality disorders use their selfobjects in more "archaic" ways and make them much more important, and in an idealized manner.

Now in order to help psychotherapy be successful for border-lines and narcissists, the so-called "primitive" personalities, the therapist has to provide this glue in a Winnicottian and Kohutian way.

Others would agree with you that the, let's say, rather remote attitude of classical psychoanalysis does not work well with these people, but they might also say that what you need is the basic aspects, the common factors of any kind of psychotherapy. The ones that were described by Carl Rogers and by Jerome Frank, for instance. Larry Rockland, with his Supportive Therapy for Borderline Patients (1992) *also says that what is needed is a theoretical framework (which for him is the psychoanalytic model), but what you do is be supportive. You seem to conceptualize this in a different way, isn't that true?*

Well, the support they need is defined by Kohut and Winnicott in two different frameworks. The support itself though, provides the structure and the background that allows one to work on the profound issues: the aloneness, the murderous rage, the intense sadness and depression that is often also there. And as you know, these patients very often have had terribly traumatic experiences and terrible neglect, which has to be worked on to the degree that these patients can bear it.

One man here in Boston was very important to me: Elvin Semrad (1969), who was a teacher at Massachusetts Mental Health Cen-

ter, where many of us were trained and which was in its heyday in
the mid-fifties to maybe the late seventies. Semrad came there in
the mid-fifties and died in 1976. He taught about the psychotherapy
of schizophrenia, which he deeply believed in. And like him I have
no problem with broadening the use of psychoanalytic psychotherapy to work with other so-called primitive patients. Semrad used
to talk in everyday terms. He said: "You give with one hand and
you take away with the other." This is basic to the work with borderline patients: giving with one hand is the support they need, the
structure, the containment, whatever they need. At the same time
this allows you to do the analytic or psychotherapeutic work to
address these major conflicts, dynamic issues, and deficits. Both
in my clinical work and as a teacher it's automatic for me to try to
decide at any given moment what support patients need, and to be
able to face whatever the unbearable issues are in their present life,
within the transference, or in their past.

*Would it be too much to say that where Kernberg is felt by many to
support too little, Rockland supports too much, and that you are more
or less in the middle?*

Well, in the Rockland I've read, he works on these issues too, although I'm not sure that he weighs it in every intervention. The
way I do it, automatically, is to judge, while doing any kind of intervention, what the patient needs—at that particular moment—by
my knowledge of what has gone before in therapy, what his particular problems are, what I know he can handle, and what there is
between us. If I think he may be able to stand the discussion of a
certain painful issue, I might make a statement about something
he has handled well, or some strength he has, then followed by
"However, could you tell me about this . . .," which I know is painful.

*Kohut allows the idealizing transference to develop. Might not this
approach of yours, which so clearly validates the good things the
patient does, encourage this kind of transference to develop?*

Yes, and Kohut might say that I'm manipulating this patient. And this is where I diverge from Kohut. You see, the problem is that Kernberg has tended to see idealization as a defense against envy, rage, and other things, while Kohut has tended to see idealization as a phase-specific happening that occurs in everybody. This has to emerge, to be allowed to come to fruition so that the idealizing transference can ultimately be internalized. The interaction going with this can ultimately be internalized as some of the soothing, containing, holding aspects of the "parent" or "father" imago. I think both reasons for idealization exist, but in the clinical situation it is not always immediately clear if a particular case of idealization is defensive or just something that goes with where the patient is at that moment. Now, if you confront the patient about him being defensive while actually he is having a needed idealizing transference, you undermine the transference, and you enrage the patient, who feels misunderstood, and if that happens, you confirm Kernberg's statement about the rage and envy in narcissistic and borderline patients.

Which in such a case would be iatrogenic?

Right. On the other hand, when the idealization is regressive, you must not allow it to go on endlessly. It's very hard to see which is which in the clinical situation. And when in doubt I would go on the side of not confronting. Time will tell. Actually, I think I may be too willing to go with my uncertainty, too willing to give the patient the benefit of the doubt. So I might go along with something that turns out to be defensive for a much longer time than Kernberg might. Because I feel the price to be paid for erring in the other direction would be too high.

Could it be that Kernberg would think you're spoiling the patient?

I'm sure he would. Kernberg once wrote a review of my book in the *American Journal of Psychiatry*, where he called me a Kohutian. I don't consider myself a Kohutian. I look at myself as an eclectic, someone who is attempting to synthesize a lot of what's there and then trying to bring my own contribution to it. I just try to integrate developmental theories and other theories about borderline and narcissistic pathology.

I once chaired a meeting here in Boston. Anna Ornstein was there, and Stolorow, and I heard Anna Ornstein say about me to Stolorow: "He is not an enemy!" (grins) Kernberg too once said to a colleague: "He is a semi-Kohutian, but he is not an enemy." So while I'm not welcomed in any camp, I'm not seen as an enemy. It would be too easy to just label me as one or the other and then dismiss me.

Does this round off the overview of your approach or is there anything more to add?

Oh, I would like to mention the extremely important concept of projective identification. The projection by these patients of feelings they cannot handle onto their therapist, the provocation of that projected part, which the therapist already has within him, and the reliving of that, and the ultimate internalization of the interaction that deals with the containment of what the patient projected and provoked. That interaction is ultimately processed, interpreted, and internalized as an important part of the process of change.

Which personal motives have led to this specific choice from the various psychoanalytic approaches and to the treatment of this category of patients?

Well, when I worked at Massachusetts Mental Health Center I enjoyed working with schizophrenics and with borderline patients, although at that time we were only just beginning to call them that. I was offered a job by one of my supervisors to work in the prison system, and I loved working with those people who were acting out, character disordered, some of them armed robbers, some of them murderers. I found that exciting work. I ultimately felt they were a variant of borderline patients, and some were severe narcissistic patients. So somehow I just drifted into this area.

It doesn't sound like that. It sounds like you feel attracted to tackling the problems the toughest cases present.

I do, yes. There is a competitive side in me—so that if something is tough, I want to be involved with that. Also, when I was 17 years old, going from high school to college, I first got involved in psychoanalytic treatment for myself. As I was becoming an adult, the separation issues in me led me, before I knew it, to be lying on a couch. It turned out that the analyst I had was beginning to write papers about patients whom we would now call borderlines. I think an identification with him was a major reason for going into psychiatry. After deciding that I was not going to go into my father's business, which I decided after graduation from college, I went to see my old analyst and said, "I want to do what you do." I was going to go and get a Ph.D. in psychology (this was way back in 1951), but he said, "If you really want to do what I do, you'll have to go to medical school," because psychologists had no stature in those days. I figured out that if I did that, I would be 35 years old by the time I finished my training. It took two years longer, because I liked medicine so much that I took a year in internal medicine after my internship, and I also liked the leisure, the moratorium that taking premedical courses gave, so that I took an extra year doing that. There was also the influence of Elvin Semrad, another idealized figure, although I do see him as a very human person with many human failures. But as a teacher and a very gifted human being there was much to idealize in him.

Could you give us some of your private thoughts about psychotherapy in general and about your place in that field?

Well, you're speaking with somebody from the United States, and in this country psychotherapy is in deep trouble. Managed care has taken over, supporting short-term treatments, and preferring cognitive-behavior therapy and psychopharmacology. I don't oppose any of these, they can all be very good in conjunction with long-term treatment for people who need it, and I would do all of them myself when needed. Still, I think it's important that we preserve parts of our structure, and teach good psychotherapy and psychoanalysis. Because over time the literature on research will show that, in the long-term, psychotherapy—the psychotherapies—including long-term psychoanalysis, is cost-effective. We are currently working with a project called GAP, the Group for the Advancement of Psychiatry, where we are putting together all the literature on cost-effectiveness to demonstrate to health care organizations that this is a good way to go.

There are indeed research data for interpersonal psychotherapy, cognitive-behavior therapy, and Dialectical Behavior Therapy (DBT), that prove they are cost effective.

Right, and we are going to use those data.

But would that convince those institutions that the same cost-effectiveness goes for psychoanalytic treatment?

Well, first of all I think that what Marsha Linehan does with DBT is on a continuum with what I would do, and with what I would supervise. There really is a large overlap between what she does and what Dan Buie and I have done and are doing.

Oh? Marsha says that she is 90 percent behaviorist, with Zen and validation added.

I actually wrote a review for the *Journal of the American Psychoanalytic Association* of a book by John Clarkin and others in which she has a chapter. I spent half of my review discussing Marsha's work and pointing out that one could translate a lot of Marsha's validation work in terms of a Kohutian framework. Also, I think that Marsha's *limit setting* is very, very important and related to what I say about the personal limits of the therapist. You see, many borderline patients and some narcissistic patients are ultimately going to demand much more than any human being can offer. The therapist has to define limits. I don't like the term "limit setting," because it tends to be used punitively. I like to talk about the personal limits of a therapist and about the importance for the therapist to clearly define who he or she is and what his or her personal limits are. Marsha does that too, in her own elegant way. And she has a lot to teach us about how we define the boundaries of how much an organization, for example her organization, is willing to offer and how much any one person within it is willing to offer. I learned from Marsha that we had better be firm on these things. I did this before, but she has helped me to do it even more, to say, for instance: "You know, the way things are now, you either go to the hospital or we can't continue treatment." Or "If you have to call me in the way you do, I can't be your therapist." On the other hand, what I think we psychoanalysts have to offer Marsha is to work much more with fantasy exploration. I would focus much more on the specifics of the painful past, present, and the transference situation. I would think that an ideal treatment would be by a Marsha Linehan who is dynamically trained. From my vantage point she is a good way there. She could be even better if she brought in more of the psychodynamic approach. But you know, I think she does more exploration than you would think. She does a lot of play-acting kinds of things with her patients, and Zen and other things, and I think that's fine. If you're comfortable with this approach, that's the way to work. I feel somewhat comfortable with it, but not as much as she does. She brings in all kinds of adjunctive things and I'm all for that. I don't do it myself, but I have no problem hooking people up with therapists who do offer that for those who need it.

I would like to go back to our discussion on the research data, which obviously are required nowadays if you want funds for what you do. John Clarkin is doing research on the psychoanalytic treatments, but the most unequivocal facts are on the outcome of the cognitive approaches, are they not?

That's correct.

Do you expect your side of the field to catch up with that?

Well, what's needed are studies that can evaluate real personality changes. And changes in the quality of life in conjunction with symptomatic relief.

Larry Rockland quoted Wallerstein's "Forty-Two Lives in Treatment" (1986), with research showing that many patients who had had only supportive therapy turned out to be changed quite impressively, while some others who had had uncovering, exploratory treatment had not changed as much as had been hoped for.

I think it's more complicated than that. Because I think one of the things that Kernberg has done to complicate our literature is to talk in terms of supportive therapy versus exploratory therapy. And when you talk in those terms, especially when you did that twenty-five years ago, a lot of things that I would call "somewhere in the middle" would have been lumped with "supportive." I think the good work that has been done in the field is a combination of both. The supportive therapies described in Wallerstein's book are really such a combination. They are what Semrad used to call "Giving with one hand, and taking with the other." In the 1960s and '70s those were "no-no!"s and in the eighties and nineties they are "okay"s and "must!"s—they are the way to go about it. And I must say that this includes psychoanalysis for healthier people. Relational theory and intersubjective theory change many of the ways we do analysis. It's still an exploratory approach, but offers an interactive essence that is necessary for optimal treatment for a lot of people.

You mentioned having learned from Marsha Linehan's approach, concerning the setting of limits. Have there been other major changes in your approach over the years?

I think I've understood a lot more. I think I began as a "classical" analyst who tended to be silent with everyone. That lasted about a year. It took me about five or six years to become "me." The "me" is a relatively active person and what has helped me was to be part of the movement that tried to understand the interactive, intersubjective aspects of transferences and relationships—that helped me form a kind of framework that justifies the skills you need for the work I do.

And during the last ten or fifteen years I have come to understand the usefulness of the concept of projective identification for understanding the process of change in psychotherapy of these patients.

Do you think that your approach has any limitations? For instance, are there specific areas where it should or should not be the choice for therapy?

I think it's important to define, as best one can, which of these borderline and narcissistic patients are treatable and which are not. Of course a patient may be treatable by one person and not by another. It's a matter of matching too, but also of theoretical framework. One of my concerns about Otto Kernberg's approach is that he limits the number of patients who can be treated by his framework. For example, in my review of that book by Clarkin and others, I also take up a research paper they have in there, where within a period of one or two years something like 60 percent of the patients dropped out of treatment. They say, "That's what happens with these patients." I say, "That's what happens with these patients when you use Otto's approach." They also claim that the dropouts were with therapists who were not experienced psychiatric residents—students and so on—that the more experienced therapists do better. I think Otto does better, he is very skilled. But I think Otto is such a very gifted man and has such an idealized reputation that this is curative in itself. I think patients will tolerate or even love what Otto does, while with other competent and even very skilled psychiatric residents the same interventions would not work. Some of them have said, "It's an interesting theory, but it doesn't work well for many of us." Incidentally, Otto's basic formulation about borderlines is a very useful one, no one contradicts that. It's what he does with it in the therapeutic framework.

When you see him in action though, he's much more supportive than his writings would lead you to expect.

It's interesting that you should mention that. I was part of a group instituted by the National Institute of Mental Health, the NIMH, which held a conference on borderline research. Otto was there, and we watched a tape of his, and when I saw that, I said, "Otto, you are really quite supportive in that tape!" He said, "You know me, Gerry, you know I can be supportive." I said, "Well, most of the time I think you can be, but the rest of the world does not know that." It's such a pity he has not written about that side of him.

Which professionals have influenced you especially, apart from Elvin Semrad, whom you already mentioned?

I would like to say something more about Semrad first, if I may. He stressed the importance, over and over again, of always having a psychodynamic formulation. And he stressed the importance of being exploratory. "Investigate, investigate, investigate," he would say. He would also be very alert to the ways in which what I've called primitive people may feel things without knowing them, and then somaticize those feelings. The problem with him was that he could not put it into an intelligible theoretical framework.

But to mention some others who were important to me. There was Paul Myerson, who was my chairman from 1965 to 1979. He was a traditional psychoanalyst and actually my first supervisor, but he was much more than that. He was also a scholar and a careful listener. He essentially taught me to value scholarship and reading and thinking. Even to this day I think of him. Even though he was well established as a psychoanalyst in standard analytic theory, he was always reading the current issues about psychoanalysis and thinking and writing about them. Borderline patients were far from his interest, yet he appreciated my work and Dan Buie's, supported us in what we did, and critiqued our papers in very useful ways.

Could you say something about any specific successes or failures that you have had?

I have worked with many patients where these principles really did apply. They would go through long periods—months, or even years—where they felt this regressive rage about not remembering me. In the middle of a regressive transference they would call me up on the phone and say: "I'm calling you because I can't remember you." Of course they had the cognitive capacity to remember me, or else they wouldn't have called me, but what they were talking about was that they had lost the affect of the introject, the felt presence. And when eventually that stage passed, I considered that as a success. The failures have come about in two ways. One, not confronting enough, or rapidly enough, in patients who in retrospect were probably not treatable or perhaps not treatable by me. Someone who could have contained much more in a limit-setting way might perhaps have had more success. There were a handful of those. Two, I think that these patients need very careful evaluation to decide whether they are treatable at all, by the usual intensive psychotherapeutic means. These patients might benefit from a Marsha Linehanian approach, often in institutional environments, or in something like what Otto offers in Westchester, which has a day hospital, or in different kinds of work programs—a very structured environment where, for instance, twice-a-week psychotherapy might be only one part of it, and where an intensive therapy would bring out a "malignant" kind of regression that can be handled by the setting. Over the years I learned to pay a lot more attention to who is or who is not treatable. I think Otto is the best in defining these people who could not benefit from any kind of exploratory treatment: malignant narcissists, or the ones who have malignant regressive aspects of their borderline personality.

Would you add dishonesty to that list?

Oh, yes. You need truthfulness for any kind of treatment. Very impulsive people would also be hard to treat.

That's a problem! Impulsivity is at the core of borderline pathology!

Yes, but I'm talking about the extreme cases. They might be treatable in prison settings though, or other very structured environments.

Which two or three books, not written by yourself, would you advise the reader to study?

Number one: one of Otto's books: *Borderline Conditions and Pathological Narcissism* (1975). That book includes his seminal paper, given in 1966. Incidentally, the first time I ever saw Otto, I was sitting in a meeting of the American Psychoanalytic Association and listening to that paper and thinking: "Wow! This is a magnificent contribution!"

Then I would recommend at least one, if not all three of Kohut's books: *The Analysis of the Self* (1971), *Restoration of the Self* (1977), and *How Does Analysis Cure?*, which was published posthumously in 1984. It would be a toss-up for a third choice. Either John Gunderson's book (1984) about the state of the art in the treatment of borderline patients, which gives a coherent synopsis of many different approaches, or Marsha Linehan's (1993a) book, because I think she brings her conceptual framework to bear very clearly in a way that can be useful to many therapists and be integrated in the work of psychodynamic psychotherapy.

Are there any aspects of your work that we haven't discussed and that you would like to say more about?

Well, I think that in the limited space we have this more or less summarizes it.

The Situations

In the middle of the night, you're called on the phone by a patient who threatens to commit suicide. What would you do?

A patient of mine? Then I would know something about him and it probably would not come out of the blue. Knowing something about the dynamics of the person, what's going on in his life and where we are in the treatment, I would obviously take it seriously and wonder why I was getting this call at that time of night. If I really thought we were dealing with a life-or-death situation, I would be willing to talk with the person then. Not in the office, but on the phone, even for longer than half an hour if it were necessary. That has not happened more than maybe once or twice in my entire life though.

What if this was acting out by the patient? Or if the suicide threat is just to get your attention, or maybe it's somebody who has lost the evocative memory of you in the way you described?

That happens much more often, and then just the sense they get that I'm not angry with them because they called restores the soothing, holding selfobject they need. That takes only five or ten minutes, usually. Incidentally, my patients know what time I go to sleep at night and they know that if they call me during certain hours, say up to 10:30 at night, they rarely wake me up. So those patients who need it can do that. The patient who calls in the middle of the night usually is desperate. The "why" of that has to be clarified. Occasionally, of course, there are people who take advantage of you.

How often do you allow them to call you in the evenings?

If the person is in the middle of regressive issues, twice a week would be okay. But I would negotiate my terms with them. I have a private life and they may have to wait an hour or two before I can get back to them. If they are so needy that they can't stand such a delay, I take that up with them. "I can't offer this in a way that you really might need, so we have to work something out."

There are many therapists who say, "Look, my office closes at six, you can't call me after hours."

For some patients that's fine. But some patients do need something more at certain moments, and I think a therapist who limits his accessibility in such a way will not be helpful for those patients.

As Harry Truman would say: "If you can't stand the heat, get out of the kitchen."

Right.

A patient comes to the appointed session obviously inebriated. What would you do?

I have a basic principle that I don't see inebriated patients. I don't throw them out, and if I think they're in trouble I would do something to be sure they are safe, but obviously you can't do useful therapeutic work then. The inebriation is often an enactment of some sadistic thing going on between us, and it's useless to talk about it at that time. With some patients I always sort of sniff at them as they walk past me through the door and if I smell alcohol I won't even see them. I can be wrong sometimes, and then I apologize. I explain that it is my responsibility that we do useful work, and that I may sometimes be mistaken, going from the past history of a patient. But I do have a good sense of smell!

Michael Stone would say in all such cases: "Go to Alcoholics Anonymous, because if alcohol is such a problem for you that you drink when coming here, even once, you've got an alcohol problem and I can't solve that for you."

Basically that's a fine principle. I would give the person the benefit of the doubt though, and warn him. "You can't do this and if you do it another time, you really should be in an alcohol treatment program," AA being a superb one.

If the patient didn't think this was necessary and didn't follow your advice, would you stop treatment?

I have occasionally done that, and said, "You can come back when you're in a treatment program."

Here's an amusing illustration: I had sent one of those patients away a few times. She was one of those people who go to AA but don't do it well. That takes time. So on one of these occasions she said, "Just let me stay for a little while, I have to tell you something now." I said, "Okay, I'll listen." And then she said, "Adler, I wanna tell you that you are not as great as you think you are!! And what's more, you are getting old!!!" I said, "Okay, let's talk about this when you come back next time." (laughs) I think she needed the drink to be able to say that to me. Next time we talked about this, but having said it while drunk didn't help her at all, because she still could not discuss it with me while sober.

You meet one of your patients at a cocktail party and he or she wants to use this opportunity to have an ordinary social meeting with you for a change, and starts to chat with you. What would you do?

Well, I try to allow a certain ambiguity within the treatment, but also I try not to come to conclusions prematurely. I go with the flow, feeling "Here we are in a socially awkward situation. I can't tell whether this person is aware of this, and we both did not ask to be here." Under these circumstances one makes small talk. Also, some people benefit from an interaction that we did not set up, so I would go along with the social situation. I would simultaneously be monitoring the situation for any messages that might pertain to the therapy. If the patient doesn't bring this up in the next session, I would certainly do so myself and explore whatever it might make clear. In my evolution as an analyst I've learned the hard way that you can offend people in really hurtful ways by not being willing to give them the benefit of the doubt. If you find yourself in the elevator with a patient you are going to see some minutes later, and there are only the two of you, you are being dumb and offensive, even harming the treatment, if you don't make small talk. I monitor what I say too, though. Because, being a friendly guy, I may have said something I should not have, and I want to remember that.

A patient turns out to be in the neighborhood of your front door every time you come home. Just standing in the street. What would you do?

I would see that as something potentially very serious. I want my privacy—I demand it—and this is really an intrusion. Usually people who do that are very disturbed. They often have a lot of violent fantasies as part of who they are, so this would be totally unacceptable. However, a confrontation that implies "What the hell are you doing here!?" is destructive, and since I hypothesize there's something potentially dangerous for me or for my family, or perhaps for the patient here, the last thing I want to do is antagonize him. So I would use every skill I possess to try to explore with the patient whatever this is about and ultimately get through to him that he cannot do this and be in treatment with me. I'd try to do it in such a way that it would come across as supportive, as interested, as caring, as trying to understand it from the patient's perspective, while simultaneously, internally I would be very concerned. And of course it would have to stop, although I would accept it if it took a couple of sessions to have it stop. If necessary though, I wouldn't hesitate to involve the police. I wouldn't hesitate, either, to have the police go to a patient's home and break in the door if that person was really suicidal. Knowing that I would do that is felt as helpful by them.

You discover that something from your office has been taken away by a patient—"borrowed," stolen, or just picked up on an impulse. You know who did it. What would you do?

I'll give you a clinical illustration of that.

Some years ago, my wife and I had offices on the same floor of a building. One day she told me that a very favorite Museum of Modern Art umbrella was missing from the coatrack. I didn't know for sure, but there was one woman in my practice whom I suspected. She is basically an honest woman but she had this hysterical flaw to her. So I asked her in a roundabout way, the way I usually do such things when I'm not certain. There was this umbrella that disappeared, and had she perhaps seen it when she left the last time? She turned red and told me that she had taken it, because she has one just like that and it had disappeared, and she assumed that this one was hers and that she had left it there. But as we talked about it she began to realize that this was a rationalization, and that indeed she was not at all certain that this one was hers. She also thought that such a very special umbrella could only be owned by a very special person like herself.

All this led to insight, but I'm giving the example to illustrate the way I would handle such a situation. Because one of my problems is that it would be very hard for me to be certain, and to say, "I know this was here before you came, and when you left it wasn't here anymore." If I were really sure though, I would say it much more directly. Because if I believed it happened and would not say so, the therapy would be ruined anyhow. Fortunately this sort of situation never came up.

> Once, when I was a resident in a psychiatric hospital, a borderline patient, being very angry at me, smashed a window in the office. I told her that I would not treat her unless she paid for the damage. We are talking about the limits a therapist has to set. Once I had a patient who left so many messages on my answering machine that she filled it all up. I said: "If you do that again, you are automatically out of treatment for a month. And if you do it again after that, there is no way for you to come back into treatment." When she did do it again, the treatment stopped.

Our final question: Could you describe the setting in which you see your patients?

It's an office, about fourteen by fifteen feet, with a lot of contemporary furniture in it. The couch is not an original, but a classic copy of a Mies van der Rohe couch, the table is contemporary, the two easy chairs are contemporary Norwegian, everything is design. Some people consider it too spare, too cold. These people ultimately see me as too cold. I deliberately have my chair and the patient's chair identical, because even though there is a disparity between the therapist and the patient, we are equals within the room. The chairs can turn on a pivot so the patient can either look at me or away. There are two footstools. I always use mine, the patient can do so if he or she wishes.

That would make the whole situation very relaxed, would it not?

Oh, I think it does. One thing I don't really like is the distance between the two chairs. Aesthetically it is as it should be, but for good contact it's too far. I tell people, "Feel free to move your chair forward if you like," and some people do. My chair is directly next to the couch. Out of sight of the patient in the classical position, but much closer to the headrest than usual, because the patient has to experience me as close, to cut through the defenses when we work on intimacy issues. They can hear my voice inches away from them.

There is a large painting on the wall, an abstract painting that some patients find very disturbing because there seems to be a lot of anger in it. Most of my patients are not so sick that this painting really disturbs them badly, though. I don't work with schizophrenics anymore. For most of my patients it's a sort of Rorschach. There are other pictures, some aerial photographs that really look like abstract art, a Khazak on the floor that is over a hundred years old, and there is a bookcase. The bookcase used to be jammed with books, but I took most of them out. There are some I refer to regularly, and there are some that are still in there because at the time when I moved to this office there was a patient who got very disturbed at the change of setting. I let her choose some of the books that in the old situation she would stare at during sessions when she could not look at me, and put them in there for her in the way of transitional objects.

2

Salman Akhtar

Biography

Salman Akhtar was born in Lucknow, India, on July 31, 1946, in a highly cultured family that had for generations produced many renowned poets, politicians, and writers. Seeing all his family members' names constantly in newspapers and magazines led to a very early ego-syntonic identification with writing and publishing. These gifted relatives at the same time often were erratic, confusing, and idiosyncratic, which raised questions in his mind about human nature and led to his choice of psychiatry when he entered medical school; the choice brought the literary side and the troubling, quizzical side of his childhood together in a harmonious gestalt. In 1973, after finishing postgraduate training in psychiatry in India, he arrived in the United States, re-did his residency training over the next four years, and came into contact with many psychoanalysts, notably Dr. Vamık Volkan, who was a mentor to him and who remains a very good friend, and Dr. Otto Kernberg, who was first a hero from a distance, then a role model to be emulated, and finally an intellectually and professionally helpful senior colleague.

Being an immigrant has had a profound effect on Akhtar. It fueled the already existing tendency of his thought toward the synthesis of contradictory themes, showed him the relativism of many rigidly held postulates about normality and abnormality, and gave him a broader perspective on human conduct and its variations.

The creative gene continues to exert its effect: Doctor Akhtar's son is an upcoming and already quite successful editor of films and television in Los Angeles, and his daughter is a blossoming artist, an avid equestrian, and a fine poet. As for himself, he is now integrating his interest in poetry and psychoanalysis at a deeper and more theoretical level.

The Interview

Doctor Akhtar, we would like to start this interview by asking you if you could give us a brief outline of the basic tenets of your approach.

My motto is to practice psychotherapy from an integrated approach. This is actually the result of the way my own development in the field has gone. I started my work in psychotherapy by reading Otto Kernberg and finding his views to be very useful, especially because I was dealing with sicker, often hospitalized patients. Later on, as a person, he was extremely helpful to me and I owe him a great deal. That became an important part of my mind. Unlike most people in the field of psychoanalysis, I had my training upside-down. I read a lot of Kernberg *before* I did my psychoanalytic training. When I started my training I discovered that mainstream North American psychoanalysis was a different ballgame altogether. Dominated by ego psychology, the clinical approach I then learned was slow, piecemeal, achieving little by little. That departure from a more "aggressive" psychotherapeutic style shook me up. As if this was not enough, a friend introduced me to Winnicott, which again meant a different set of ideas, a different approach.

This clash of traditions challenged me, particularly since I was an immigrant; I was trying to put the culture of India and the culture of the USA together in my head. Add to that the fact that I was trained as a psychiatrist in India in a very descriptive way, and that my U.S. psychiatric residency was psychodynamically inclined. So I had what you might call a large number of intellectual splits in my mind. Of course, personal stuff also lay underneath all this. Therefore I was striving to heal myself and to put my mind together, both professionally and intellectually. I thus developed a need to put all kinds of theories together and to create an integrative approach.

I was supervised by a lot of people and became quite influenced by them for a while. But I'm not the kind of person who stays with one position in a sustained way. I take something, discard some of it, and keep the rest. For instance, I agree with Kernberg on about 90 percent of what he says, but not on all things. It's the same with Winnicott. I take into account both sides of this equation. Let's take idealization as an example. You have borderline and narcissistic patients who are looking for some kind of guru, or a perfect lover, or a wonderful city to live in, or a wonderful employer. The question is, "What does this mean?" There are different theories about this. Some people believe that this need of a patient is pathological to begin with—that it's a defense against aggression. In other words, "As long as I idealize you, I don't have to really know you, because if I did, that would inevitably mean ambivalence and mobilization of aggression." Idealization might also be an attempt to avoid feeling a failure oneself, since by clinging to manic hopes one can deny imperfections not only in others but in oneself as well. I think this theory is right, but I think idealization can be more than that. It can also be a remnant of the normal desire of a child for a strong parent. In idealization, there can also be healthy elements. It's a variety of love, too. It cannot be said that it is either this or that. In listening to patients, I try to hear both sides.

What is the position of your approach in the main field of theories concerning the treatment of severe personality disorders?

I'm not really somebody who makes a big effort to push his work, although I'm an ambitious person and enjoy being known. I don't keep repeating my concepts over and over. I don't publish the same

paper, so to speak, again and again. More importantly, I don't claim
to be an "expert." Unlike some other people who go to hundreds
of meetings and present the same material over and over, my work
is beginning to be known largely because of my teaching. For
instance, somebody heard me at Harvard, and that led to a weekly
series of workshops in Washington. One thing leads to another,
like my teaching here, at Zon & Schild in the Netherlands. This
came about, I think, upon the recommendation of Otto Kernberg.
I have given lectures in twelve of the twenty-eight institutes of
the American Psychoanalytic Association in the last two or three
years. Also pretty much all over the United States. I think that
my biggest strength is teaching. Anybody who listens to me in-
vites me again, and often there is someone in the audience who
will invite me to a new place. My way of thinking has spread by
word of mouth.

*Still you do publish a great deal. Strangely though, not so much of
all that is on the subject of personality disorders, which is the subject of your special knowledge and experience.*

Well, as I said, there are people in the field who will write on the
same subject again and again, which for an academic career is very
useful, even if in all those publications you just keep on repeating
yourself and don't really add something new. Now, I once wrote
an article on narcissistic personality disorder. That led to many
invitations to talk about this and write more about it. I said: "I don't
want to do that again, but please let me write on the schizoid
personality disorder." Next invitation, I requested that I write on
the hypomanic personality disorder. I did all that, then moved on
to other syndromes. All this led to my book *Broken Structures*
(1995). Another example: I just wrote a paper on immigration,
which became a "hit." Best paper of the year award, that sort of
thing. Many journals wanted me to write something for them on
that subject. But I said, "No. I'll write on something else." Because
I want to apply one kind of thinking to as many different clinical
problems as I'm dealing with. Perhaps that lack of one kind of focus

prevents one from seemingly becoming an expert on something. You don't become an expert by repeating yourself, but by a special way of thinking that you can apply to different areas.

You are not interested in developing something like your own school?

No! To me, treating somebody with a personality disorder is not really different from treating any other patient. On the other hand, the fact is that where many people look at pathological behavior in a way that implies only sickness, I look at its adaptational value to the patient with comparable valence. And I constantly challenge myself by taking on new things to approach from this point of view. For instance I was once asked to discuss the problems of children from Asian, Indian, Chinese, and black cultures. I picked the black child because I had not read so much about black children in the USA (to my shame). I thought this was an opportunity. Now I know more than I did before.

Could you let us know some of your guiding principles in this basic approach?

Well, as I said before, you have two kinds of approaches here. On one extreme is the psychoanalyst who, when greeted with "Good Morning!" looks at the patient and thinks: "Aha, an interesting disguise for hostility!" He sees sickness in everything. On the other hand, there is the analyst who sees health in everything. If you disagree with him, he will say, "Wonderful, he takes me seriously enough and cares enough about me to be honest with me!" My motto is that you should listen to the patient, not to a theory. And don't just listen to the words spoken by the patient, but also to what he is feeling. You listen for the reasons he may have for feeling this or that. And then you might make the patient aware that whether or not you agree with those reasons, you respect them and can see where they're coming from. I learned this from my own analyst. Whatever I said, he practically never responded with a "No." He always said "Yes!" But then he added something that got me to thinking. And after that "Yes," I was more receptive to listen to the rest. Step one: the patient must feel understood by us. Step two: he must learn to understand himself. Step one alone would make him feel good, but step two is essential for psychic growth. Empathy is a prerequisite and not a replacement for interpretation.

Another major guideline is that one has to be brave, and free of shackles. There is far too much anxiety about such things as "What would my colleagues say?" You shouldn't be looking over your shoulder all the time.

> I remember a patient who insisted on sleeping with a loaded gun under her pillow. And everybody was scared she would kill herself or somebody else. So was I! But somehow it felt right that she insisted on this behavior and I kept on accepting it, no matter what other people might say, or the trouble it might cause me. Because I felt she needed to induce the terror it caused me and everybody else, and to know that I could suffer. Like a baby that bites mother's nipple. You can't slap the baby or throw it away. I think that sometimes your patients need to hurt you and you must be able to stand the hurt. Eventually I got so pained by it that I told her and asked her to give up the gun. She said that she would not give it to anybody else but me. I took the gun and the bullets, and kept them in my office behind a lock, without anybody knowing about it. For years there was a gun in that drawer.

Did you start like this or develop this attitude gradually?

Gradually.

> For example, I once treated a patient who was extremely sensitive to any kind of separation. I started treating her like Otto does, but that was really only hurting her. Then I changed, and at certain times told her where I would be.

Even that was not right. I then told her, "Look, I'm giving you carte blanche. From now on, whenever I change an appointment, if even for an hour, or sometimes for many weeks, you can ask me anytime for the reason I have for that." After that, she has never been in pain again at a change of appointments, and never asked why I did it.

The principle behind this is the developmental principle: if mother locks the door when the child is playing outside, the child will be curious and will want to know what's going on and want to get back in. If she leaves the door open, there's no problem.

Isn't this approach a very personal one, and wouldn't it be very difficult to teach people this way of thinking and working with patients?

Your question resembles one I was asked recently during a course. A student asked me if I was teaching psychoanalysis or my own character. I was taken aback for maybe five seconds and then I told her: "Look, if you see four extremely good tennis players, all four people are playing tennis, and they each play in their own way. So the question is, "Is this tennis, or is this them?" Of course it's both. Obviously I teach psychoanalysis, but this cannot be outside my character.

In this regard, Kernberg says that there is a difference between technical neutrality and anonymity. In classical analysis these two often get blurred. You say more or less the same thing—about not trying to be anonymous—don't you?

Sure, because I think that in classical analysis people have come to glorify silence. That can sometimes hurt a person. On the other hand, we are not there to just please people, so the obvious socially expected answer to what the patient says is not always the correct one. We even have to say unacceptable things to the patient sometimes, but there are ways in which you can make the unacceptable acceptable. For instance in the case of a narcissistic personality disorder you explain that he was raised in a condition of too much praise, too much attention for his talents and not enough attention to his humble and human self. As a result of such early training the child becomes ashamed of that normal and humble part of himself and becomes addicted to that special self. Such people then develop a defensive contempt for ordinariness, even their own humanity. They thus become a beautiful machine, but it's very painful, because they are so preoccupied about keeping themselves going that they appear uninterested in others and may be mistaken as being unloving because they are so worried about themselves most of the time. We have to learn how to talk; then we can say anything.

What are the preconditions to be able to work this way? Because it obviously has some explicit risks.

First, a long period of apprenticeship. A long period of continued absorption, admiration, and even idealization of the pertinent literature, reading, practicing, and so on. And then gradually freeing oneself from the specifics of the received wisdom. Then one would find one's own voice, develop one's own style. However, one should never be secretive about what one does. Because then megalomania, corruption, or perversion may seep in.

Second, the practitioner has to have basic decency and ethics, because within reasonable boundaries of civility one can do almost anything. For instance during the analysis of a patient once, it was raining cats and dogs. So I offered the patient an umbrella that I had lying around. There is nothing terrible in that, I think it would have been terrible not to do that. But always share such things with colleagues, check out what they think of it.

John Clarkin says what good psychotherapists for borderlines have in common is that they consider the responsibility for either living or dying to lie ultimately with the patient. Do you agree with that?

Well, then I'm not a good therapist because I don't fully agree with that position. I think mostly that is true. However, there are times when one can say the responsibility equally belongs to both parties. At still other times, the therapist might have to take on even more responsibility and should be willing to be available twenty-four hours a day. I have one particular patient who can occasionally feel extremely dejected, and become desperate and suicidal. In that state, if she needs to see me at twelve o'clock at night, I might see her. Many others would not do that. Maybe this difference is because I was trained in a developmental tradition that, combined with my deep love of children, led to this sort of approach. I approach these people from a developmental viewpoint. A little child can't do everything by itself. Somebody has to pick it up to help it get something that's way up high, for instance. Similarly, a therapist has to be at times an auxiliary ego for the patient. I once wrote a review of the book by Yeomans, Selzer, and Clarkin, *Treating the Borderline Patient* (1992), where it says that if a patient is absolutely suicidal at night, you tell her that it is her responsibility to commit suicide or not. I do not agree with that. I think it should be: "You must call me." They would consider this to be the omnipotence of the analyst. They will point out that you make yourself out to be an all-good object but will sooner or later fail. They might suggest that there is masochism in the analyst if he does what I am suggesting. I think differently. I believe that this is a developmentally optimal availability of the therapist, just like a parent should be available to a child in times of need. Loewald (1960), and, more recently, Tahka (1993) and Settlage (1989, 1993, 1994) have emphasized the parallel existence of therapeutic and developmental processes in any in-depth psychological treatment.

In this respect an analyst will have to be very good at judging correctly whether a particular demand of the patient is manipulative or not.

Sure! There will be times when you say, "No, I won't do this for you." Just like a mother or father will! If you let yourself be exploited, it *is* masochism.

And it helps to avoid being exploited if you share with colleagues what you do with your patients?

Yes.

> I once had a patient who had been beaten, ignored, and called a monster during her childhood, and, frankly, throughout the beginning of the treatment, she looked like one. She lived in extreme self-deprivation. After two years of seeing her in psychotherapy, I moved my office and she could now see a particular painting that had been in the office before, but not in her line of view. She asked me to move that picture. I was taken aback for a second, then I said, "Hey, I'm flattered that you should ask me this. Because I know that you are not the kind of person who asks easily of people to do things for them. So I'm touched. But you see, I like this office to be the way it is. I will therefore make a compromise. I will take this painting off the wall during your sessions, so you will never see it. But when you leave I shall put it back, because then the office will be mine and I like it the way it is.

Notice that I did not ask her what it was about the picture she could not tolerate. I was tempted to do that, but thought it inappropriate at that time. When a hitherto thwarted developmental tendency becomes manifest as a result of interpretive work, you don't reduce it to its constituents, you just let it be. Sam Abram's concept of developmental interventions is pertinent in this context.

Take for another example your son, who's wearing your shirt when you come home, and he's talking to a girl. You don't ask him, "What are you doing with my shirt!" No, you let him wear it. Then maybe four days later, sitting in the backyard with a gin and tonic, you can say: "By the way, I noticed that you were wearing my shirt the other day. How come?"

The fact is, that after two or three months that patient did say: "Please put the picture back where it was. It's all right." Then I asked her what had been so bad about it.

I'm collecting actions and situations like this for a paper that I'm preparing. Another one I'm going to include is the following. After twenty-three years of living in the USA, I have during the past two years had times when I was tempted to talk to my patients in my mother tongue. My first feeling is "I shouldn't." But the question of "Why?" is more important than just forbidding myself to do it. What is there in the clinical material that makes me want to speak that way? And why is this happening more often lately? What is it in me that has been awakened? Whatever it is, it should not frighten me. In this business we should always be vigilant, but never frightened of what happens within our own minds.

Apart from what you've already said, can you tell us a little more about the personal motives you had that led to your particular position?

I'm sure a lot of childhood stuff. You see, when I grew up in India in the fifties (I was born in 1946) I was taught mostly by Indian people, but the English influence upon them (and, as a result, upon me) was unmistakable. And there were Russian and Chinese communist influences on my childhood as well. Lots of pictures of Stalin, Lenin, Marx, Mao. Most children that I knew started reading fiction with British books, while I and my brother read Russian books. Moreover, a number of my family members, including, of course, my parents, were very renowned people. We were in many ways something of an oddity, and when you are an odd thing out, you begin to wonder why. Also, we were a Muslim family, a religious minority, but we were not religious at all! We were thus a minority within a minority. Also, my mother and father were separated for two or three years, for political reasons, not for personal ones. To have a father some nine hundred miles away, is a very powerful influence upon a growing boy. A topographical split of that magnitude cannot but get internalized.

Don't you think that this approach of yours, where you always think: "I might do this, but on the other hand something else altogether might be more appropriate," is something that will be very hard to learn for beginning therapists? Isn't it more for experienced therapists?

I think you're right. The beginning person is better off being in one camp or another. One better start in a very conservative way. I had very rigorous conservative training. For instance, one of my supervisors told me to never accept a check that had not been signed by the patient himself. So for ten or fifteen years I refused to accept any check signed by someone else. Then it became clear to me that the different signature was not the issue, but the question as to *why* the check was signed by someone else. Another one taught me to never use the words "my wife" while talking to a patient. When a patient fantasizes about her, you should respond with: "Well, I wonder what are your fantasies about this woman of mine that you have in mind." I did it exactly like that, for years! But now I can do it this way or any other way. Sometimes speaking directly is better. At other times, a certain formality of language has technical advantages. Going back to the one-school-or-many question, let me say this: You cannot have a child raised by a Jewish mother, a Hindu uncle, a Catholic father and so on. The child might get all confused. It's better to be raised in one religion and later on to discover that there are alternatives. You know, your question makes me think that there are some teachers who are good for junior people, and others who are good for those with more experience. And I might have gradually moved from the first to the second category. Thank you for facilitating this insight!

Rules are used to facilitate behavior, but they can sometimes become rigid and then they become restrictive instead of facilitating.

Certainly.

Take this patient that I had in analysis. At one point she developed a nearly delusional transference that was just not responding to interpretive efforts. Ultimately, I asked her to sit up during the sessions, thinking that this might facilitate correcting her quasi-delusional ideas better than the rule that she should stay on the couch. She did do that, but then refused to look at me. So I said I would only continue with the treatment if she looked at me. I had to draw a wedge between the transference and reality, so that the transference could be analyzed.

The point is that it's excellent to use unusual techniques, but that you should be very much aware of the risks, and know why you deviate from standard practice.

Of course. You know, it occurs to me that there is a very nice chapter, called "The Concept of Interpretive Actions," in Thomas Ogden's book *Subjects of Analysis* (1994). The clinical examples are unfortunately not very good, but the ideas are. Ogden emphasizes that no matter what the analyst does, it should always be accompanied by his putting its potential message into words for himself, even if he will never discuss it with the patient.

Have there been any major changes in your development?

No sudden ones, it all evolved quite gradually. At first I was 100 percent on the side of Otto Kernberg. You know, this reminds me of an interesting anecdote. I was in a taxi once, with Otto, in Amsterdam. He asked: "Do I have it right, that you're shifting a little toward Kohut's approach?" Well, he was giving me a ride, and I didn't want him to shove me out (you know I'm joking), so I said, "No! But I am reading Winnicott and his views do interest me." That was five years ago. I graduated from the psychoanalytic institute in 1986 and had been incorporating many things very gradually, and then at some point in time it all had become a different gestalt altogether. I was free from it all. I mean, as free as one can be or one should optimally be. Bob Michaels has written about this kind of growth in an analyst. In any case, it wasn't only important for my own development, but for my patients as well.

Does your approach have limitations?

Well, my clinical experience for one. I have not treated many psychotic patients. I haven't treated patients with multiple personality disorder either, or people with severe perversions. Most of my patients are more or less midway sick. I have only one who is really very, very troubled. Another problem is that I am recommending an oscillation between affirmative and interpretive modes, while the fact is that I myself tend to get restless in the affirmative, supportive mode. After awhile I want to get back to the interpretive mode and that isn't always good for the patient. Actually the limitation isn't in the approach, but in the titration of the various modes. The temptation is that you think that you can do it both ways. But actually this back-and-forth movement can be quite tricky. I sometimes find myself getting a bit greedy and wanting to do more in a session than to remain in just one mode. You see, this integrative approach is only five or six years old in me, and I am only now beginning to master handling it.

Do you remember any failures?

Yes, one very bad one. Neither one of us got anything out of the treatment. The reasons are not all clear to me, but there certainly was the matter of bad selection. The patient should not have been put on the couch for analysis at all, something I realized only in hindsight.

What do you do when a treatment isn't going the way you want?

I might seek advice from colleagues. Or I might ask the patient to seek another therapist, at least for consultation. One patient even saw another therapist for one session a week while she was still in analysis with me, five times a week. I accepted that and continued the analysis. Soon the patient stopped seeing the other person. Frankly, I think that this acting out had adaptive aspects and helped the patient. However, as I said before, such cases should always be presented to one's peers in a study group. The problem is, most of us are only one kind of person, and to find a multiple kind of relating and conceptualizing is a very difficult thing to do. You can be very good at playing tennis *and* basketball, but you shouldn't try to do both at the same time.

Which two or three books, not written by yourself, would you advise the reader to study?

I would think they should read Kernberg's 1984 book *Severe Personality Disorders.* The earlier two books by Kernberg are hard to read and not that relevant for nonspecialists. This one is. Another book would be *On Learning from the Patient* (1985), by Patrick Casement, who is a very good exponent of Winnicott's ideas.

Another one would be *The Basic Fault* by Michael Balint (1968). And some papers of Winnicott, such as "*Hate in the Countertransference*" (1949). Finally I would recommend a paper by a Norwegian psychoanalyst, Bjorn Killingmo, entitled "*Conflict and Deficit: Implications for Technique*" (1989). And a paper entitled "*The Romantic and Classic Vision in Psychoanalysis*" (1989), by a Tel Aviv psychoanalyst, Carlo Strenger.

Are there any aspects of your work we have not yet discussed and that you would like to say more about?

I think I've said plenty!

The Situations

In the middle of the night, you're called on the phone by a patient who threatens to commit suicide. What would you do in such a situation?

One of my ongoing patients? It *has* happened. I would stay on the phone as long as it takes. If he's deadly serious, with a gun in his hand, threatening to blow his head off, I might ask him if he thinks it would be helpful for us to meet; that would simply be moving to another location, as it were, the kind of inconvenience that the patient is introducing anyway. There are times when such therapeutic actions are necessary. That offer in itself is so powerful and significant that it can rattle the patient and create a situation of hope, and diminish the anger, the revenge fantasies and what have you. Secondly, if he is being obnoxious, I would ask him if he would object to giving me names or telephone numbers of relatives that I might call to help him. If he doesn't want to do that, then I would have to resort to other measures. I would say: "You know, by calling me you have given me responsibility for what happens, so I am now going to call the police and make sure that they protect you and take you to the hospital." So it may be anything from calling the police to seeing him in person. If somebody is in bad trouble, there is no reason for not seeing him, even if it is at an odd hour of the day (or night). Other specialists—internists, gynecologists—do.

And if this happens more often?

Well, you can't be masochistic. You can't perform surgery while the train is moving. If it's a life-or-death situation, you might do it. But when you're asked to do it regularly, something is being missed in the treatment or the treatment offered is perhaps not the appropriate one in the first place. The whole situation has to be reevaluated then. But when you're asked to become a train-surgeon and do it regularly, then you have to decide whether this will be your specialty or not. And you have to interpret it: "Why do you ask me to do this? Why do you get suicidal regularly at two o'clock in the morning?"

How would you react if a patient comes to the appointed session in a state of obvious inebriation?

A glass of wine is one thing, but if someone is actually drunk, there would be no point in continuing. I would say: "How come this happened? But I doubt that we can even discuss this meaningfully at this moment so I'll abort the session right now and we will discuss this next time."

You meet one of your patients at a cocktail party, and he or she wants to use this opportunity to have an ordinary social meeting with you for a change, and starts to chat with you. What would you do?

I would certainly chat with her for a minute or two. But I would talk only to a certain extent. That wasn't always so, by the way. I used to become frozen.

What do you think Otto Kernberg has said to this question?

I would think that he would be on the very conservative side.

Well, like you, he was one of the few who would have no trouble chatting for a while. As long as the patient behaved appropriately.

I'm pleased with that.

A patient turns out to be in the neighborhood of your front door every time you come home. Just standing in the street.

This has happened! My reaction would depend on how intrusive this is. When your little son or daughter climbs on your lap, too tired to walk, it's all right. But then, when the child also pees or shits on your trousers . . . You see? A burden is all right, but there are limits. Don't worry about burdens. That goes with the job. Some people call it masochism, but I don't. You cannot be a psychotherapist if you want to avoid psychological burdens. But—how much of a burden can you stand? That differs from temperament to temperament. Some people can carry one suitcase, others can carry two. If it's burdensome and painful, it has to be stopped. First the behavior has to be stopped, then you can start interpreting.

What would you say to such a patient?

I once said to a patient who was doing such a thing, "You should know that I'm concerned about you and that I have good feelings for you. And I care about you. Now, if I'm going to continue to be of use to you, to truly help you through your problems, I have to feel okay myself. Your presence here at my door every day makes me feel not-okay. We must discuss how we can contain this situation, so I can return to a position of feeling okay and continue working with you. Because if this goes on, I could not."

In another situation, when I felt less burdened, I responded differently to the patient. I said, "Obviously you want to see me more than five times a week, and I'm sorry that I didn't recognize that need. Now you've found a way to show this need and of getting in touch with me." I could do this, because it wasn't bothering me then.

Like Marsha Linehan, you stress the need of discussing any behavior of the kind she calls "therapy-interfering behavior."

Exactly.

You discover that something from your office has been taken away by a patient—"borrowed," stolen, or maybe just picked up on an impulse. You know who did it. What would you do?

It would depend upon how psychically valuable the thing is to me. If it was a letter that was written by my parents, or a book that was signed by Sigmund Freud, or my daughter's painting, or a copy of my son's movie script, these are treasures. But if it was one of my books, that's a different case. No, seriously, what actually *has* happened is a patient took one of my scarves. I'm pretty sure she took it from where, along with my overcoat, it was hanging outside my office. I expect that this scarf will turn up years later. It's not such a big thing, you know, a scarf. In a way it's flattering also. It's certainly annoying because I liked that scarf, but it is a sign of love, in a way. I'll just sit on it, even if it has to be for a couple of years. To see how and when it will pop up.

You will not bring it up with the patient?

No, because I'm not sure it was her.

If you were, what would you do?

I would wait to see, but it would depend upon the value. It's the degree of pain that's at stake here. There's a story about Harold Searles. The patient says, "Can I bring my dog to the next session?" and he says "How big is the dog?" It's a funny thing to say, but look again: What Searles is doing is attempting to establish a reality base and to limit suffering in the countertransference. If I don't mind too much, I'm willing to wait it out. If I do, I would say: "Listen, I'm pretty sure that you took this and I'm very upset about it and I cannot work in this situation. You have to give it back. We will have to talk about why you did it, but only after I get it back. Right now I'm too disturbed to work with you."

Ultimately, at some time, you would do something about it?

I would hope so! Hopefully the progress of interpretive work itself will create a situation where either the scarf or the subject will come up.

How do you like to work with your patients? Is there a desk between you, or are you sitting more or less opposite from each other, or maybe more side-to-side? Are there any easy chairs, or fairly comfortable ones? Are there many personal objects in your room or office? That sort of thing.

My room is a little too big for my taste. I'm in a medical school and they give you an office. I don't have much choice. I like a somewhat smaller office. I've tried to make my current office smaller. The whole floor has a big oriental rug that my daughter helped me pick out, and two walls have bookshelves all over them, filled with a thousand books, and they are a very dark wood, and there are two big windows that are never opened. So the office is quite dark. There are a few lamps. It actually looks like a French restaurant with an Indian touch. There's a couch, my chair, and everything is very dark. (Paradoxically, I like my home to be as light as possible.) There is a second chair near mine, for vis-à-vis therapy, and there is a small table between those two chairs with a little lamp on it. There is a desk as well, and a sofa, and a small coffee table.

Why do you have such a dark office?

All kinds of reasons! At the deepest level, my mother was hospitalized for a long time when I was a little boy, and I used to go and visit her there. My memories of that hospital are of a very dark room. So the darkness of the office is connected to me and my mother. And to my early reparative longings toward her. And then I was dating a young woman in medical school and I was madly in love with her. In India it's very hard to have any physical contact with girls. But there was this French restaurant, called *La Bohème*, and there you could do anything. So that might be a second source of my office decor. Also, a British analyst, who reminded me of my father, had a very dark office. So there is a mixture of all these things: mother, father, sadness, reparation, sex. By the way, with some of my students and colleagues (and one particular patient) my office is a little bit of a joke: they call me the "prince of Darkness."

3

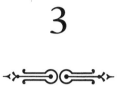

Lorna Smith Benjamin

Biography

Lorna Smith Benjamin was born in Rochester, New York, on January 7, 1934. Her father's family emigrated from England in the 1700s, her mother's family emigrated from Holland in 1917. Her grandparents were farmers in upstate New York. She was raised in the Presbyterian faith. Her father was an executive in Eastman Kodak, her mother was a schoolteacher. She has one younger sister, and a foster brother who joined the family during World War II. She went to Oberlin College, where she graduated in 1955, and received her Ph.D. in 1960 from the University of Wisconsin, in Madison, with Harry F. Marlow as her major professor. Then followed four years of internship and postdoctoral training in psychiatry at the University of Wisconsin Department of Psychiatry, where she progressed to become full professor. In 1987 she moved to an Academic Psychology Department at the University of Utah, in Salt Lake City. Since 1965, she has had a private practice as well. She is the mother of two children and the grandmother of three, and apart from that she enjoys skiing, hiking, mountain biking, cooking, drawing, and photography.

The Interview

Doctor Benjamin, we would like to start this interview by asking you if you can give us a brief outline of the basic tenets of your approach and of the consequences thereof for psychotherapy.

In twenty-five words or less? (smiles) Well, the most important thing in therapy is, I think, that interventions should be directed at what's wrong. You should know why you are doing what you're doing, based on assumptions of psychopathology. So there should be an organizing theory that is testable and refutable, and not just in general but on a moment-to-moment basis. So the value of integrating science and clinical intuition is very high. It means that the approach is data-based and very much contingent on what is important from moment to moment. That characterizes the *style* of the approach. The assumptions that are then used to *organize* the approach are developmental and biological in a behavioral sense. I think biology includes behavior as well as structure and chemistry and physiology. It's an evolutionary approach and it starts with attachment theory, which John Bowlby (1969, 1973, 1980) told us about. Attachment is primary in primates and humans. The approach really focuses on the importance of attachment and its impact, not only on the developing child but on the adult as well, including the personality-disordered adult. I think that pathological processes are in essence normal, it's just that they have run a different algorithm, have a different content.

I think that early attachments set the patterns that affect the adult, whether they are normal or pathological. There are direct links between them. The chief complaint can almost always be framed in terms of copying the important attachment objects: mom, dad, older brother, uncle, aunt—to be like him or her (otherwise known as *identification*), to act as if he or she were still there which I call *recapitulation*, maintaining the role you always had, and/or *introjection*, Sullivan's idea of treating yourself as he or she did.

And those copying processes are startlingly direct. You can track the connections, using the Structural Analysis of Social Behavior (SASB) model, which strips down interactions (interpersonal or intrapsychic) in terms of *focus*, that is: on another person, or on the self, or turned inward; in terms of *love and hate*; and in terms of *enmeshment and differentiation*. If you use that lens you can see those links, those copy processes. The pathology then is reflecting early patterns rather directly. The implication of that is that you have to decide to stop trying to work along the old patterns. That brings us to the question, "Why would people want to do that?" I think it's in the primate's hardware—to copy. I like the concept of psychic proximity, the intrapsychic version of Bowlby's lesson that the toddler derives security by going back to the parent or the early object, derives the courage to go out in the world and be healthy, or clings, or is ambivalent, or whatever. Copying the old ways is a way to get closer to the internalization and thus is a way to achieve psychic proximity. So when you do maladaptive things, you do them in order to get closer to the loved one who is associated with those patterns. So therapy means giving up the old fantasies of "kiss and make up," or "if only it had been better," or "to do it again," or to wreak revenge. If you can do this, you really separate from the bad object. Therapy is just a learning process, but the hardest step is giving up the old patterns.

Therapy has five main steps. These five steps cut across schools of therapy—you can use client-centered therapy, Gestalt, psychoanalysis, as long as it sticks to these five steps, in relation to the case formulation based on this attachment theory and the copy process idea. One is *collaborating against the problem patterns*, which does not mean that when the therapist and the patient are kind of friendly, they are collaborating. It could be enabling a problem pattern if they're having a good time. The second domain that is correct is that anything you can do to *help the person recognize these patterns*, who they are copying and what for, is good therapy. The third domain is *blocking maladaptive patterns*, and that can range all the way from suicidality or homocidality to subtle undermining of therapy, like talking about irrelevant things. The fourth domain is the most important one: anything you can do to *enable the will to change*, and that is the hardest one. To get on the unconscious level to the willingness to let go and grieve about the old wishes and fantasies. This takes the most creativity and it is where the therapist and the therapy relationship are the most crucial. The fifth domain is *learning new patterns*. A lot of what is called the behavioral technology is great, but they don't do anything until you have done the homework on the preceding steps.

Keeping those five steps in mind enables you to evaluate on a moment-to-moment basis whether you are on track or not. If whatever you do doesn't fit one of those categories, you probably are not well focused and you're probably wasting time. The hypotheses about the links are absolutely concrete enough so that an independent observer can look at the interview data and say, "Those copy processes are there or they are not." The patient and the therapist have to agree to the presence of these processes before I consider it to be a valid case formulation.

Do you think your work resembles Jeffrey Young's schema-focused work?

Well, I think that it does. I've been borrowing shamelessly from an awful lot of people. Actually this approach I've been describing is not anything new at all. I like to think of it as a way of codifying good clinical wisdom.

This reminds me of George Kelly's (1969) construct theory, where he says that everybody always works from a theory and constantly adapts it to new data. Do you recognize that?

Oh, yes. His was another way of organizing object relations. His methodology is a little more open-ended than mine.

You mentioned the term SASB, but perhaps for our readers this needs a little clarification.

SASB stands for Structural Analysis of Social Behavior, and is a model for describing interpersonal and intrapsychic interactions in terms of three underlying dimensions. One dimension concerns *the focus.* Are you focused on the other, or on yourself, or are you focused internally? These last two sound familiar, but they're not. Focusing on yourself means focusing on yourself in reaction to someone else, and the third focus I mentioned is turning your focus inward. To give an example, focus on an other is "I'm going to kill you"; focus on yourself in relation to an other is "I'm afraid that you will kill me and I'm going to get out of here"; and internalized aggression is "I'm going to kill myself."

The other dimensions are *love and hate,* which everyone recognizes quite easily, and *differentiation and enmeshment.* At the one extreme of enmeshment, one person is in control and the other submits. At the other extreme one person lets the other one go and do whatever he or she wants, and the complement of that is to go ahead and do it.

So it's differentiation and enmeshment. There is a technology going along with this—questionnaires, a coding system, software—to tighten up the definition of what these patterns are, and it's very handy for seeing under what conditions there is identification and imitation, under what conditions does a person maintain his childhood role, and under what conditions does one internalize.

Which personal motives have led you to this specific choice of therapy and research?

Well, the highly socialized answer to this is that I value the integration of science and practice. So it seems to me that it's very important to put these together—science and the intuitive gift of the clinician—in order to figure out what it's all about, and that is in order to relieve suffering. The more accurate you are, the

more effective you are, and thus the more helpful you are. I did
not sort of force this to evolve, I sort of feel that I found it. There
is so much clinical wisdom, there are so many gifted clinicians!
This SASB thing seemed to be a way to describe it and the attachment theory seems to be just overwhelmingly compelling.
When you've been a parent and have seen infants, and how potent these attachment processes are—like when you see your child
doing things the way you're doing them and won't admit—the copy
stuff, and the power of the attachment. So personal experience
as a parent and as a therapist and my respect for the science of it,
those I think were motivators.

Can you share the nonsocialized answer with us as well?

Of course. At a more personal level, the love of science came from
my attachment to my father. And the fact that I fell in love with
my chemistry professor when I was a freshman at college. He was
a very charismatic guy and he described the periodic table. I hadn't
had any chemistry in high school and I thought: "Oh, my! Isn't
that amazing! You have two dimensions, atomic weight and number, and you can classify every element there is and everything is
described in terms of interactions among them, *everything!*" There
were holes in that table (this was in the fifties, a long time ago),
and subsequently they discovered elements that had predicted
attributes and I thought: "Man! The power of organization, of
describing something in terms of underlying dimensions, is as-
tonishing!" So I wanted (really, this was very grandiose) to do this
in terms of behavior. And so I was affected by the people I ran
into. My psychology professor was the first one. He was George
Heise, a behaviorist (Skinnerian), a teacher at Oberlin College.
He was fresh out of Harvard, he brought Skinner's principles in
the late fifties, and it was not at all accepted at the time. He put
his dog on the table and said: "This is Edward, and when Edward
comes to the edge of the table, he is going to stop." And I thought,
"Wow! This is amazing, he can make that prediction!" At the same
time it's obvious, but somehow George got across the idea of what

behavioral science was all about. So between the chemistry professor and the psychology professor I had those internalizations
that talked about putting things together. And there was my father as well. That's one level down!

We don't want to go all the way down, do we?

Right. But I should add Harry Harlow, my major professor. He
published a paper called "The Nature of Love." He talked about
contact comfort and attachment and he had John Bowlby visit the
primate lab when I was a graduate student there and I watched
Bowlby tell Harlow that he didn't have to abuse monkeys to create neurosis, he had done so simply by putting them in social iso-
lation. And I was there when it happened! Just take a primate away
from its attachment objects and you've ruined it. Nowadays they're
showing neurochemical changes when that sort of thing is done
to individuals. And so Harlow and Bowlby are very important in
my development too.

*Could you share some of your personal thoughts about psychotherapy
in general and your place in the field?*

Well, for the therapist's side of it, the most painful thought is that
there's a lot of therapy that's not helpful. I have sometimes been
guilty of that as well, I think. I have been not effective, not well
focused, not as helpful as I could have been, for a variety of reasons. I think a lot of that goes on, so to some extent we deserve
the bad name we've got. Also there are ill-informed theories too,
which are sometimes not helpful. For example if you have just a
technique, like facilitating the expression of anger, and you don't
do this in an informed way, you can be iatrogenic. That's why I
emphasize case formulation, and thoughtful, mindful reflection
on what you are doing and why. So that's a problem.

In a broader sense, the state of the art is wanting. Part of my
motivation is to help improve this. I think combining a gifted-
ness with a data-based orientation is the way to do that. On the

patient's side I think, more than I ever thought before, that the motives to stay ill are really potent. And, more often than I thought, eroticized!

I've written about a thing I called a Klute syndrome, something I thought was relatively isolated, and what I say in it—I am coming closer and closer to what Freud started out saying—that sexuality is incredibly important. I'm not just talking about an energy that's misdirected, I'm talking about people with severe disorders, the persistent, crazy, maladaptive ones, who have eroticized their chief complaint. It's SASB codable! As the problem pattern goes, so goes the sexual fantasy.

> For example I first discovered this when I met a schizoidal man, although I have claimed that I never really saw a schizoid. This was a sort of withdrawn, avoidant type of person, whose masturbatory fantasies were about unavailable women. I discovered this after puzzling about how he would meet someone and a relationship would start and then she would disappear. He kept on reliving this unavailability. Of course as a therapist I was the most unavailable target of his fantasies, so I had to say: "Look, you have to have three dates before you can see me again." So I put him on a contingency of succeeding in attaching to others in order to have access to me. I switched the vector, so he could not go on being avoidant and hurting and have me at the same time; he had to do it the other way around, and so he did. Eventually he got married.

The most familiar version is eroticizing masochism, for instance where degradation and humiliation are eroticized. Some people, impaired providers, have eroticized helping and giving. And they get exploited and burned out. When you look at the SASB codes of their sexual fantasies, and compare them to the SASB codes of their chief complaint and you see the similarity, it's shockingly common and dramatic.

We have worked for a long time with people who say they want to change their patterns, but they are very powerfully reinforcing their problem patterns in their sexual life. When I work with that and talk about that, it's just explosive! People will say things like: "I know you're right, but my life is so miserable that this is the only thing I have, I don't want to give it up." Then I'm stuck with the dilemma: Shall I continue to spend time with this person? You know, it's an addiction like alcoholism or drugs. Where do you set the limit? Iatrogenic therapeutic behaviors and behavior patterns of the patient that reinforce their problems, they are the two things that worry me a lot.

Now, here you ask me about my private thoughts, and I come up with my worries!

Well, that's you, isn't it? And you do something about those worries, by stressing the scientific attitude in psychotherapy.

That's right.

Have there been other influences apart from the ones you already mentioned?

Well, anyone who looks at psychopathology in a developmental way just has to acknowledge Freud. I think his paper on "Mourning and Melancholia" (1917) is marvelous, and in this age of taking drugs to feel good and to suppress your depression, I think Freud's very interpersonal analysis of depression is stunning. He talks about depression being related to someone who is, was, or ought to have been, or ought to be loved. That the target of the depression most likely was someone who was close and dear. That's anger turned inward. You never get tired of reading Freud, it's like Shakespeare. And some of the master clinicians from that era have influenced me as well: Frieda Fromm-Reichmann (1959) is a particular favorite of mine, and Harry Stack Sullivan (1953), of course, when he talks about interpersonal object relations. These are more concrete versions of psychoanalysis.

What about Alfred Adler? He influenced Sullivan.

Yes, but Adler's ideas really fall out on the power dimension of the
SASB system and that's only 25 percent. But actually all the interactive object relations psychoanalytic people have influenced me.
And Carl Rogers (1951) was very influential too. He was my supervisor for six months when I was a postdoctoral fellow at the University of Wisconsin Medical School. He and I got along very well.
I think he has had a lot of influence on a lot of people. Me included.

*Have there been important changes in your way of thinking in the
course of time?*

I think I started off as a pretty average professional, with a lot of
respect for my professors, especially the great names. I thought
they knew what it was all about. I wanted to find out from them
what it was. Then gradually, not all at once, the feeling grew that
there was something not quite right. And instead of getting disillusioned, angry, withdrawn or depressed, I thought: "We've got
to figure this out!" Actually, I was helped a lot because in the sixties I was married, so I couldn't have a job at the same university
[as my husband] and I couldn't move. I had infants and the administration did not like to see pregnant women in the hospital,
so I got moved to an office off by myself, and I had a lot of space
and time to think and I was not overwhelmed by committees. I
wasn't permitted to see patients because that was not good. I was
permitted to be a research consultant, to put out some house
publications, service stuff like that. Also that gave me a lot of free
time. I learned to use a computer, not one of those laptops, but a
huge one that filled up a room this size with its vacuum tubes
and so on. For a machine like that, you drop a box of perforated
cards, and you're out of business!

Having infants, I was learning an awful lot about behavior and
attachment, just building a wonderful background, and that's when
the SASB model hatched. Then the women's movement in America
became more influential, and the residents started to demand to

have a female supervisor. I had young children and was working half-time, and I thought it would be a good idea if I could have some clinical practice again, so I was kind of reintegrated. By then, I had had that fertile period and I'm grateful for it, even though at the time I felt frustrated and abused. I felt excluded. The supervisors would say things like: "If a man goes into therapy he has got to decide between being a patient or a man, if he has a female therapist." That helped me get rid of the idealization! And it enforced differentiation and reflecting for myself. My father used to say: "There is something good in everything," and in this case there was.

What changes have you gone through in the past few years?

I wrote a book, *Interpersonal Diagnosis of Personality Disorders* (1996). Since then my ideas have been more sharply organized around the idea that every psychopathology is a gift of love, and around the idea of the three copy processes. And I keep stumbling back onto this sexuality thing. That's not something I wanted, you see, but I do only work with the severely disordered and they are people who are very often quite gifted but are way off track and seemingly very irrational. I mean people who keep doing self-defeating things or continuing problematic behavior despite all kinds of good insight. With their behavior having become sexualized, no wonder they can't change it!

I remember Kernberg saying, "If the sexuality has gone out of people, when everything has become de-eroticized so to speak, I start worrying, while I can still work with even the most perverted people."

Well, as to the relationship between sexuality and aggression, in the SASB model they are opposite on the horizontal axis.

And should they remain opposite? As Kernberg says, they should not merge?

No, although in America they're merged all the time. Especially if you think of aggression as having a strong component of power.

I think Konrad Lorenz, the ethologist, talks about attachment inhibiting the given of aggression. In psychoanalysis, the basic energies are aggression and sexuality (Thanatos and Eros). American analysts are very much in love with aggression; for them, unless you're in touch with your anger and the basic destructiveness, you're off track. But I've gone to the other pole: I think that love drives everything. The wish to be merged with and forgiven by and to forgive the early attachments, that's what organizes everything. In fact, when aggression comes up in therapy, I usually insist that it be translated into what I think are its biological purposes, which are to implement control or distance. I don't think of it as a basic energy that has to be drained off, but rather as a servant of control or of distance, enmeshment or differentiation. Aggression is often a defense against being controlled, or against not being in control. From this perspective, getting rid of the aggression in a cathartic model doesn't make sense.

When you just talked about your severely disturbed patients, you seemed very compassionate. What do you think of Marsha Linehan's subtitle for Dialectical Behavior Theory—for effective compassion?

Well, that's a very American word. Efficacy is everything in the USA nowadays. Efficacy, to many people's minds, is in opposition to compassion and an empathic position. Empathy can both enable problem patterns and encourage a person to fight them. It's important to be on the fighting side and not on the enabling side. That way, I can understand that subtitle. Linehan knows intuitively how to be empathic in a way that discourages pathology and enhances strength. Marsha talks a lot about validating and other good stuff like that, and the purpose is to change problematic behavior. Actually we are both data-based. Different kinds of data though!

You see, Marsha is one of the few people who has actually developed an approach, implemented it, and gotten real data in real clinical situations in really tough cases, and shown effective-

ness. That's real efficacy! The measures are of parasuicidal behaviors, depressive symptoms, and some rating scales and those
are also very American: empirically based and very medical. And
I'm talking about internalizations. When you change those, you
also change these other things, but my concern is a person's relationship to himself. To get an idea about long-term change, really structural change—as I call it, reconstructive therapy—you
need a different kind of funding for your research because nowadays only short-term research gets grants. If the point is to save
money, let's take a look at the whole system for a two-year period
instead of looking for a six-week symptom change. I'm sure that
more basic changes would save money in the long run.

*Some people might worry that Marsha's method causes so much at-
tachment to the therapy—or maybe the therapist—that this will work
very well in the first one or two years after therapy, but perhaps it
might be a disadvantage in later phases of the treatment, where you
have to disconnect or differentiate from your therapist.*

Well, I think Marsha is a great "IPIR"—that is, she's strong on
important persons and their internalized representations. She is
really warm and wise and compelling. I'm sure that's an important part of the process. Whether or not this will keep people going
for a long time is a very important question, and not just concerning Marsha's approach. How do you, as a therapist, get internalized in a benevolent way without creating a dependency that's
iatrogenic and problematic? That's one of the big problems in
therapy in general. The therapist's getting internalized may be a
very good thing for the patient! There's nothing wrong with that.
The new process of internalization is the same as the earlier ones
were, only this time it's therapeutic. For that reason I encourage
patients to have relationships outside of therapy, because these
other people are going to be new internalizations. I do couple
therapy, family therapy, I mix it all up, as long as it leads to the
internalization of new patterns.

That is part of your fifth step?

Yes. But the therapist–client relationship is also part of step four, enabling the will to change. Many people, faced with a difficult situation, will have an internal dialogue, thinking: "What would therapist so-and-so have to say now?" Group therapy is very powerful in that way. I think group therapy is way underdeveloped as a method of internalization. There are so many possible implants! And it's the therapist's job to make sure they're good implants. So I'm a pretty controlling group therapist. I don't let them scapegoat. None of that catharting!

Is there any other kind of change that you haven't mentioned yet?

Well, when you're data-based and questing to figure things out, then you're supposed to be changing! To be growing. You're never finished.

Does your approach have limitations?

Sure. When someone is able to get relief from what they want by getting medication, they should take it. By all means, they should. If they can take a behavioral intervention and get relief that way, they shouldn't go into long-term therapy. That would be silly.

> I just was struggling with a case this past week. A husband of a former patient of mine, an older man who had had a serious alcohol problem, came and wanted to work through some old childhood issues through long-term therapy. And I'm kind of scared to open that up with him. This might make him go back to drinking, and he's doing so well, I'm not sure that this is appropriate. He's older, he's recovering now, and he's doing very well. I shouldn't mess with that! This stuff is serious and the outcome is not guaranteed. It's like a kid-

ney transplant: unless you're in serious trouble, you should
not fool around with it.

How intensive are your therapies? Four or five times a week?

No. I would like to do that. But under the economic constraints
that we have in the United States, the most I usually can give them
is twice a week. As you know the difference between once and
twice a week is enormous.

*Might not an analyst say, "Look, if you see a patient twice a week,
you are causing a severe transference neurosis, and that's what cures
the patient, not your data-based approach?*

So what? The theory states that it's all about attachment being
primary. Psychopathology is a gift of love, and so is health. And
so the healthy part of the patient (or client) is that he wants to go
through all this, which isn't fun. They do develop an attachment
to me, to you, to those analysts. And if the therapists are blank
screens, the attachment is to the patient's projection, but there
is an attachment. And they do internalize me, I'm not afraid to
admit that. I think I have to be palpable, so they know what they're
internalizing. Actually I think internalization, dominance, and
warmth facilitate imitation in the primate at all ages and in all
contexts. If you want to call that a transference cure, it's okay with
me. It's taking a warm, competent figure and using that to guide
yourself in better ways. It's the old question—Is it the insight, or
is it the therapy relationship that cures? And the scientific data
show overwhelmingly that it is the relationship much more than
the other. Basically the findings are that it doesn't matter which
technique, or what school.

I have not yet put it to empirical tests, although I would like
to, but all the techniques that we have should be used selectively
and in a context of case-formulation. I like to think that this attachment–internalization–copy process theory helps one to choose

wisely from all the various techniques. If you do that, it will make little difference which technique you use.

Could you say your approach is not suitable for some gifts of love? For instance, Otto Kernberg would say malignant narcissists are beyond help with his approach.

Well, I think the model is generic. But the two-person talking therapy setting is inappropriate with some individuals, like for instance antisocials. You can talk till you're blue in the face and still not touch them. But the model of internalizations and attachments works with them. You can take an antisocial and put him in a wartime situation with a tough and protective sergeant-father figure and he can be transformed, because in those life-threatening circumstances he can learn to trust others and internalize the platoon leader. Sometimes you can take quite delinquent children and put them on a survival course or in wilderness training and because of the control you have over the whole situation, you see them internalize important others.

Have you ever really failed?

Absolutely. Of course we have a tendency to say our successes are ours, and our failures are our patients', but since this is a shared process it usually works both ways. Actually I keep trying to work out how to minimize those occurrences where it doesn't work. Generically, my most common problem is being too intense too fast, getting to it in ways that would horrify analysts. On average I do have effective therapies, but this approach sometimes scares them away. On the other hand, my favorite kind of client is a gifted person who is pretty severely disordered. I have seen a lot of them doing wonderful things in therapy and really blossom.

To be more specific, a fairly recent one was a very bright professional person, a microbiologist who had been in cognitive-behavioral therapy for eight years and had been severely suicidal. She had been hospitalized three times, her functioning at work had degraded severely, she was on four classes of medication, and got referred because her therapist was scared she was coming down to another hospitalization. It's very appropriate to refer when a case gets stuck. I've done it myself a couple of times. Her self-destructive suicidal thinking was just nuts! We have worked together now for two and a half years, and her prescribing physician says she can't believe the changes in her. Her children and her colleagues all agree. It's just marvelous to see such things going on.

What was it you gave the patient that the other therapist didn't give?

My own assessment is that the self-destructiveness and the relentless suicidality were virtues, and this was supported by her religious ideas. So one of the earlier things I did was ask her to bring me a bible and show me the verses that supported this. She was so relieved, she said, to find someone who understood the importance religion had for her. Of course, she could not find any verses that supported her ideas. These self-destructive ideas were eroticized, and, most importantly, in the family she had a role to play. Her parents fought bitterly all the time and she overheard that, and a lot of it was about her. When she was born her father could not go on with his career and he was miserable about that, and it was all because of the baby coming. So she grew up with the idea that she had to take the blame for things that she really wasn't to blame for. Since her religion was that it's good to be self-sacrificing and to do good for others, this fitted in.

The cognitive therapist left out the religious part. Is that why you were more successful?

Well, I use cognitive therapy all the time, but always in this frame, that it is the atttachments that count, that reinforcements are always in terms of the gift of love. So when she was suicidal, she was recapitulating her early martyrish role, she was attacking herself as she was attacked, and she was loving those early internalizations. So cognitive-behavioral techniques are relevant when put into that frame. I do things that scare even cognitive therapists, like being very forceful when I stop a patient from doing self-destructive things or following self-destructive trains of thought. After awhile she could say the things that I would say: that she was being a lightning rod again, that she was being loyal to her parents. And then I'd ask her about her sexuality and she would say: "Not so good. I do what he wants." I would say: "How do you get rid of these messages if you keep doing that?" She made the choice to give up her sexual pleasure and try to recondition more benign images. This was very costly to her, but she decided to do it. And stuck to it! I would say that was the most important thing that she did in therapy.

Could you name two or three books, not written by yourself, that you would recommend to a reader?

The complete works of Sigmund Freud, (grins widely) just for starters. Frieda Fromm-Reichmann (1959) is great, Carl Rogers is great, and like I said: John Bowlby is great. You know, the classical wisdom is good stuff!

Are you talking about the authors in general or specific books by them?

For Rogers, *Client Centered Therapy* (1951). For Bowlby, *Attachment and Loss* (1969, 1973, 1980). Well, some authors are more repetitious than others, like Carl Rogers.

Is there anything of importance that we haven't touched on and that you would like to elaborate on?

Well, about deviating from my approach. It's hard to deviate from it because it's so flexible. Like in general, self-disclosure isn't good in therapy, but if it fits into the model it's all right! Especially self-disclosures of vulnerabilities and failures can be very useful. Not to model self-destructiveness, but to model being compassionate with your own weaknesses. I do other things that would horrify analysts, like sometimes I do a home visit—if I have to avoid a hospitalization, for instance. But then I set a limit on that.

The Situations

In the middle of the night, you're called on the phone by a patient who threatens to commit suicide. What would you do?

I would process it in terms of case formulation, I can't answer the question generically. It depends a lot on who the person is, on what is going on, and on what the therapy relationship is.

> One borderline patient called me in the middle of the night on the day that she got engaged. She said: "I have the razors out and I want to cut!" I in effect said, "Well, call your father. I think he will be more interested in this than I am." Of course I didn't leave it at that, but we discussed the background of it: she had a long history of an incestual relationship with her father. Getting married was betraying him, and she would re-create the pain that she experienced with him as a way of loving him. Then she put away the razors and we were done.

Actually the first thing to ask is "Where are you?" So that if you don't handle the call well enough, at least you know where to send the police. And then "Who's there with you?" so you know the kind of support you have, who can take the person to the hospital.

Now this patient is so excited that these few questions take twenty minutes to get the answers to. And it's still the middle of the night.

Well, I won't give them that much time in the middle of the night. I tell them my contract with ongoing cases is that if they are feeling suicidal they promise to call me and reach me and talk about it and try to contain it instead of acting on it. I don't ask them to sign a non-suicide contract: that's silly, they can't. But I just ask them to go over it with me. Just leaving a message on the answering machine isn't enough. We've got to talk. And they have to agree, also, that if we can't resolve it and contain it safely, they will come and talk to me in the office.

You do that? In the night?

Yes. Or I go to the hospital. I have a strong commitment, once I work with a person. But they'd better not fool around with me and they know that. I'll be there if they're really in trouble. I don't always do it. If they're using alcohol and they're drunk, they are on their own. They will have to go to the hospital and I'll see them when they get out.

And if they refuse to go to the hospital and keep on threatening to suicide, you send the police to them?

If I need to. I have never had to, though. Usually I ask them who else is there, and I talk to that person.

You mentioned quite a few rules for crisis management. Are you familiar with that field?

Yes. In the sixties I formed a crisis group, and we worked with the police. I also have been in charge of an emergency room, both in-patient and outpatient. But these rules are not really anything else than basic good sense, aren't they? My preferred way is dynamic crisis handling, but it has to be within a safe setting. Then I usually make it clear to the patient, "Listen, this is not therapy we're do-ing. Therapy is like learning to swim. And if you have this crisis stuff, we are just preserving the option to learn later. In the mean-time, I'm only keeping you from drowning." If they still keep up this stuff, I make it clear that our approach isn't working. That way I usually get "control" of suicidal acting-out very quickly. Again, I sometimes cut them off too soon and they go to somebody else. Paradoxically, by this long-term approach (which is important for a holding relationship to develop), I get good management in a month or two. This way, they want to maintain the relationship and know they risk losing it if they don't get it together and get to work.

What would you do if a patient comes to the appointed session in an obvious state of inebriation?

I had that a few weeks ago! Again, it's a matter of case formulation. This was the first time it happened. It was a complicated situation and so I had the session with her. I heard some things that she wanted to say that she could not say otherwise. At the end I asked her if she was inebriated and she said she was and asked what I thought about that. I said I thought she should not have done it and would she agree not to do it again. She said "Yes." If it's just acting out, I would say, "Well, I think we're just wasting time."

Do you understand that some of the others we interviewed would say, "I would stop the session right away"?

Well, it's a good rule and basically I believe that. Ordinarily I wouldn't even agree to work with people who use alcohol as the solution to problems, because psychotherapy is a learning pro-cess and you can't learn when you're under the influence. Unless they're committed to control that. I would like it a lot better if they went to AA or NA to solve that problem. I threaten all the time that I will stop treatment if they don't. But I haven't quite figured out yet exactly how tough to be in such cases. There were periods in my life when I used different approaches.

You meet one of your patients at a cocktail party and he or she wants to use this opportunity to have an ordinary social meeting with you for a change and starts to chat with you. What would you do?

Chat! Ordinary living-room tact is never a mistake.

A patient turns out to be in the neighborhood of your front door every time you come home. Just standing in the street.

My house is kind of isolated, so that situation would be really bizarre. But I understand the meaning of your question. I would talk about it of course. It would depend upon what the patient's problem was. If it's just an ordinary neurotic, I'd just talk about it. If the patient is murderous, or homocidal or suicidal, I would be a lot tougher about it. "You cut that out, or we are finished."

What if he did this because he wanted to know all kinds of things about you and your private life? No bad intentions, but an adolescent-like being in love, for instance?

I would talk about that in the light of his or her internalizations, and how this relates to problem patterns. In any case, I try to avoid a power struggle if I can help it.

You discover that something from your office has been taken away by a patient—"borrowed," stolen, or maybe just picked up on an impulse. You know who did it. What would you do?

Talk about it, why not?

Would you demand it back?

It might depend on what it was. If it was something really personal or sentimental, I probably would. It would be too much of an invasion in my private life, and a breach of trust.

What if the person denies it and you are certain?

There would be nothing I could do. I'm sure that if this therapy would go along, we would discuss it later and then we would work it out.

You would not stop therapy because of the breach of trust?

No, colleagues do worse things all the time! You know, life is tough. Like Harry Truman said: "If you can't stand the heat, get out of the kitchen." If you work with people with severe disorders, they are primitive people; you have to take some hits.

Our last question: Could you describe the setting in which you see your patients? Is it a private room? Are there any personal things there, like pictures of your family or works of art, to name a few examples?

Right now it's an office in the university and I don't see patients at home. It's a large office, comfortably furnished. There is a couch, but I don't have people lie down on it, though I have done that in the past. It's not intense enough. You don't get the internalization and the hot therapy going that way. There are pictures of my family. Art objects, but nothing expensive or fancy. Personal things, little gifts from patients over the years. A lovely little plaque that says: "Life is lived forward and understood backwards." Posters of the Utah mountains. That's about it, I think.

4

John Clarkin

Biography

John Clarkin is a Professor of Clinical Psychology in the Department of Psychiatry of the Cornell University Medical College, and the Director of Psychology for the New York Hospital at both the Payne Whitney Clinic and the Westchester Division. In this role, he is the Director of a large clinical psychology staff and is in charge of two predoctoral internship programs and specialized postdoctoral training programs in psychology.

Dr. Clarkin's clinical research has focused on the assessment of individual and family treatment within several patient populations. For the last twelve years he has directed a large-scale clinical study of the effect of psychodynamic psychotherapy with severely disturbed borderline-disorder patients. He has obtained a National Institute of Mental Health Treatment Development grant to further this work. Funded by a grant from the NIMH, he also conducted a clinical trial of the effectiveness of marital treatment as added to standard pharmacotherapy for couples in which one member suffers from bipolar disorder.

Dr. Clarkin's academic publications are numerous and multifaceted. His research publications are on the phenomenology of personality disorders, especially borderline personality disorder, and in the clinical outcome of family therapy as applied to seriously disturbed patients. A major area of academic interest has been the delineation in several textbooks and in books of clinical cases of the principles of differential treatment planning in psychiatry.

Dr. Clarkin completed his Ph.D. in clinical psychology at Fordham University, Graduate School of Arts and Sciences, in 1971. He completed internship training and further research training at the New York State Psychiatric Institute. He has been with the New York Hospital-Cornell Medical Center since 1970.

The Interview

Doctor Clarkin, we would like to start this interview by asking you to give us a brief outline of the basic tenets of your approach. Since you are better known as a researcher, and not as the proponent of a specific theory, your answer will probably be guided by the research you do on the work of others. Is that right?

Yes. Historically I was trained as a clinical psychologist, in cognitive-behavioral therapy, in interpersonal treatment and in family and marital treatment. Actually, some of my research and a lot of my work at Cornell is with couples. Historically my orientation has not been psychodynamic. But over the years my basic orientation has been to assume that there is no one perfect treatment, but rather that there are many treatments. There are many different kinds of patients, different kinds of situations. One of my first publications was with Allen Frances (well-known for his work on *DSM*) who was my colleague at the time, and Sam Perry, who has since died but who was a revered colleague at Cornell and did a lot of research on HIV. We (Frances et al. 1984) wrote a book called *Differential Therapeutics in Psychiatry*. Our opinion then was that different people should get different kinds of treatments. This was 1979. We were amazed that at that point in time we couldn't find in psychiatry any differential therapeutic manuals, so you couldn't tell the residents "Go look up the differential therapy for this specific disorder."

I ran the outpatient clinic, and Al Frances was head of the walk-in department and the emergency room. This was the Payne Whitney Clinic on the East Side of Manhattan, a clinic for all comers. Back in that time, when we asked our residents in psychiatry to interview a patient and make a treatment plan, they were wonderful at doing an in-depth interview and making a diagnosis, psychodynamically formulated, but when you asked them which treatment they would recommend, they would at first be astounded. Then they would advise either the medication dispensed from a clinic, or long-term psychodynamic psychotherapy. There must be other alternatives! So we started looking at the indications and contraindications for all kinds of therapies that were current back in the seventies, and then we would ask them "When would you give this treatment to this person?" That kind of reflects my own training in various kinds of treatment.

My basic tenet is also a research one. I have always assumed that the answer to each of these questions should be embedded in a research study, and in research evidence that this approach for this patient is effective. Since then there have been numerous studies that show that specific treatments are in fact successful with specific patient populations. Then, and still today, we will never have all the research that we need. So you have to train psychology fellows and psychiatry residents to use the research and their own head. In the USA with managed care now, you have to defend those decisions with a lot of information, and many of your decisions are being co-opted because they are reducing the length of the treatments. To summarize, there is no one treatment that fits everyone. There is probably an armamentarium that can be used and whenever possible we should get data to substantiate what we are trying to say.

Do you nevertheless have a favorite approach?

Well, there is an interesting split in my own life about that. I enjoy and do a lot of marital therapy. For reasons of referral these tend

to be middle-aged couples in some difficulty and in a relationship of some duration. I try all kinds of approaches with them,
from cognitive-behavioral to a kind of object relations approach.
The other side of the split is studying Kernberg's treatment, which
is very clearly an object relational, transference-focused, psychodynamically oriented approach.

Do you still do therapy?

Yes.

Which tenets do you use then?

I try to gauge the level of interventions that my clients can be
comfortable with. For example, some couples will initially seem
to clearly want a concrete, problem-solving approach. Others
would see that approach as simplistic, as common-sense, as something that their grandmother could tell them. They want an expanded understanding of what's going on, and why they interact
that way. I use my assessment of where the couple is at, and I try
to be flexible and take the lead from the couple.

What is it in you, to make you adjust to what they expect?

You could trace that kind of behavior of mine in other realms of
life. You could safely say that I'm consistent. I was a first-born,
who certainly had his turn at trying to negotiate between his parents. I am a director of psychology and I try to direct by sniffing
out where people are going to go anyway, and then use that to
bend it a little bit to where I think they should go. I'm also doing
research with an individual who in many ways (and I mean this
respectfully) knows what the answers should be and it seems to
me that my position should be as the one who does not know
where the answers are, just to listen and accommodate to how
the data come out.

Is this sort of diplomatic attitude a reason for your position being so broadly accepted among researchers of all kinds of approaches? You are accepted by Marsha Linehan, by Otto Kernberg's team—professionals all over the world accept your knowledge in this field.

I would like to think that's because they know that I listen very carefully and I try to understand what they're saying. I would not like to think that it's accommodating just to accommodate. I have my pet arguments with each of them. But they also know that I try to use what seems sound to me in each of their orientations. I believe that when you look at expert therapists, like Dr. Kernberg or Dr. Linehan, you can always find very powerful and accurate things they're doing. I get a thrill out of finding things that they do alike, but describe in quite different metaphors. Because when you look at one level they are doing quite different things, but at another level they may actually be doing the same thing. For some reason that kind of intrigues me. I don't believe there are as many really different therapies as the literature suggests.

We met you while attending a research meeting at Cornell in White Plains, where we were impressed by your capacity to listen to the other person's needs. Do you recognize that?

Yes. It seems to me that I've been very lucky to work with a very talented group of people at Cornell in psychotherapy research since 1970. Each one of these people is quite talented, an expert in his or her own right. The only way you keep a group of people like that together, rather than have them split off and go their own way, is by trying to make sure that each one of them has a respected role in the group, that they all feel in a real sense that they're contributing to their own development and that of their group.

If that doesn't occur, the person will either create problems in the group, and that can be quite difficult for the group, or he will leave, which sometimes I think may be the best thing.

Do you think your own tendencies to be a prima donna are less well developed than in others?

I wouldn't say that. I suspect that if somebody else wanted to play the role that I play, I could get quite upset about that. But it hasn't occurred. Maybe I'm lucky! (laughs)

Maybe you have a good way of selecting your colleagues. Or you're better in doing this job of directing. You have a very well-developed capacity for listening. You are to some extent the perfect counselor. Somebody presents an idea to you and discusses it with you, and you help them understand their own ideas better.

In fact that's a role I've enjoyed a great deal with Dr. Kernberg. When I first read his earliest books in English, I felt they were basically Germanic (with the verbs almost at the end of the sentence), and over the years I have repeatedly said, "I don't understand this, be more concrete!" And I don't need an excuse for that, because if I have to measure this or that, I need concrete information. The best illustration of that is the treatment manual. The first version came out in 1989 and we now have the second manual (Clarkin et al. 1998). I think the manual has grown tremendously from 1989 till now. I don't think this is because Dr. Kernberg knows his theory better. The theory is the same, but I do think that because of constant questioning it has been amplified and made more concrete. Also, the manual has been tremendously improved as we actually do the treatment with different therapists and different personalities, and consequently use different ways of applying it.

There's an interesting paradox in this. Most of my European fellow researchers do not believe that you can manualize a treatment. Certainly not a treatment that is not cognitive, that is, psychodynamic, and one that is longer than twelve or thirteen sessions, say, a year long. And they have a point, for they think a manual is like the book that fits into the glove compartment of your car and tells you where the carburetor is and how many pounds of air you put in your tires. That is a different kind of manual. Our manual is specific enough to help in training therapists.

That is actually another theme in my life. I am director of psychology, which means we have a large number of psychiatric residents, a number of psychology interns, and so on. I don't think we teach people how to do psychotherapy very well. I don't think we're concrete enough about it. Most therapists, at least in the psychodynamic tradition, are supervised on the notes that they make and that they think describe the sessions that they had. Whereas the part of the session that they cannot put down in notes and that they missed is often the most important part, which you could only see if you had audio or video tapes. I can't prove this, but it's my impression. So the closer you get to the material, the more specific your supervisory interventions will be.

You describe yourself as the perfect helper, and you started as a therapist. Then gradually you became interested in data and now you focus on research instead of helping people. Why?

Well, keep in mind that the training of a clinical psychologist is very much oriented toward data, but despite that it's also true that I went into it looking more for clinical work. The first part of my career was almost entirely that. At this point in my life I would say that it's partly related to the fact that my father was an engineer. I believe in wiring. I believe that your brain and your temperament are wired in certain ways. I think there are two kinds of clinical psychologists and I always try to have both kinds in my faculty. One is the therapists. Give them a choice and they'll do another therapy session, and they are very attuned to everything that's going on. The other kind has a good relationship with their mother and an engineer for a father. They are people who both appreciate the interpersonal aspects of life and also have a sense of data. My journey went from being more therapy oriented to then wanting what I considered to be more the real thing—that is, the answer to the question "Where is the truth?" Well, truth is also an illusion, (laughs) but it's a helpful one.

Do you think you might be bored doing more therapies and less research?

If I did only psychotherapy I would be bored. In fact, I have never done that. It's always been a combination of administration, psychotherapy, and research. And of course teaching.

Could you explain how this developed over the years? We now know that you have a personality trait that's helpful in doing the things you do, that is, your receptiveness. But that doesn't explain everything. What else has played a part?

I have several immediate thoughts. The first is that one is heavily influenced by the environment. I've been with Cornell Medical School since 1970. So I've had as colleagues people like Allen Frances, who has published a great deal, a lot of which he and I did together, on personality disorders. Tom Widiger was a student of mine who then started working with Allen and me on personality disorders. Another student, Tim Trull, has done the same; Michael Stone has been a colleague throughout the years. I guess you could ask the same question: Why did this group stay together? I think it was a shared belief that personality and personality disorder provides the foundation and the context in which other things occur, even Axis I disorders. And certainly the context in which psychosocial functions go on, get developed or destroyed, and the context in which treatments are either grabbed and utilized or destroyed. This was a guiding belief for us.

Could you name two or three professionals who influenced or are influencing you very much?

I like that question! It sets me to thinking about things like "Where will personality disorder research be ten, fifteen years from now?" One area that I think is being developed is the whole area of biology and neurology, the whole body foundation of personality disorder. There's a colleague of mine at Cornell, at the university in Ithaca, Richard Depue (1996a) who has a chapter in my book (Clarkin 1996) on major theories of personality disorders. For me he provides a theoretical orientation to the rather complicated biological systems that interact on temperament and other kinds of behavior. He is one of the best ones. Certainly he's in a league with Larry Siever and Emile Coccaro, but he puts it in a context that's broader and better. I try to keep up with these theories, because any way that we can take psychological phenomena and behavioral phenomena and see those as phenotypes of what's going on in biological systems, I think that's going to push this field ahead.

Another area is represented by a man named Paul Ekman (Ekman and Davidson 1994). He has studied emotions and the expression of emotions. I think that the knowledge of the neural networks of emotions—emotional expressions and cognitions—has come a long way and will develop further. This is central to understanding the personality disorders.

Another one is Otto Kernberg (1980). I think his object relations theory (well, not his theory, but his rendition of it) has made a lot of the data come alive and be understandable. We should look at the intersection of his theories, the neurobiological systems, and the emotion theories. His theory is very congruent with Ekman's work on emotions, because Dr. Kernberg has always talked about the internalization of object relations and of course the affect that integrates them. That's very consistent with the current emotion theory.

Will you share some of your private thoughts on psychotherapy, apart from what you've already said? For instance, do you think psychotherapy will survive all the current attacks, like managed care, financial limitations, and so on? What are your thoughts on the future of psychotherapy? Will it still be the treatment of choice for these disorders twenty years from now?

Managed care would like to have a manualized brief treatment for the predominant disorders. They would like to have the least expensive person possible delivering that manualized treatment. To exaggerate a little bit, preferably a B.A.-level social worker who is one day out of training. I think at its worst the manualized treatments they hope for will be like the manual in your car. Well, I don't think that will succeed. For many reasons—one of which is that most patients do not have a single disorder, and also because the skill needed for doing these manualized treatments is underplayed by the notion that anyone can do it. I also believe that the more seriously disturbed the patient is, and the more complicated the situation, the less it fits in the single focus of manualized treatment. The pendulum will go to the extreme (treat everything with a mono-focused manual), and then they'll find out that it doesn't work and, moreover, is not cost-effective. They are short-term in their focus. Managed-care institutions are being bought and sold at a rapid rate, and their leaders want their money in a short period of time, but in the long range the pendulum will swing back. Then they'll discover that a sophisticated manual (with some guidelines but not describing everything one has to do) in the hands of a sophisticated and experienced therapist will pay off in the long run.

The sad thing is that our field doesn't have those data now; we haven't focused ourselves enough to assemble these data at the present time. I would love to be among the group that begins to collect those data. We think there are certain combinations— especially of Axis II disorders (particularly Cluster B)—that will define for you a very costly group of people who come into your delivery system very sick, they don't work out in your treatment, they behave against medical advice, then they go to the emergency rooms, again don't take the medication, and so on and on. We've got to isolate groups of people, and Cluster B would be a good place to start, which shows that if you don't treat them it's going to cost you more. We can begin to isolate those groups, change their treatment, and begin to expand its effectiveness. My work with Dr. Kernberg at the moment suggests that we are quite good at treating borderlines who are not antisocial, with two-times-a-week treatment. I'm not so sure our treatment is really that effective with patients who have both of those two personality disorders.

Will there ever be a workable treatment for these people?
I think we can push the field forward this way.

Is Marsha Linehan's approach more attuned to that group?
The answer is in the data. My understanding is that Marsha is now running into borderlines who are also antisocial, because she now has the money to work with borderlines who also are drug abusers. That's where she will find that very difficult group. Maybe a behavioral approach that has immediate rewards could be quite effective with that group. We'll see. I do not think Dr. Kernberg's treatment is that effective with these patients, at least with the data we have now, partly because the patient has to be somewhat motivated, which implies being attached to the therapist and wanting to understand how he or she operates. There are a lot of antisocial people who have neither of those attributes.

Have you gone through major changes in your development, apart from the shift from helping people to research, which we already discussed?
A major one has been working with Dr. Kernberg. Let me give you the context of that. In some ways it was sort of accidental. I was the director of psychology at the Payne Whitney Clinic and Dr. Kernberg was at the Westchester Division. Our paths did not cross. Then, around 1980, the Westchester Division needed a director of psychology. They did a sort of national search. I didn't apply for the job, I was happy where I was. They interviewed people, they were not happy with what they found. Our chairman, Dr. Michels, came and said, "John, I think it would be a good idea if you interviewed for that job." I said, "Really?" He said, "Yes. It's a larger group of psychologists, there might be some advantages." So I said, "Okay," and went up and interviewed with Dr. Kernberg. I was offered and took that position. At that point there were groups of people who were trying to form some research around borderlines and Kernberg.

I had already done personality disorder research with Allen Frances and was interested in it. A psychologist, a very senior person who shall remain unnamed, warned me, "John, don't ever work with Dr. Kernberg!" I said "Why not?" and he said "Because he's the medical director, that is your boss, and if you do research on his theory and find data that suggest that he's wrong, people have a tendency to shoot the messenger." Given the level of this psychologist, I thought I should pay attention to this, but caution has never been my greatest attribute, and I was never very suspicious, basically. So I wanted to check it out anyway.

Actually, I was not at all impressed by psychodynamic theory— I did not believe in it. What impressed me was that Dr. Kernberg really did, in a videotaped session, what he had said he was going to do. And even more: I could see it, I could rate it! I was very impressed by that. Furthermore I found out that if you asked him why he did what he did he could give you reasons. I liked that too! So our research began on that. Gradually over time I have seen successes. Some of the patients have responded dramatically. So I began to believe more in some of the psychodynamic theory and that's been a big change for me, because a lot of the theory is so abstract that it sounds more like philosophy. So now the task is, can we get it so specific that we can measure it? An interesting challenge!

I must admit that if we find that Marsha Linehan's treatment is as effective as psychodynamic therapy, or even if we find it a little more effective, I would still be drawn to the psychodynamic side. Because I like the complexity of it. Cognitive-behavioral treatments can get to be kind of boring, at least the way they are taught in the United States.

Your favorite position is an eclectic one, and you are much less active as a therapist. But what is your opinion about the limitations of the major approaches?

If you choose one approach with a certain patient and it goes well, this may be for quite different reasons. We are actually only just beginning to find out what's going on. So a major limitation is that our own points of view tend to be rather limited and we tend to focus on clinical cases that can have many interpretations.

Do you think therapists not only overestimate the value of their theories, but also their own skills? You said earlier that you were so impressed by Dr. Kernberg because he could tell what he did and why he did it. Does that mean that in your experience many others could not?

Certainly. I have come across many therapists who were reputed to be outstanding, but there was a striking discontinuity between what they said they did and what they actually did. I have also seen, in this research project of ours, senior clinicians who were supervised by an expert clinician, and I think sometimes this supervision was difficult, because it pointed out difficulties and insufficiencies in even very experienced therapists. I am not deprecating these senior therapists. I think anybody who treats these borderlines is in for humbling experiences. This is a very difficult group to treat. The affect-storms and the identity diffusion are such that they can throw off even a very experienced therapist. That's somewhat humbling.

Talking about limitations—Do you think therapists in general are flexible enough to work with these patients?

Let me reframe this. There are many mildly disturbed people, let's say neurotic level individuals, who come for psychotherapy. The level of skill they demand is not terribly great. Don't get me wrong: some of these people may not be helped terribly well by less experienced or less talented therapists, but these will not do much harm. I do believe that as the patients get sicker, the skill demanded in the therapist increases dramatically. There, I think, therapists can actually make mistakes that have consequences.

What are the qualities needed? Well, flexibility is one. But let's talk about borderlines, because that's the focus of your series of

interviews. Just for the fun of it, let's focus on Dr. Linehan and
Dr. Kernberg. They are both quite experienced therapists with
borderlines, working from totally different metaphors. But there
are similarities. They are both convinced that they know what to
do, they both are tenacious—neither one gives up on a patient—
they love the challenge, and the potential for suicide does not
frighten them. Now, try to teach that to a third-year resident! And
that's what we try to do! In part this is ridiculous, but we try. And
after several years they're beginning to get it. With that group of
patients those attributes of these two people are crucial.

I would not say that with another group of patients, for instance
the bipolars. There a good therapist might need different characteristics. Again I'm suggesting differential therapeutics in a way.
Here, too, you can't generalize about what makes a good therapist. The major question is, "What is a good therapist for which
kind of patient?" I think one of the things good residents in psychiatry learn is which kinds of patients they are comfortable with
and are good with, and they begin to learn which ones they are
not good with, and I hope that begins to shape their career path.
Unless they want to be heroic and do treatments with people they
are not so good at.

*Do you think that those specific qualities needed for working with
borderline patients can be trained? Isn't it to some extent a question
of talent, of the way you are, of your own defense mechanisms, which
can only be trained to a lesser extent? In other words, should we se-
lect aspiring therapists better?*

I do believe that we have at least anecdotal evidence, in our own
work, that many residents and psychology trainees can learn to
work psychodynamically with borderline patients. There are also
some who cannot. For psychodynamic treatments you need to be
perceptive, to have some innate skill in perceiving how somebody
else is treating you in the here and now, and be able to reflect on
that and be able to put that experience into words. Some people
have difficulty doing that, to others it just comes quite naturally.

The other thing that is quite crucial is that you have to be able to do all that in the context of aggression from the other person. So you have to be able to tolerate aggression and handle your own counteraggression. Again, some people are not comfortable with that.

Would you say these traits of therapists have more to do with temperament than with character?

That could well be. To rephrase it, temperament and character get so interwoven that it's hard to split them apart. Both are contributing to whether or not a therapist is feeling comfortable and free enough to really intervene.

That's a touchy area, and as researchers we are actually creeping up on that. The review board that decides if we get grants for research has pointed out that what we are in essence researching is the therapists, not the patients! Because what we should find out is whether the therapists are delivering what they promise. So the therapist has to sign a release form, agreeing to be one of the two subjects and to be rated for his or her behavior. Now the second step would be when you start assessing the therapist by instruments, like you assess the patient, and we're gradually working up to that. In fact this year we gave the Adult Attachment Interview (AAI) to the patients when they first started the treatment and one year later. But we also gave that interview at the end of one year of treatment to the therapist and the patient, individually, focused not on their paternal and maternal figures, but on the therapist's attachment to his or her patient during the last year. And we interviewed the patient about his or her attachment to this therapist over the past year. The therapists at Cornell all agreed to this, although one of them has somehow managed to be difficult to get a date with for this interview.

So indeed, we must begin to look at aspects of the therapists. That's a delicate thing that our field has not been strong on. In fact part of our work at Cornell is very unusual in that Dr. Kernberg, who is a renowned psychoanalyst, simply says that we are going to videotape the therapists. He doesn't believe that by videotaping you are vitiating the psychodynamic process. There are many others who would insist that that should not be done. So it takes leadership even to get that!

In Holland, we are inclined to do group psychotherapy with border-line patients, rather than individual therapy. Do you have any idea why this is different in the USA?

This is an assumption: the transference in the here and now can take center stage in an individual treatment, and the analysis of it with one patient can proceed with efficiency and clarity in direct focus. If you do that in a group setting it might be less efficient or less clear. On the other hand, we at Cornell are now beginning to use a group treatment in our psychodynamically oriented day hospital. I think that shift was in some aspects occasioned, if not forced, by managed care, but our group is going at it with enthusiasm. So my guess is that group treatment with borderline patients will grow in the USA as well as in Europe.

I have the impression that group psychotherapy may be an alternative for individual psychotherapy in your setting, whereas in our case we consider it to be an addendum. Most of our treatments are combinations of group and individual therapy, sometimes by the same therapist, sometimes by different ones. We use the group for all the acting-out parts and the interference with other persons, and this way we can dilute the transference.

Right. I think you may run into a technical problem, though. All my research suggests that borderline patients are quite heterogeneous. They are a mixed group, even on the level of aggression. I have a colleague who does groups that are cognitive-behavioral, with patients who have been sexually abused early in life and have recently experienced some kind of sexual abuse. The data indicate that when she has an aggressive borderline patient in one of her groups, that group does not improve, including both the hostile woman and the other members of the group, whereas when there is not such a hostile person, the whole group improves. It could be that the level of hostility in groups might be something you want to look into and titrate.

Can you give us one or two examples of people who participated in your research and who deviated from their own approach? "Sinned" against their own beliefs, so to speak?

One example immediately comes to mind. When you have a borderline patient who is self-destructing, cutting herself or making parasuicidal acts, a real battle of wills and reinforcement issues will be going on between the therapist and the patient. When this behavior is going on, the therapist should be even more intensely concerned about the current transference than ordinarily, and interpret that in depth.

Some of our therapists, experienced people, don't do that. They get supportive in technique at those points. It is my impression from a few cases that this is at the back of some therapies that do not work out well. Actually these are some of the cases that get worse at that point. Their acting-out behavior continues in face of the supportive techniques. If the supervision can get the therapist to be psychodynamic at that point, I've seen the patient's behavior improve. This is an example of a therapist who ostensibly is doing a psychodynamic treatment, which is easy to do when there is no threat of self-destructive behavior. In the face of self-destruction some of the therapists get supportive. Now some psychotherapists say: "That's just what you should do." Our data don't suggest that. But keep in mind that I'm not working with large numbers. People don't always do what the theory says they should do. Especially under threat, under stress. And a cutting borderline patient scares most people. Some therapists believe in a theory only up to a certain point. When they get supportive, they really believe that's what they should do. From one point of view they are reverting to their own mode of action and don't do what they have been taught to do.

*To give an example, in several interviews of Dr. Kernberg's that we've
videotaped, we've had some behaviorists who were viewing the tapes
say, "But that's behavior therapy! He tells the patient exactly what
he should do!" Now the question is, is Dr. Kernberg deviating, or is
this typical of his regular approach?*

I don't think it's totally accurate to call this behaviorist. Dr.
Kernberg does not tell the patient what to do. An interpretation
or a confrontation is not telling people what to do. It is a statement about the motivational structure as to why the patient is
doing it. But Dr. Kernberg's approach absolutely is a structured
approach. It is not psychodynamic treatment as it is often thought
about, but it is psychodynamic treatment, even if it's jarring to a
lot of people and not what they expect.

Let me give you an example about another therapist.

The therapist goes away on holiday. The patient says she
is in a crisis, she doesn't like talking to the covering physician. The therapist comes back. The patient comes in for
the first session. She says, "I had a terrible time! And by
the way I cut my wrists in the bathroom at work, but things
are going okay now." The therapist says, "Wait a minute!
You did what?! You know it's in our contract that if you do
that, before we can have another session you must go to
an internist to see if the cut is clean, not infected. You get
a note from that doctor, and then you can come in for the
next session."

The patient tries to wriggle out of it. The therapist says
"We have to end the session now. Go to an internist." She
says, "That's silly! I hardly even cut myself!" But the therapist says "No," and cuts off the session.

The therapist revealed in the supervision that it was extremely hard for him to do this. He was very experienced,
and yet he had never before kicked a patient out of his office.
That therapist was beginning to follow the structure in the

treatment. And from that point on that patient has improved. I can't prove that she improved because that occurred, but I can show you that when the supportive techniques occurred before, her behavior continued.

So I have kind of what the psychologists call an A-B design. That does not prove something, but it does show that that therapist is beginning to follow the dictates of the treatment, what the behaviorists would call structuring, I guess. That is, following the contract. It feels for the therapist that he is doing something terrible to the patient and is punishing her, while in fact he is trying to structure the interview differently, because there is a contract that simply says, "If X happens, Y follows."

Can you name one or two books, not written by yourself, that you would advise people to read?

Yes! Paul Ekman, whom I talked about before, his book on emotions, *The Nature of Emotion* (Ekman and Davidson 1994). And I would also strongly recommend Richard A. Depue's *"Neurobehavioral Systems, Personality and Psychopathology"* (1996b).

Is there any important aspect of your work we haven't yet discussed?

No, I think you hit the crucial things. Obviously we are not only trying to study the treatment of these patients, we're also trying to develop the instruments that will get at some of the psychodynamic constructs. I feel that the psychoanalysts have not been able to measure the constructs they talk about. They would say, "Well, that wasn't our job!" I understand that, but in the current era one almost has an obligation to do that. Otherwise I'm afraid psychoanalysis, at least in the USA, could die! I think it has to begin to measure its constructs so it can come into the marketplace of the university.

The Situations

In the middle of the night, you're called on the phone by a patient who threatens to commit suicide. What would you do in such a situation?

That depends on what kind of patient we have here. If it's somebody with a major depression and not somebody who I know has a borderline personality disorder, I would do something differently than with a borderline who uses suicide as a way of life. In that case, our manual says you refer the patient to the contract. You say, "Look, you and I both should do what's in the contract. If you can control your impulses, we'll talk about this in the next session. If you think that you can't do this, you should go to the emergency room right now. And follow the advice of the psychiatrist in the emergency room!"

How would you react if a patient comes to the appointed session in a state of obvious inebriation?

Again, in our contract-organized treatment, if the patient had done this in a previous treatment, it would be part of the contract. It would be understood that we would stop the session then and there, because being inebriated would destroy the session.

And when the patient starts sending out all kinds of suicidal messages? "Doctor Clarkin, if you send me away now like my mother always used to do, I'll kill myself"?

Well, I would say: "How are you (the patient) treating me right here and now? You're threatening me. You're the bully, the victimizer, I am the victim!" So in part you would address that theme, but probably not in depth, because you previously said that you would end the session!

Also, quite frankly, I would use my sense of this patient and see what happened before. If there is a history of doing these things and indeed making suicide attempts, I would call the police right then and there and let them take her to an emergency room.

You meet one of your patients at a cocktail party and he or she wants to use this opportunity to have an ordinary social meeting with you for a change, and starts to chat with you. What would you do?

One of the great things about living in New York is that this rarely happens! It does happen, though, and it has happened to me several times. What I would do would depend on the kind of treatment I'm trying to do. If it's a problem-solving, cognitive-behavioral treatment, I would not be concerned about trampling on transference and so forth. In a transference-oriented treatment I might say some niceties and then get scarce. I always let patients do the first move. I would not go to them and start chatting to them, even though there is clear eye contact. It's always interesting to see which patients will acknowledge you and which patients won't.

A patient turns out to be in the neighborhood of your front door, every time you come home. Just standing in the street.

At the very least I would talk about this in the next session. I would begin to wonder about what kind of patient this is, and about his reasons.

You discover that something from your office has been taken away by a patient—"borrowed," stolen, or maybe just picked up on an impulse. You know who did it. What would you do?

I would confront the patient with it. Even if I couldn't really prove that this person did it, I would still feel compelled to talk about my suspicion and discuss this. Because it would be at the back of my mind, and that would disturb the therapeutic relationship.

Even when you're not sure?

Yes, I would indicate that.

How do you like to work with your patients? Is there a desk between you or are you sitting more or less side-to-side? Do you have easy chairs or fairly comfortable ones? Are there many personal objects in your room or office? That sort of thing.

It has enough space for couples. They can sit on a couch that's big enough for three people, or on individual chairs, if they choose to sit there. Space and choice are the major variables.

Do you have patients in a room that is part of your private space?

Not anymore. My wife, who is a clinical psychologist, has a den that's an office. One of the reasons we bought this house is because you can walk into the house, right into the den. For me it's simply more convenient to weave the patients right into my regular work in the hospital. But I have done it, and have no problem with it. It would be more difficult to do this if you see borderlines, rather than neurotics. Historically I have seen neurotic-level people at home. These people will inherently respect your office, which borderlines will quite often not do. With them there is a real risk that they will violate the boundaries.

5

Robert Cloninger

Biography

Robert Cloninger was born on April 4, 1944, in Beaumont, Texas, as the first child of his recently married parents. His mother was an aspiring actress and his father was a military pilot whose parents were farmers. He lived with his mother on her parents' farm in Texas during most of his childhood, and has always closely identified with his mother's Italian roots. He was the only child until he began school and the first of three sisters was born. He had a healthy and happy childhood except for one year when he was 10 years old; during that year when his parents divorced, they moved to another town and he changed schools and friends. His mother was remarried five years later to a successful business-man and stock investor, with whom she shared a mutual love for English literature and theater. This marriage has been happy and stable, providing a supportive environment that placed high value on academic and professional achievement. In school Cloninger had an equal love for science, mathematics, literature, and phi-losophy, but decided to become a physician when he was 12 years old. He majored in philosophy, psychology, and anthropology.

Cloninger was fortunate to attend a research-intensive school of medicine at Washington University in St. Louis, Missouri. He began research in psychiatry doing diagnostic interviews with criminals as a junior medical student with Sam Guze in 1969, the same year he married his wife Sherry. Cloninger wanted to un-derstand why antisocial personality disorder, substance depen-dence, and somatization disorder were so often associated in the same individual and in the same family. The research led to longitudinal studies with these subjects and then family studies. The findings led him to study quantitative genetics with Ted Reich in St. Louis and later Newton Morton in Hawaii in order to better quantify and test hypotheses about the inheritance of psychiatric disorders.

In the late 1970s he worked on modeling complex patterns of inheritance using path analyses to allow for both genetic and cultural inheritance. This gave him a better appreciation for the nature of complex phenotypes, and stimulated his interest in adoption studies. Since 1980 he has collaborated with Swedish investigators on the inheritance and longitudinal development of alcoholism, criminality, and somatization. The studies showed that each of these disorders was influenced by both genetic and environmental factors. They also made clear that the risk of acquiring these disorders, as well as their covariation, was primarily the result of heritable personality traits that were measurable in childhood and moderately stable throughout life.

Consequently, in 1985 Cloninger began work on a comprehensive model of personality, guided by his own research findings in family and adoption studies, as well as by his reading of the literature of psychobiology, including neuropsychopharmacological studies of motivated behavior and the evolution of learning abilities in animals. As he developed this model theoretically, he also tested it in clinical practice. In this way, Cloninger has always simultaneously been engaged in basic molecular genetic and neurobiological studies of personality, as well as studies of clinical correlates of personality. This combination of theoretical and clinical work has been crucial; for example, by 1990 he realized from his clinical work that his initial model of temperament neglected those aspects of personality that distinguish mature humans from other mammals. These are also the character traits that distinguish individuals who are maturely adapted from those with personality disorders.

More recently Cloninger has focused increasingly on the practical clinical applications of the seven-factor model of personal-

ity that he has developed, including its utility in predicting response to treatment with medications and psychotherapy.

The Interview

*Doctor Cloninger, could you start by giving us an outline of the basic
tenets of your approach and of the consequences of these tenets for
psychotherapy?*

I think it's important that we bring a scientific basis to psychiatry
and psychology—at a level that goes beyond the level of description. In order for us to advance systematically, as for instance
chemistry and physics have done, we need a specific theory of
the person and our nature of being. As a result of that I have tried
to work out such a systematic model, and have progressed by
stages to more and more inclusive theoretical frameworks. The
basic position I have now is that we have to see the whole person
as more than a collection of disease states: a person is composed
of multiple elements of body, mind, and spirit. And each of these
has to be carefully defined and measurable, so that we can avoid
fantasy and speculation and have testable models that will lead
to a progressive clarification of wrong assumptions we have made
in the past. With that general sense, we need to emphasize measurement and testability.

What has become more and more clear to me is that people
have a natural integrative tendency that leads to health, and that
disease emerges whenever there is a block. Blocks can come from
a genetic predisposition that interferes with natural development,
or from social learning, or from prior experiences that are unique
to the individual. Therapy then involves several stages. First, trying to measure and assess the patient's understanding of who he

is, and then to provide a clear mirror or description of that, which the patient and the doctor can share and clarify over time. That process can also communicate to the patient that you accept him as he is, which helps him to accept himself and get a clearer, less distorted picture of who he is.

That process includes education about the nature of the genetic predisposition of personality, what the nature of traits are that may influence patients, so that they get a better understanding of their emotions and what triggers those emotions, and clarification of their concept of themselves, who they are as individuals, who they are in their relation to other people and to the world in general. That itself goes through several stages. That recognizes the fact that patients usually need to make small changes in states of calm, so that they can be more and more free of distortions of their understanding of themselves and their relationships—until they get a clearer sense of the personal meaning of their relationships, their thoughts and their desires, and the consequences of those. That awareness, without self-criticism or the urge to change, has a power of transformation that the therapist can release within any individual. So the therapist himself has to be able to see in a fairly undistorted way, to facilitate the patient's process of self-change. Because inherently I see that people are fundamentally healthy and self-organizing and that the tendency for self-organization is interfered with by our false assumptions about ourselves, and about our relationships. The therapist then is more a provider of a facilitating environment and a relationship that allows a progressive clearing of the distortion of the assumptions and fears.

This sounds very much like something a psychodynamically oriented psychotherapist or a humanist-oriented one could have said, while you are best known for your work on the biology of personality disorders.

Well, you have to see the course of my work as how I tried to begin with as simple a model as I could. I have been forced by my falsification of my own initial assumptions, step by step, to have a more and more inclusive model. You see, I began with a model of temperament that was very much based on behavioral principles of stimulus-response, trying to understand the biology of the brain. I assumed that everything would follow from that as natural corollaries. Then I was confronted with reality: people who were extremely similar in temperament-configuration were nevertheless extremely variable in their level of maturity, so that any temperament configuration could be very mature, or very immature. I had entirely left out the basis of individual differences in maturity. I then developed this in terms of a more humanistic model of character, which captures in a quantitative, dimensional way aspects of ego and superego, the dynamic framework.

Self-directedness in my model of character is very closely related to measures of ego strength in psychodynamics, and very related to the predominance of dysfunctional attitudes in cognitive therapy. My trait of *cooperativeness* includes aspects of the ego-ideal, and conscience, which is very much a quantitative measure of superego, and those together are only two of the three character dimensions, the third being *self-transcendence*, which leads to a more existential understanding of who we are as beings. That is something classical analysis has rejected, and that classical neurobiological approaches have rejected also. I only included this out of a desire to not make the assumption that we could ignore it. I said, "Let's measure it and see what the significance of it is. If it's not significant, we can put it aside. Otherwise we will have to deal with it."

Temperament is an aspect of the body in relation to the basic emotions. Character is a way of dimensionalizing and quantifying the mind, which includes both more complex emotions and our level of thought. Then there is this other aspect of spirit, which is still poorly understood and dealt with, self-transcendence, which gives us the capacity to be self-aware, without conditioning from axiomatic beliefs, and involves more intuition.

I have moved from a more temperament-based to a more thought-based to a more awareness-based approach, so it is a progression from behavioristic to more dynamic to more existential. None of these is wrong, each of them is right within certain parameters, in certain cases under certain circumstances. But for us to communicate with each other, to appreciate the limitations of different strategies, we really have to have as inclusive a model as we can. This poses serious challenges to us. To understand, "What is this, our nature?" so that we can avoid the kind of stagnation that has been characteristic of purely descriptive sciences. That handicapped physics and chemistry while they still had very strict notions of objective matter. Especially with the mind, we have to understand the more subtle aspects of mental functioning. We all recognize that we need to have a very humble approach. We have to recognize that we don't know the truth from the start, so this all leads to being open-minded and humble and testing our hypotheses—because we just don't know the truth.

How many years has this development taken you?

In the professional record you can see that my work on temperament was my model of human nature from 1985 until 1992. I really worked stubbornly to see how much we could extract from three or four dimensions of temperament that were heritable. Then from '92 until '95 I worked exclusively on understanding character structure. And then from '95 till the present I worked on the existential aspect. I must say I have written very little about this yet—there are only three papers or so about this aspect. This had grown out of the application of the temperament and character model in patient care. I don't know enough, frankly, to formulate ways of measuring these rather subtle questions about being in spirit. And so I have experimented essentially in therapy to have patients teach me what helped them transform.

Actually, I wondered myself where this motivation came from. When I go back and look at my interests in childhood and adolescence and in college, I recognize that in college I had already revealed my interest range, because I have three majors. One is in philosophy, in which my primary interest was in phenomenology and Immanuel Kant's work. I had a second major in experimental psychology, in which I worked on learning in animals and did some work also with clinical psychologists as a research assistant, and I have a third major in cultural anthropology. That really expressed the way I like to think about people. But then I was rudely taken from this rather humanistic approach and stuck in a department of psychiatry that was very anti-Freudian, very antipsychotherapy, but had the great strength of emphasizing measurement and classification and testability. So I immersed myself in that approach, sort of forgetting about these earlier roots from 1969. I began research as a medical student in psychiatry, doing structured interviewing, until I sat back and saw too many inconsistencies in diagnostic classification and a lack of progress in the categorical approach to classification, which saw health basically as just the absence of disease. And that did not mean progress to me.

We did not have methods that allowed me to describe to the medical students and residents where my intuitions came from about patient care. I always knew where the person was, but it was always something that I did intuitively. I saw that these intuitive interests in the person as a whole being were often quite undeveloped in a lot of the students that I was supervising, and I did not know how to communicate to them what it was that came naturally in me. So then I went back in earnest to studying the measurement of personality, in 1985.

I had tried this when I started research in the seventies, when I did studies of criminals. I tried measuring personality as it was then fashionable to do, and I found I didn't get meaningful answers. So when I wanted to try it again, I began working on temperament, because I had the feeling that we had to begin with this neurobiological basis as the underpinning of everything else that came later. The reductionistic approaches, both to psychology and neurobiology, just did not make enough progress.

How did people react to your huge shift from biology to awareness and transcendence?

Well, I'm not really aware of much criticism, but Peter Kramer (1993) in his book *Listening to Prozac*, called my early approach a humanist nightmare. By the time that book was published I had developed my concept of character, which, as I was very much aware of, was more or less a humanist dream! Then I got reactions from people who were very interested in transcendental psychology, thanking me for including the dimension of self-transcendence. I just did it because I wanted to be inclusive, and because some aspects of personality could not be covered without this dimension.

I remember when I worked with Norman Zuckerman on comparing the seven-factor model with other dimensional models. He suggested we leave out that dimension, because that was rather spiritual and we didn't really need it in a biologically based model of personality. I said: "If we leave it out, we change the psychometric properties of the test, so let's leave it in!" He respected that argument as a psychometrician. And it turned out that just that dimension had a lot to do with susceptibility to psychosis, and it also had a lot to do with the potential for creativity under other conditions. And now, remarkably, the people who I collaborated with in Australia have shown that the heritability of self-transcendence is between 30 and 40 percent! So it would have been an error, from a biological standpoint as well, to leave it out. This is a lesson in humility. That we just almost never know enough to make assumptions on what to leave out or not. We're better off to be inclusive, even if tentative.

Which professionals have influenced you in this development?

At the very beginning, when I trained as a psychiatry resident, I began working as a quantitative geneticist. From 1975 till 1985 I had a research scientist award from the NIMH for studying population genetics. That included working with multivariate models. Then I met a biologist, Saul Right, who was one of the three founders of population genetics. He was one of the people who reconciled Mendelism and Darwinism and developed ways of modeling the evolution of human populations as what are now called complex adaptive systems. He developed the mathematics for that, and I now find myself using them. Because most of what we now know about biological systems is that they are inherently nonlinear, and his mathematics can be used for studying that. The real breakthrough will come when we realize that simple structural models, linear models, actually do work but that they are only right for certain individuals, under certain conditions. Our job, as more complete therapists and scientists, is to understand the more complicated picture, the comprehensive view. The major question is: "Under which circumstances can we use which technique for which symptom of which patient?"

The strongest influence at the beginning was the work of Hans Eysenck on temperament, and Jeffrey Grey's more open-minded approach on testing Eysenck's model. I knew Eysenck personally, though not very well, and I very much admired his book on the biology of personality, as an experimental paradigm. But even at that time I knew very well that there was a lot more to it than he thought. Then I was exposed indirectly through a Swedish psychologist, Daisy Schaling, to the psychology of the Swedish psychiatrist Henrik Sjöbring, which helped me to add a third dimension, *reward dependence*, to the two I already had identified, *novelty seeking* and *harm avoidance*. In my work on character there were many influences. Abraham Maslow was one of them, certainly for self-transcendence and cooperativeness. Of course there were influences from Freud, and as far as the distinction between temperament and character is concerned, there was Immanuel Kant. Then there was Viktor Frankl for the existential aspects (Daseinsanalysis), Fritz Perls, and perhaps most importantly, Jiddu Krishnamurti (1973).

You have to understand, though, that by my nature of working I have to take all these theories and ideas, then digest them in my own work and observations, before I'm comfortable with how to put them together as a system.

You're a very independent thinker. How are you on reward dependence?

I would score rather high.

But at the same time you're very autonomous, you're not just a follower of others.

I am, however, a good listener. I do struggle to keep myself free from making early assumptions blindly. Although I'm high on reward dependence, I realize that just trying to be approved of will postpone the pain of seeing the truth. This doesn't mean that there is a struggle between aspects of my temperament and my character. You can see it that way, but there need not be a struggle unless you make it one. The natural way is that we all are intrinsically self-organizing. If we will just let ourselves be free in our expectations and judgments of other people and ourselves, this will probably lead to the resolution of neurotic tendencies, and to happiness. This is where dynamic theories fail, in my opinion, because they remain defensive, inherently seeing life as a conflict, while it need not be.

Which personal motives made you choose this development?

I already partially answered that question. I can see that this momentum has been there from my early youth. My parents were very interesting and they reveal a lot about this. My mother was an actress, very psychologically minded, my father was an English teacher, a very literary person. Our family life was very much organized around discussions during dinner, which invariably were psychological analyses of people who were important in our lives, and what they were doing and why, so I grew up in a basically very psychologically minded environment. It was natural for me to look for the internal dynamics behind the superficial behavioristic level. Many of my colleagues in training were not doing that. Later on I was given a lot of opportunities by distinguished teachers and professors to read a lot and study on my own. That way I could do again what I had done at home, but at a higher level. Going to medical school after that was a shock, because of the emphasis on memory work. It lacked all these things that I had found so enjoyable about understanding people. And yet I saw a great strength there that I would perhaps not have come to by myself. It would have been very natural for me to go into psychoanalytic training, but that would not have disciplined me to go into neurosciences and genetics, which now helps me to move the field forward a little bit. This combination of various backgrounds has helped me to develop my theories.

This approach to psychotherapy that resulted from your theoretical position—is it broadly applicable to any personality disorder, or are there any limitations to it?

Well, part of the answer has to do with another question: "What is a personality disorder?" In the traditional Western view, those with personality disorder are considered to be low in self-directedness or ego-strength, and to a lesser extent to be low on cooperativeness. What that leaves out is the inflexibility that is characteristic of personality disorder. Self-transcendence actually has a lot to do with flexibility, but it often is not manifest in our particular culture, which does not emphasize it until people begin to face old age, physical and mental illnesses, and death. So self-transcendence is a very important aspect of healthy adjustment in older age, or perhaps earlier if you get faced with crises or diseases that are beyond your control. This implies that we have to deal with all three character factors as aspects of healthy adjustment, while currently we are only emphasizing the first two, or primarily the first one: self-directedness.

The virtue of my approach really is, that it not only includes the behavioral component, or a more dynamic component, but also both of these plus a more existential component. Now with each patient we will have to decide which of these three is most applicable. I think a plausible hypothesis might be that the more severe personality disorders require supportive techniques and more behavioral techniques with a lot of repetition and drill. As self-directedness increases, there is still often a gap in the development of the capacity for intimacy or cooperativeness. Then the more psychodynamic approaches and the interpersonal ones are more applicable, because there is already a foundation of self-directedness.

Finally, if we have a capacity both for loving and working, there may still be conflict, a sense of a lack of fulfillment, of not understanding what we are all here for, of who we are as beings. There, some existential work is required, or it may be required for people who are facing uncontrollable losses, suffering, and death. So what I have been doing is to first try to understand this progression and to define eclectically what the techniques are, from existing approaches that we can graft onto my schema for character development. And then I moved back more recently to trying to understand more fundamentally what the ingredients are that actually allow us to essentially have a more integrated, unifying understanding of personality disorder.

These consequences for psychotherapy are less well-known than my theoretical work, because I've only written two or three papers on this yet, while unquestionably my work on genetics and temperament are much better known. The implications for psychotherapy that we just talked about are already there, spread through many of my publications, but it is now time for me to put them all together in a monograph. In my personal work with patients, I have now come to the point where I can hardly bear to proceed unless I've first done this systematic assessment, because we can learn so much more by having psychometric precision.

What is your expectation of the ability to grow toward self-transcendence in people with severe personality disorder?

I'll give you some facts that are not yet well known, but they are there. One is that the techniques as practiced by cognitivebehaviorial therapists do not lead to structural changes in the cognitions of these patients. The best predictor of success is really the level of self-directedness. If it's low to start with, you are not very likely to achieve it with the therapies as they are currently practiced. So getting success with psychotherapy is very much a matter of selecting patients who score high on this to begin with. This also goes for Dialectical Behavior Therapy, (DBT), Interpersonal Therapy (IPT), and even the use of antidepressants! I don't know the figures for dynamic therapy, but in general if you are highly harm avoidant and low on self-directedness, you do not respond well to available therapies.

So if you have a borderline personality organization in Kernberg's terms, or are low on self-directedness in my terms, or if you have low ego-strength in Freudian terms, you are not going to respond! And then we might as well do supportive work, or deal with crises, or work on a particular problem, or teach a particular skill.

We can, however, go beyond that, as I found in practice, although I have not yet proven it. All experienced therapists know that, even so, you will have some severe patients who do get better, while others who seem equally severe don't. So what's the difference? We do not as yet know. This does, however, warn us not to give up hope of positive results even before starting therapy, just because somebody's Three Dimensional Personality Questionnaire (TPQ) profile predicts nonresponse. We just do not know enough at this point.

What we must do, is to be always realistic about the expectations with any particular patient, but to always remain open to the possibility of there being an exception. Other things to remember are that people will only change in a state of calm, when they are not being pressured. And this change comes in small steps at a time, each step leading to a new state of balance.

Could you mention two or three books, not written by yourself, that you would advise the reader to study?

I already mentioned Viktor Frankl's *Man's Search for Meaning: An Introduction to Logotherapy* (1959). It had other titles—there are various versions of that book. Then I would advise Kauffman's book, *The Origins of Order, Self-Organization and Selection in Evolution* (1993). That's very much a statistics book about non-linear systems; he is one of the leading people in the mathematics of nonlinear systems. It's not close to psychotherapy, but it gives you the necessary background for even beginning to think scientifically about the psychotherapeutic process. Another one is Krishnamurti's *The Awakening of Intelligence* (1973), a compilation of his writings on the way he saw personality change in my terms, from the point of view of existential psychology.

Are there any topics of importance that we haven't yet discussed and that you would like to say something about?

Well, I'm still looking for even better instruments that may help us to identify all these factors we've been talking about, especially in a more detailed way for the healthier patients. For the more disturbed patients that would not be practical.

The Situations

In the middle of the night a borderline patient calls you on the phone and threatens to commit suicide. What would you do?

This unfortunately is something that comes up all too often. I don't think there is a general answer that you can give across the board, because it very much depends upon the seriousness of the threat. You have to assess the circumstances of that call. If I don't know the patient very well, for instance if it happens at the beginning of the therapy, I may not be certain of what the significance of it is. I will tend to be more conservative and might encourage the patient to go to the emergency room for direct evaluation, to see if there's a need for hospitalization.

What if you've been working with that patient for a couple of months already?

I would always begin by simply listening to the patient, being very attuned to why he chose to call. I'm listed in the phone book, but I don't generally give my number to the patients. I would only on rare occasions tell patients that they can call me at home, but I don't put a barrier to them being able to get through. Then I would try to get the patient to relax. I may do some relaxation techniques with him over the phone, such as deep breathing, being quiet for a few moments, and then ask him again to tell me what may have been the precipitating factors, to see what he was thinking of and if he's done anything, to assess the dangerousness of the situation. I would try to reassure him, if by knowing him I knew what the pressures were, and offer him a consultation within a few days if such an appointment had not already been made.

What if this has happened so often before that you suspect this to be a maneuver of the patient?

I have seldom had it progress to that kind of problem. Because once this happens the first time, it will be a major topic of discussion in the next session. Was it appropriate to call? What are other resources, what is the family situation or the support system in general? So the next time he calls, I can remind him of those resources. Once it's clear that the patient is overly dependent or trying to express a sense of distress or aloneness this way, I would let those calls be increasingly short. I don't want to reinforce the patient by allowing it too much. Generally, by letting patients know that I take them seriously, and that if they really need me I will be there, there will be no need for them to let it escalate.

A patient comes to the appointed session in a state of obvious inebriation. What would you do in such a case?

Well, I've done a fair amount of work on alcoholism, so I've seen a lot of substance abusers. And substance abuse is very often a way of coping for people with a personality disorder. I always emphasize to patients that they can't get better, can't learn, can't benefit from psychotherapy if they're intoxicated. If someone comes in and is grossly intoxicated, I will say: "This is not a good situation for a session," and will just let him go home, after finding out how this happened. When he is sober again, I would look at the question in depth, to see if this was a chronic problem, in which case I would try to get him into some sort of therapy for substance abuse, if I were not going to do that myself I regard it as impossible to do it myself, if I want to work on serious changes of a personality disorder.

You meet a patient at a cocktail party, and he or she wants to use this opportunity to have an ordinary social meeting with you for a change and starts to chat with you. What would you do?

That is a very interesting question that raises a lot of issues. I am personally not as uptight about maintaining neutrality in therapy as I think a lot of people with a strict psychoanalytic background would be. But I've also found from experience that it makes for a lot of problems if you have much social contact and if you go beyond the therapeutic relationship. I remember reading that Freud was phobic and did not like looking at patients and did not like them looking at him. So I think a lot of the strictness about neutrality came from his own personal feelings about what he was comfortable with in relationships. And yet there is a lot of wisdom in it, which led to its still being taken seriously. Because the more severe the personality disorder is, the more important the patient's knowing about your personal life is, I believe. And because it gives more opportunities for various boundary problems, and for manipulation, that is not going to be helpful for them. So to me the problem is really that this creates more work in the therapy, that it's going to be more problematic for the patient.

I honestly don't think that it's really a problem for the therapist if he is not afraid of the patient seeing who he really is. But there are a lot of therapists who I think hide behind the need for neutrality because they are not what they would like to be themselves. I say this because there is a tendency for people to think that they are perfectly objective and godlike in their approach to therapy, and that's not very constructive, so if you hide behind neutrality, the patient won't find out the discrepancies between what you say and what you live. Even if you were perfectly healthy and had no reason at all to be afraid of people finding things out about you, if the patient knows it and is immature, then that will create a lot of issues that will have to be discussed, because they will tend to say things that they think will please you and that will then have to be gone through, and it's just a lot of work. For them to know much about you is, at best, a practical inefficiency. And at worst it will lead to distortions of their presentation to you and it might lead to your gratifying your own needs with them within the relationship, and that's not going to be of any benefit to the patient.

I don't think it's a sin to have a short chat if you happen to bump into a patient at a party. The chat might be longer the healthier the patient is, and this has also to do with your understanding of how he views you. I have one patient, not somebody with a personality disorder but a rather mature, older, obsessional patient. Because of her relationship to the university I've bumped into her two or three times and actually for this patient it's helpful, because she sees me as one of her doctor-sons with whom she can be honest. While she can't tell her children about her obsessive-compulsive disorder, she can tell me and she very much sees me as a confidant child, who happens to have expertise. But I'm not really doing very much psychotherapy with her.

In general, one must not be rude. However, you must be aware of the fact that even innocuous-sounding remarks about the weather may have all kinds of hidden meanings that you will have to deal with in the therapy. And chats may easily escalate—"How many children do you have? Where are they? May I meet your wife?" And so on. That makes work.

A patient turns out to be in the neighborhood of your front door every time you come home. Just standing in the street. What would you do?

I haven't had the experience of dealing with such a situation, actually. If it would happen, I would see it as a serious problem. It could involve something like erotomania, or some persecutory ideas, or dependency—this could be the representation of a whole variety of very, very serious signals. Of course trying to understand this would be a major focus in therapy. The therapist just cannot satisfy all the needs and wishes and curiosities of the patient, so when they need more than they are getting this will have to be dealt with by trying to find other ways. In a case of erotomania the therapy may have to be broken off and another therapist may have to be looked for.

You discover that something from your office has been taken away by a patient—"borrowed," stolen, or maybe just picked up on an impulse. You know who did it. What would you do?

This has not happened to me either. I have knowingly had books borrowed and not returned, but I have not acted on that. I would certainly remind, but sometimes the patient might be reading something around the time of termination and I would just decide to let him have it. Knowing myself, I think that I'd probably be rather tolerant to this happening, and maybe ask a general question like, "I think you were the person who borrowed this or that. If you're done with it you can return it," but it may be that it's not something where you can ask that question gracefully. For instance if it had obviously been stolen, like a cigarette lighter or something else that he had no real use for, I would want to understand if the patient did this kind of thing very often, and why. I would not just ignore it, because I think it's a serious breach and you need to understand why the patient is doing this. We see our patients in a rather artificial environment, so we do not really know much about this kind of behavior, which they may not want to reveal to us. So even if there's no graceful way to do so, I would still discuss it and try to understand the background of this action.

What if it's an object that you value highly? And the patient denies taking it?

That's a problem. I would want it back. I would have to present the problem to the patient this way: "You know, I'm concerned that this has happened and I really, truly believe that you took it and I can see that this means a lack of mutual respect. Yours for me, and I'm beginning to doubt if I can continue to respect you." The basis for therapeutic change is credibility and honesty as much as possible, although we all tend to lie to ourselves in variable degrees. We have to talk about it, because otherwise the therapy will be undermined and I cannot go on with this at the back of my mind. This is an explosive situation that may end in the patient leaving prematurely and to you feeling wronged, and if it was something of great material value, I would go as far as calling the police about it.

To round off this interview, we would like you to describe the setting in which you see your patients. Could you tell us something about the way you sit during sessions? Are there any personal objects in there, and so on.

I have a rather large office, where I see patients for about fifteen hours a week. The patient enters and sits down in some chairs that are in front of my secretary's office, her desk. When the patient walks into my office I have a couch with a table in front of it and chairs on either side. Generally I sit with the patient facing me across the table, and we're looking face-to-face; but there are some patients who prefer to sit on the couch. They look forward, not necessarily at me. I generally indicate to them to sit in front of me but some patients like to avoid eye contact. As the relationship improves, generally they change and sit in front of me directly, which I prefer. The office is lined with bookcases and there is a desk. The phone system is arranged in such a way that I can't be disturbed during sessions, although I allow one intrusion: from my wife. My secretary knows how to use the short cut too, but she usually doesn't.

Are there many personal objects there?

Not a lot. Some photographs of my family and some groups of friends. There are some objects that have been given to me for awards, and some diplomas, but the setting is fairly comfortable and not too personal. There is a painting that I like and some lamps, a pedestal I have from Japan, with a Korean Buddha on it. I am not a Buddhist, but I did study Buddhism. This one was selected by my wife for its artistic merit. I retained it because it has the image of harmony.

6

Arthur Freeman

Biography

Arthur Freeman was born in New York City on February 14, 1942. His parents, Abraham and Helen Freeman, were the children of Jewish immigrants who came to the United States some forty years earlier. His maternal grandparents came from Minsk, Lithuania and his paternal grandparents from Kiev in Ukraine. Freeman is the middle of three children; his brother Stanley was born five and a half years earlier, and his sister Marcy was born seven years after him.

He grew up in the Bronx, New York. His neighborhood was at that time a middle-class area, with many small stores, local schools, and houses of worship. His father was a skilled worker in the women's garment industry, a major industry in New York. His mother was a housewife.

Arthur spoke very early (by 1½) and by his mother's statement has never been quiet since. He loved reading and spent as much time as he could in the library. In fact, one of the advantages of being hyperactive in the classroom was to be thrown out and sent to the library to "cool down." This was in fact very reinforcing of both his reading and his hyperactivity. In 1951, when Arthur was 9 years old, his father died suddenly. This was obviously a major loss for the young boy, and influenced his life forever. The effect of his father's death on Arthur was noted by his teachers because the normally exuberant child became quiet and depressed. In fact, the teachers were worried because Arthur now sat quietly in class and never got sent to the library. He recovered his exuberance over the next two years, in part because of his social needs to be with other children, and also his need to begin to establish himself as independent.

He attended high school in New York and was graduated at the rather young age of 16. He then went on to New York University, where he earned his undergraduate and first graduate degrees. He then attended Columbia University and earned his doctorate. His early training was psychoanalytic, and it was later that he moved to a more behavioral and later cognitive-behavioral model of treatment. His major work involves the teaching and training of clinical psychologists in the clinical psychology doctoral program at the Philadelphia College of Osteopathic Medicine, a program that he started and now runs. Freeman travels extensively throughout the United States, South and Central America, and Europe, presenting workshops at major local, national, and world congresses. He has published twenty books and his writings have been translated from English into nine other languages. He is on the editorial boards of several international journals. Freeman is the past president of the Association for Advancement of Behaviour Therapy, and the president of the World Congress of Behavioral and Cognitive Therapies, which will meet in Vancouver, British Columbia, in 2001.

Arthur has three sons and four daughters. He and his wife Sharon enjoy travel, decorating their home, attending auctions, and collecting antique cars.

The Interview

Doctor Freeman, you have published a lot about the cognitive-behavioral approach to personality disorders. Could you tell us what the main tenets of that approach are?

The basic model of cognitive therapy has two roots. It has one foot firmly planted in dynamic therapy and another in behavioral work. The idea is to help individuals more efficiently self-monitor their thoughts, actions, and feelings, and to look at the antecedents for these thoughts, feelings, and actions. We find that the sources, the major antecedents, are (not always but quite often) cognitive; they have to do with the way people process information. So in this way the model is computer-based. What we want is to let individuals look at the manner, the content, and the style of their information processing. And to then look at how this affects their thoughts, feelings, and actions. And to make those antecedents and basic ideas conscious, to bring them into awareness. This will help people take control and become more self-efficacious.

I can see this as being effective with people with depression or other symptoms—they are usually well-motivated to get rid of symptoms. But how will this work with people who will have to change all the way? Isn't it the whole world that's wrong, instead of them?

Well, the issue is not that they have to change everything they do. They don't have to change all the way. If you ask patients to do that, they would say, "No way!" If you say, "There are certain things that if you change them you become more effective, happier. Just certain things," they will be motivated. We don't try for all-out changes. One, because we just don't have the technology, and two, I think we don't even have to be that complete. As an example, when I work in corporate consulting with managers who may be narcissistic, what I do is give them a presentation entitled "How to change what you do without changing who you are." What we know is that once you change what you do, you are different. In their own opinion these managers are successful because of what they are. They don't want me to take that away from them! But if I can help them identify those pieces that need modification or revision, they can be more successful.

There are some psychoanalytic people who would disagree with you when you say, "We don't have the technology for helping people change all over."

There's a movie in America, called *Jerry McGuire* (1996). He's a sports agent and has one client and he keeps calling this football player and saying: "Look, I think we have a deal!" The football player replies, "Jerry, show me the money!" You know, psychoanalysts have been making promises for a hundred years, but I say, "Show me the money!" I'd like to see the data! There are some studies, like Lester Laborsky's work on psychoanalytic work, or Mardi Horowitz's work, and Otto Kernberg has done some research, but the data for classical analysis are nonexistent. The data for psychoanalytic approaches are much more promising. But at this point when they say we've got the technology, I don't believe that. I haven't yet seen it.

So you think that the psychoanalytic approach really isn't any more effective than yours?

I haven't seen any compelling data.

Nevertheless, when you have a borderline patient with very disruptive behavior, I can imagine that to some extent it is strategy to say, "You don't have to change," but it seems to me that with such a patient there are so many areas of behavior that need to be changed. How do you go about that?

One part of my approach is a need for specificity, and you are not being specific. Are we talking about a mild case, a moderate one, or a severe one? Do we have a mild borderline patient who has occasional episodes that may be specified to interpersonal relationships? Do we have a moderate borderline where the problems are more pervasive and affect more parts of their lives? Or a severe borderline patient who is cutting and slashing and so on? These are three different patient types.

I was talking about the severe ones.

Such people may not see the need for change because with them the problem is usually ego-syntonic. Then the question is, before we talk of changing, "Can we offer them some kind of motivation? A rationale for change?" There's no guarantee that we can. Depending upon the level of severity, even a severe borderline is trying to be successful in a way. Their methods sometimes work, so if what they want is attention, they slash and they get attention, in ways that are far superior to what they can get in any more so-called realistic or normal, ways. No one will ever notice them as much as when they come into the emergency room dripping blood on the floor. They see themselves as guaranteeing relationships, because they say, "If you leave me, I'll kill myself!" So part of the problem we have to deal with is how to convince them that a very successful method, though self-damaging and self-injurious, could be given up.

I've had the greatest success when I could help an individual find less self-damaging ways to get what he wants. With certain patients there is no way we can match what they win with their impulsive, self-injurious behavior. That's what I mean by "We don't have the technology." I think Michael Stone would agree that this is probably an issue of hyperreactivity of the central nervous system, and probably genetically based. And probably for that severe borderline patient, when we get better and smarter techniques, genetic engineering would be the best way. At this point the most we can do is offer them other methods to be successful, if that is at all possible.

Could you give an example of how somebody who keeps her relations in check by blackmailing them could change her technique and do it by other methods?

Again, it's a maybe. If someone says, "I don't want to be left!" what I would want to do is work with her to identify ways of *decreasing* the possibility and probability of being left. One way is to make better choices, which is a problem with borderlines. Don't choose someone who by definition is going to leave you! That makes sense. There's a quote I'll always remember, by Albert Ellis. His description of neurosis is: "stupid behavior on the part of nonstupid people." A borderline is not stupid, and in fact may not be a borderline all of the time. But when certain stimuli are presented she loses control. I'd like to help these people realize what those stimuli are, so they can take action before they lose control. In the midst of this borderline drive it is very difficult to stop. For example I may tell her, "If you don't want to be left, first, make better choices about who you engage with, and second, go out of your way to find out what are the things that will keep them close. If threats keep them close, great! If blackmail keeps them close, great! But if those things don't work well and sexual seduction works, okay! Cooking a good meal may be another thing. It's an issue for borderlines, in direct activity, of being in a drive-reduction mode, or better, a need-reduction mode, and once they are in that mode, nothing will stop them. So what we want to work on is to teach them to be aware of when they are getting into that mode. That's the place to stop. Even the most severe borderlines in hospital have rational moments. They are not demented, not retarded. They'll often say, "I don't believe what I did. I did it again . . . Why do I do that?" When they come into therapy they are often remorseful, even penitent. But if you give them the same stimuli, they will do it again. So part of what we'll do is much more of the behavioral work, stimulus control and response prevention, preventing them from responding in certain ways, giving them alternatives.

I'll give you an example.

I've been working with a man who, when he was upset, would do things that had the potential to kill him. He would get involved in highly arousing activities. He would drive his car at high speed at night with his eyes closed. He'd look at the road and then drive as long as he could. Or he would aim his car directly for a bridge support and he'd say: "Ten, nine

. . ." And his idea was not to kill himself, but to see how close he could come, because the need was for arousal for his overstimulated or hypersensitive central nervous system. What we looked for were other ways of achieving arousal. And he found several activities that were not as arousing, but enough so that he did not have to get involved in the dangerous ones.

You're saying that when someone is extremely novelty seeking (Cloninger 1987), that is biologically based, so what you want to do is teach somebody to live with it?

Yes, by going skiing for instance—there are lots of things. My 17-year-old son has always had difficulties in school because he has an attention deficit—he's hyperactive, as am I! And the two sports that he has come to are skiing in the winter and sailing in the summer. I sail for pleasure, he sails competitively, he's a racer. And during a race he's doing seven things at once! So he's using his problem, that's a sublimation if you wish. He is compensating, adapting, to use his attention deficit in a more productive way. This is what I want to do with this kind of borderline patient. Can we *use* their characteristics instead of banging our heads in fighting them? Most of these patients, when they come to us, have not been very successful, neither in life nor in therapy, or after therapy. So what we say is, "Let's go and see if we can use what's troubling you."

How does this relate to Marsha Linehan's work?

Well, Marsha talks about how we can help the patient—as an example—control her "therapy-interfering behaviors." In such cases you don't just regard it as a matter of transference, you say explicitly, "Look, you do things that mess up the therapy. They mess up all your relationships. They've got to stop." Marsha's model and Marsha herself don't dance around the issue. She says, "One of your problems is that you involve yourself in therapy-injurious behav-

ior. Let's talk about how to stop it. Because if you don't stop it, you'll
be out of here and visiting still another therapist."

*So does Dr. Kernberg. He makes a very tough contract when some-
body has messed up therapies in the past to prevent it from happening again. Perhaps this is something all therapists and therapies with
tough borderlines have in common, don't you think?*

It does count for Kernberg and Linehan, but I'm not sure it goes
for all these therapists. I think lots of people will interpret, while
we would say, "You do these things because you have trouble with
boundaries and limits. Let's set the limits. And if you violate those
limits, there's a price to pay." In this way I see Kernberg as using
contingency management, a very good behavioral technique. So
Kernberg is becoming a behaviorist, that's good to see! (smiles)
But all effective therapists do have this in common, yes. I think
all therapists who understand borderline pathology would set limits, but sticking to these limits is harder than setting them! Because it may come to a point where you have to say: "We shall
now have to stop the treatment."

   You have to realize however, that much more than limit setting is involved in being effective with this group of patients. Do
not underestimate charisma and personal style as an important
variable. With all due humility, I have a quite outspoken personality and visibility and I do very well with these patients because
I am who I am. So does Otto, and so do for instance Michael Stone
and Marsha Linehan. But I'm not sure that everybody can get away
with what Michael Stone does, or what Otto Kernberg does.

So that's more important than the frame of reference a therapist uses?

Sure. But it's very difficult to codify. We all write books describing what you should do, but what we are really saying is, "This is
what you should do if you were me." People try, and then say,
"This doesn't work so well!" But of course! They're not me! So the
problem is how to take what you do and take it down in a step-

by-step fashion, so that it can be used by everyone. If psychotherapy is an art, then some of us are Rembrandts, some are van Goghs, and some of us are monkeys, just putting paint on a page. If you're a Rembrandt, it doesn't matter what you do, it'll look good.

Many people say, "It's the nonspecific factors that make psychotherapy work." Are you saying that these factors will work if you put them to the patient in the right manner?

Well, I think psychotherapy is more than just providing a supportive, accepting environment. Those three factors of Carl Rogers— those are important but not sufficient. There are different types of therapists. You have the theoreticians, they just sit in an ivory tower, don't do therapy but theorize and don't even know if what they say will work in practice. The second type is the politician, who sees therapy as a kind of political maneuvering. There is the rhetoritician, who just talks about it all the time, lectures, but doesn't actually do it. Then you have the magician who has magic. He says: "Spend an hour a week in my aura, and you'll be cured." For some people that's true! I once had a supervisor, very big, 240 pounds. He was good with any patient, because he would fill a room with his body and his personality, no matter what he did. Then there's the clinician who has a theoretical model, can offer the kind of emotional support that's needed, and has a technical expertise. That, I think, is essential. It's not just the acceptance, the supportive environment. Priests have been doing that for years, parents do that. Even Carl Rogers, at the end of his life, moved away from the idea that all you needed was unconditional regard.

Jerome Frank stressed the point that what you need over and above these common factors is offering a patient a myth he can believe in and it doesn't really matter which myth.

I would disagree. The idea that all therapy works simply isn't true. Does primal scream therapy work? There's evidence that certain therapies are more effective than others. And that has to be looked at. So therapy isn't really an art, it's a science. And we can teach people the science of therapy.

And some personalities help.

Right. There are some people who work really well with children, because of their style. Some people can tolerate the high arousal of a borderline. I am a high-arousal individual and this high arousal of the borderline patient doesn't offend me or scare me. I'm probably more high arousal than most of my borderline patients! I understand people who are more or less all over the place. I find Cluster C patients boring. I work with them if I have to, but I don't enjoy it. I work with antisocials, narcissists, histrionics, borderlines. With them I find therapy really enjoyable.

Talking about charisma, earlier on you mentioned Albert Ellis. What do you think of his approach?

I would like to differentiate two things. One is his current approach, which he now calls REBT (Rational Emotive Behavior Therapy). I think Ellis is probably one of the most brilliant clinicians we have had in psychotherapy. And sensitive. The problem with his model is that people think that what Albert Ellis does with his model is the only way to practice REBT. REBT is important, because it was one of the very first cognitive behavioral models. Ellis credits the work of Alfred Adler and Karen Horney as the basis for his model. What he did, very early in the game, was to look at the way people think and process information. That wasn't new. Kelly, Frankl, and Adler did it before him. The problem was, though, that these people were not discrete in terms of technique—they never spelled out exactly what to do. Ellis did just that. He identified techniques that effect change. Probably the greatest flaw I would find in his work is that he has never fully explicated what he does. Albert is a strange fellow. He lives above his clinic, gets up in the morning, takes the elevator to his office, sees patients, goes up for lunch, goes down to his office, and so on. He hardly ever leaves his building. The reality of Ellis is quite different from all the rumors you hear about him—like he's supposed to have been married twelve times, while he's lived with one woman for more than thirty years! Now, he has been very good at describing techniques, but he has never written about why—and how—he uses these techniques. This may leave a bad impression when you see him in action. For example he starts making interventions and interpretations after only five minutes of contact, which horrifies experienced therapists! He is able to do that for several reasons. One, he's been doing it for fifty years. And two, because of his character; he is very focused and doesn't have a lot of other interfering issues in his life when he does therapy. He is therefore able to listen far better than any of us can, he hears nuances, subtleties. I had the opportunity to ask Ellis if he really was able to conceptualize about the patient within seconds, and he said "Yes!" But he has never really spelled out how he does that.

Actually this is something every inexperienced therapist comes up against when he watches an experienced one. A little information may right away be enough for the expert who has noticed slight details without even being able to specify them and the pupil will be amazed at how the expert came to his conclusions.

We have already discussed some things about other therapies compared to yours. Now we would like to go into this a little further. For instance, what are the similarities and the differences between your approach and the one of your former colleague Jeffrey Young? Young told us that you have been working together, with Aaron Beck.

Well, in what he calls "schema-focused therapy" Jeff has identified eighteen so-called "early maladaptive schemas." Well, I don't think schemas necessarily have to be maladaptive. For instance, if I have the belief that I need the help of others to survive, that isn't necessarily maladaptive. If I find a spouse who takes care of me and a job working for a government, any government, I will be taken care of, and that's not maladaptive. Calling it maladaptive presupposes that there is some sort of perfect individual and such a person just doesn't exist.

Take me for an example. One of my basic ideas is that it's important to be noticed. That's me. I was a middle child, so I learned very early that I couldn't be as big and strong and smart as my older brother, who is five and a half years older, and I couldn't be as cute as my baby sister. My mother has always said to me: "You spoke very early, and you haven't shut up." By speaking I could get noticed! I wasn't quite 2 years old and when people came to visit I was just talking away! Everybody was complimenting me and I learned I could get noticed by my verbal ability. And in school I loved getting noticed, so I would speak out in class, which caused all sorts of difficulties because teachers don't like that sort of thing. But as an adult and a professional, speaking out in public has helped me become very successful. The idea that it's important to be noticed has then become translated into finding different ways of getting noticed, such as writing books and choosing a career not as a therapist sitting in an office all day long, just seeing patients, but a career in teaching. So I come to Holland, I go all around the world, standing in front of groups and being noticed. It's not a good or bad thing, but how well it fits.

In the examples you gave earlier, you showed that you focus not just on the maladaptive side of behavior, but on the adaptive side as well. And you seem to be less moralistic than others.

Yes, and I think Jeff has become moralistic. I want to look at what the strengths are, because we have to think of what we can use before we throw everything out. Not everything will have to be changed. I would bet for instance that the head of security at Schiphol Airport is probably a paranoid personality disorder and the reason he got to be the head of security is because he doesn't trust anybody.

Is there anything else you'd like to add about the field of psychotherapy in general?

Yes, I think every theory should be held with its feet to the fire and be checked empirically. It's "put up or shut up," the time for free theorizing is over. I would like everybody in the field to be held to that demand. If it works, show us!

Who has influenced you the most?

Personally or professionally?

Is there a split between the two?

Well, I've been very influenced by the work of Alfred Adler and have taught Adlerian theory in Chicago for several years and published in Adlerian journals, and I've been a keynote speaker at the Adlerian conference. My study with Ellis has been an important influence and my study with Beck (Beck et al. 1990) certainly has been of importance as well. Probably the most important personal influences were being a middle child and the fact that I had to fight my way all the time, which gave me a great drive, but also the fact that my father died when I was 9 years old, so I had to learn a high level of independence rather early. My mother was focused on surviving herself and on taking care of three children. When I was about 13 the counselor of my high school, who had been a childhood friend of my father's, called my mother to school one day and said, "We have a problem here. Arthur isn't doing well." Now, I was doing okay, but I wasn't doing up to my potential since I should have been getting the best grades instead of middle grades. He referred me to a therapist who really was an important influence in my life. Here was an adult male with whom I could identify! I think my choice of psychology and a career as a therapist was probably molded by that influence. I wanted to be like him! Having a successful adult figure who was supportive. When I went on to college I would consult him from time to time, he would be aware of my doing nicely, and would watch me having success. He would send me notes from time to time, referring to publications of mine that he had noticed, congratulating me, and so on. He still is a source of support to me.

And then after college, how did you choose the training you had?
You've been in analysis, but that doesn't seem to fit you.

(smiles) Well, this therapist was analytic, so this is what I learned and it made sense. Also, I studied at a psychoanalytic institute in New York, the Metropolitan Institute for Psychoanalytic Studies, and they followed the work of Theodore Reik, who had done the first psychoanalytic dissertation at the University of Vienna in 1912. That was the model I was trained in.

I was running a group at that clinic, of patients who were of different therapists. They asked me to take somebody into my group, a very tall fellow, very skinny, almost white hair and very blue eyes, and he spoke in a falsetto voice, which was very noticeable. His therapist explained that he had an unresolved oedipal confict and was unwilling or unable to get a man's voice because he was afraid of castration. At this point I believed that. He had been in analysis for two years, three or four times a week. After a while I began to wonder and asked his therapist if there might not be anything wrong with his voice. Medically! I was less concerned about the patient than about me maybe missing something, and him dying and the newspapers shouting: "Freeman is an incompetent, he missed something and his patient died!" He said, "I don't think so, I never asked." So he asked the patient, but he also told the supervisor, who told the head of the institute, and he called me on the carpet. "What are you doing? This patient's problem is not medical, it's psychogenetic! Take my word for it, because I say so." I was still worried, and informally this therapist and I kept on talking about it. And then he had his patient checked medically. The family doctor said, "There's nothing wrong with your voice, but I would like to refer you to a specialist." This was an otolaryngologist, who agreed and then referred the patient to a speech pathologist. And in six sessions of speech therapy he learned to speak in a lower voice and terminated his analysis. So I got called in again and was told that I had ruined this man's life! I thought to myself that this made no sense. The patient had come for the purpose of learning to speak with a lower voice, and he could do that now.

Maybe simple is good! I began thinking on this and eventually I ended up on the board of our institute and we had these long analytic board meetings and I was so bored! Well, you know I don't like boring things . . . Once we had a discussion, all day long, about the question of whether candidates for our institute could be in analysis four times a week plus a group, instead of the regular five times a week. I finally raised my hand and said: "If the person's problems are intrapersonal, he needs five times a week. If they are interpersonal, I think a group is helpful." There was this endless silence, and they looked at me and said, "You don't understand the theory!" Well, they were talking theory and I was thinking practical. I said to myself, "There's something wrong here," and I started looking at other models at that point.

I started with behavior therapy. This was in the early sixties, when behavior therapy was very mechanistic. I felt uncomfortable with that. Then I looked at Adler's work and studied it, and then I heard about Albert Ellis. I heard him speak and I was very fascinated by what he had to say and took courses with him, which really transformed what I was doing. This was about 1971 and I was finishing my doctoral thesis and I was stuck. Every night I came home and I did nothing on it. Week after week, month after month. So I went back to my analyst and said: "I need some help to get my dissertation finished." He said, "Well, I happen to have a group, all people who have trouble finishing their dissertations" and I joined that group. In that group we would complain week after week about our not doing anything to finish the job. After several months I felt I wasn't getting anywhere. I needed to get this finished! Nobody was saying "All right, next week you have to come in with this much work finished," because the idea was that when we were ready, we would do it. Then I called Albert Ellis and went to see him for therapy. I had had him as a teacher, but not yet as a therapist. I sat quietly (which is hard for me to do!) and he said to me, in his way, "Art, what can I do for you?" I said, "I need help finishing my dissertation." He said, "Why haven't you finished it?" Having been in analysis all that time I was ready for that question. I said, "Well, you see, I had an older brother. He and I always have had conflicts and it's a matter of sibling rivalry. He's a dentist and has the title 'Doctor' . . ." and he said, "Bullshit! Why haven't you finished your dissertation?" I thought maybe he didn't hear me well and repeated what I said. He said "Stop with that Freudian bullshit!" And I was appalled. My analyst had never once said "shit"! Then Ellis said, "I'll tell you why you aren't doing it. It's because you are too fucking lazy!" I said, "I resent that!" He said, "Okay, why are you resenting it?" "Because I'm not lazy." He said, "Then why don't you do it?" I was stuck for an answer, not being lazy and being smart enough. Well, within three months I had it finished and submitted. It was done!

It impressed me that this straightforward, reasonable approach felt right. I moved to Philadelphia in 1975 and I said to Albert, "Who can I contact there, to work with?" He gave me Aaron Beck's phone number and I called Beck and started working with him.

Have there been any important changes in your way of thinking since then, like during the past ten years?

Well, when I first started with Beck, cognitive therapy was very new. Jeffrey Young was a doctoral student there at the time, and we were all kind of new at this business. Beck and I had been analytically trained, Jeff and several others were not. Since we did not want to be accused of sticking to old stuff, we tried to avoid using any psychoanalytical terminology. I now do work with analytical concepts, trying to approach them from a cognitive perspective. Like the broad area of resistance. I don't like the term "resistance," which is very loaded. I like to call it "impediments to therapy." These come from four places: the patient, the therapist, the environment, society—and from the pathology. Much "resistance" behavior is only a part of the disease. Of course you cannot deny the existence of several fundamental building blocks of psychoanalytic theory, but if you put them into a cognitive-behavioral framework, you can then raise the question, "Now what are we going to do about it?"

Would you agree that there may be a fifth factor in so-called resistance, namely matching problems?

Sure, that too. An interesting point. As an analyst I learned that a good analyst can work with any patient. That is just not true. Some people just are better with some patients than with others.

Do you think there are any limitations to the usefulness of cognitive therapy?

I don't think there are limitations to the cognitive approach. They are only in the creativity of the therapist. When I first started working with Beck, in 1976, '77, we only worked with depression. If a patient came into our clinic with an anxiety disorder, we would refer him out. Then Beck said, "Wait a minute, let's see if this stuff works for anxiety as well!" Then in the middle to late eighties, we even started treating people with personality disorders, taking our model that we knew worked for certain groups, from our work and the work of others, and since then we have come to work with couples as well. And with groups, with schizophrenics, with bipolars, PTSD—so the model really is a very ubiquitous one across different disorders. It really works well. I don't think it's limited by culture either, like psychoanalysis is. In some cultures there is no such thing as an oedipal complex. In China, where everybody lives in one room, what about primal-scene trauma? They watch their parents having intercourse and still they don't have that trauma. Cognitive therapy is culture free because the goal is to help an individual to understand the rules he lives by. Now these may be different in all kinds of countries. If I were to work with a Dutch patient, my goal would not be to work from a set of rules that I know about, but rather to have him understand his own rules, which he knows about.

Could you give us an example of yourself sinning against your own approach?

Well, I think it's less helpful to tell a patient what to do. The Socratic dialogue is much more effective to help people reach understanding. But . . .

> I have a patient who is very needy and dependent and he was involved with a borderline woman who was very excit-ing. He had never found anybody that exciting! She broke up with him. Now, only a few days ago he said, "Well, it's her birthday and I sent her a card and she called me to thank me and I asked her out to dinner and she said yes. Do you think I ought to go?" (grins widely) Well, I started off pretty well, by asking him what we had been discussing in the past. He said, "Oh, you don't think it's such a good idea?" I said, "No. *We* decided that it would not be a good idea." "Do you think I ought to cancel?" "What do you think you need to do?" And so on, and finally I said, "You know what? I think it's nuts for you to go out with her. She's going to embarrass you, to humiliate you, you are going to get suicidal. Why on earth would you want to do that?" And he said, "You're right." Now he won't do it and I will have protected him. I would much rather he sees the error of seeing her, than him leav-ing it to me. I would like to excuse this by saying I needed to get packed because I was going on a trip, but actually I was fed up. The same old stuff again . . .

Which two or three books, not written by yourself, would you advise the reader to study?

Probably the best book for understanding borderline personality disorder is not a professional book at all, but a novel. *Scarlett* (1992), by Alexandra Ripley—it's kind of the sequel to *Gone With The Wind*, the story of Scarlett O'Hara. When I first read it, I found myself getting so annoyed that I wanted to slam it shut and throw it away. But then I picked it up and started reading it again. Again I closed it and put it down as I got so annoyed at Scarlett. Then I wondered why I was getting so annoyed with a character in a book. Of course it was countertransference. She was a borderline personality and I was responding to the things she was saying and doing. I think it's so excellent, because it shows Scarlett sometimes as a reasonable, caring, and stable individual. At other times she drinks and abandons her children. The author has given us her internal dialogue, her cognitions. She would think, "Oh, if only I could get Rhett back again! I would do anything for that . . . " Then there's a knock on the door, she asks who it is, Rhett calls, "It's me!" and she shouts, "Get out of here, I never want to see you again!" Afterward she is remorseful and self-critical, and this is exactly what borderlines are about: they're not nuts all of the time. This is the best book on borderlines that I know of. At the end she gets Rhett back again and he tells her: "Look, you and I will never have a home. We'll travel around the world because we need excitement," so it's clear he recognizes her need for arousal and activities. I give it to my residents and ask them to make up a treatment plan for her. I say, "It's now six months later. They're fighting again, they come for therapy, you know all this information about her, about them, about their lives. More than you'll ever get about a patient. What is your treatment plan going to be? Do you do individual therapy with them both? Do you do couples therapy? If they have a child, do you do family therapy? And there are questions about the future too—when their 6-year-old daughter is, ten years from now, an attractive 16-year-old, how is Scarlett going to deal with the competition, the jealousy?"

Are there any other books you would suggest reading? Professional ones?

I think Theodore Millon's works are pretty essential for understanding personality disorders. I think a very influential book is

Stone's work, *Abnormalities of Personality* (1994). He has, by the way, quoted from my work about fifteen times, so I know he is a man of impeccable taste. I like Stone, because he takes the dynamic work, and then he takes the cognitive-behavioral parts and the need to understand the dynamics. Linehan I think has been very important and has influenced my thinking a great deal. These are the major ones.

Are there any recent developments you would like to mention in this interview?

Yes. I've just become really excited about antisocial personality. Everyone says these people are untreatable. Well, either they're biologically and genetically untreatable, or we just haven't been smart enough to figure out what to do with them. I was asked to do a book on antisocial personality, so I've had to do a lot of reading on the matter and the more I read, the more angry I get. Everybody claims there is nothing you can do, but then why write about it? But looked at from the cognitive-behavioral perspective, what we are lacking for adequate treatment is specificity. What we've done with borderlines, seeing them as just one big homogeneous mass, we are also doing with antisocials. There are different styles of borderlines and after having differentiated them we started developing different methods for treating them. So I'm now speculating about developing a typology for understanding diverse types of antisocial pathology that will allow us to target treatment. Now Thurstone wrote about such an approach in 1926, looking at antisocials along a continuum, and I want to develop these ideas a little more. I have some students who work in prisons and I want to see if we can intervene, based on this new typology.

Did you know that Michael Stone has recently changed part of his working week and is now visiting prisons as well? He said, "I always wrote about them, and now finally I am going to see the real thing."

Hey, that's interesting!

The Situations

In the middle of the night, you're called on the phone by a patient who threatens to commit suicide. What would you do in such a situation?

Has this been going on every week? Is it a common occurrence? In that case I'll say, "Oh, this is your weekly suicide attempt." I would want to remind him that it's been an issue in therapy before and I would remind him of what has worked before. If he says, "Nothing works! Nothing is going to work!" then I'll say, "You have to go to the hospital." If it is the first time he has done this, I deal with it differently. I would want to talk with him briefly. My goal would be for him to get to a place of safety. That means with someone else, or if there is no one else, to a hospital.

How long would you give him? This is three o'clock in the morning.

Well, this is limit setting we're talking about. I would start by saying, "Listen, let's take ten minutes for this." If he says, "I need more than ten minutes!" I would say, "Okay, here's my notebook, I have room for you at ten o'clock tomorrow morning, I'll see you then. Right now, I'm not available for more than ten minutes."

I don't tell my patients that I am ultimately, absolutely, totally available to them.

By the way, we talked about breaking my own rules, and now we're talking about setting limits. Well, I once had a borderline patient who wanted to sit in my lap because that's what she needed, she said. I said "No" and she said, "Why not? There are therapists who do that!" I said, "We talk, we don't touch." But then something happened: she had been trying to do something, and she finally accomplished it. I met her at the receptionist's desk and she said, "I was successful!" I said "Congratulations!" and shook hands with her. She came into my office and she said, "You bastard! When I needed physical contact, you didn't give it to me. Now I don't need it and you're willing to give it to me!" She was right: I was just not sensitive enough to what I was doing, you know—it was only a handshake . . . But when the rule is No Touching, I should not have shaken her hand. You may say, "Well, you acted normally," and I did! But I violated a rule I set myself.

Anyway, talking about suicidal patients, I make it clear that I cannot and will not take the responsibility for anybody who wants to kill himself. And actually, in thirty-three years of practice, I have never had a patient kill himself. This doesn't mean I never do anything. I called the police once or twice when the patient refused to do this himself, and I took somebody to the emergency room twice when the patient was confused and might not have been able to find the way himself.

How would you react if a patient comes to the appointed session in a state of obvious inebriation?

The first time, I explain, "This is unacceptable. I will not meet with you when you come in high or inebriated. So when you do, I will end the session immediately and you will have to pay for it anyway." If they do it again, I just send them home, I won't see them. Not because I'm rigid, but there is such a thing as state-dependent learning. If they pick up anything during a session when they are inebriated, they will only remember it when they are inebriated!

You meet one of your patients at a cocktail party and he or she wants to use this opportunity to have an ordinary social meeting with you for a change, and starts to chat with you. What would you do?

If we're in the same social circle, it's quite possible that we'd meet at a cocktail party. It would be unrealistic for me to say, "I'm sorry, but no." Again I would set parameters. If he were to go into therapeutic stuff, even vaguely, I would say, "This is not the time and place for that." The reality of life is that you are a person, you have a life, you meet people in social situations. There is something you might call therapeutic narcissism, where you consider yourself to be so much above "these people" that you don't want to meet them. I have a great respect for my mechanic because he can do things I can't. He has a magical way with my cars, so I respect him. There are times when we talk about cars. Now if he says, "Hey, are you going on a vacation?" I won't say, "Sorry, we only talk about cars!" Would a gynecologist talk to his patient? Sure he would! Then why not a psychotherapist?

Well, people worry about transference and countertransference, projection and so on. And not only psychoanalysts.

I don't. Not in a situation like this.

A patient turns out to be in the neighborhood of your front door every time you come home. Just standing in the street.

That won't be a patient very long. It's a violation of rules. We meet in my office, we meet at specified times, and on specified days. So this is inappropriate. The patient may say, "But I'm a patient!" but that doesn't mean he can get away with behaving inappropriately. When something is offensive to me or my family, that's the limit. And if he keeps it up, I'll end the therapy. If he still goes on, I'll call the police and have him arrested.

What if he doesn't do anything, he's just standing on the opposite side of the road, not talking to you. It's a public street.

I would still call the police. If I perceive harassment, it is harassment. Of course the police will just say, "Hey, go on, man!" And then, if he refuses, the police will make trouble for him.

You discover that something from your office has been taken away by a patient—"borrowed," stolen, or maybe just picked up on an impulse. You know who did it. What would you do?

I would confront him. Explain why I suspect he did it. Then I'd say, "I didn't see you take it, but I have to ask you: did you take it?" If he says "No!" all I can say is, "Well, if you did take it I would like it back and then we can talk about it." If he says, "I only took it for a while because I wanted to show it to somebody," I would say, "Okay. But you know, if you ask this in advance, I might say 'yes.' But this way I do not agree with. It's against the rules to just take stuff." If he keeps on denying, there's nothing I can do!

You might stop the treatment.

Well, there have been times when I misplaced things, myself. So the first time this happens I may have made a mistake.

But if you're sure the patient is lying about it, could you still work with him?

If I cannot trust a patient, while treatment is based on trust, maybe therapy has to stop.

You seem much more hesitant than others in this respect.

Well, I'm just not as certain of things. I've been certain of things and turned out to be wrong after all! Now, if this would happen the second time, I would surely say, "That's it!"

Our final question: Could you tell us a little bit about the setting in which you see and treat your patients?

The room is a personal space in my home. It's not simply an office but a study and in that study there are lots of things. One wall is bookshelves, wall-to-wall, floor to ceiling, there are windows on two sides, and in daylight you can look out on a backyard with flowers, bushes, a swimming pool. Above a large couch there are diplomas on the walls, mixed with family pictures. There is a stereo cabinet, a TV, an antique table, a large comfortable chair (with an ottoman) that I sit in with my feet up. The patient sits on the couch. When he walks into the house he sees my living quarters.

7

Glen Gabbard

Biography

Glen Gabbard was born in 1949 in Charleston, Illinois. He has one brother, eighteen years older. Growing up in a small university town in the midwest, where both his parents were drama professors, he was educated at a laboratory school at the university, where he had exceptionally fine teaching and the opportunity for independent study. Following his parents' footsteps, he majored in drama as an undergraduate at Northwestern University in Evanston, Illinois, and at the University of Texas in Austin. He then entered Rush Medical School in Chicago, and did his psychiatric training at the Menninger School of Psychiatry in Topeka, Kansas. While a resident there, he also started his psychoanalytic training; he finished his professional education in 1984.

He now is Bessie Walker Callaway Distinguished Professor of Psychoanalysis and Education in the Karl Menninger School of Psychiatry and Mental Health Sciences, and clinical professor of psychiatry at the University of Kansas School of Medicine in Wichita. He is also a training and supervising analyst and the director of the Topeka Institute for Psychoanalysis.

Dr. Gabbard is the author or editor of twelve books, including *Psychodynamic Psychiatry in Clinical Practice: The DSM-IV Edition* (1999), which is an all-time best-seller. In addition he has published over 150 scientific papers and book chapters and has been actively involved in psychotherapy research on borderline personality disorder. He is associate editor of the *Journal of the American Psychoanalytic Association*, and is a member of various editorial boards of other professional journals. As a result of all these activities, he has become the recipient of numerous awards.

In his spare time, he is an avid theater-goer, plays golf and enjoys wildlife, and is very interested in the cinema. Together with his brother, who is the chair of the Comparative Literature Department at the State University of New York at Stony Brook, where he teaches film, Dr. Gabbard has published *Psychiatry and the Cinema* (1999), which has just come out in its second edition.

The Interview

Doctor Gabbard, could you start this interview by giving us a brief outline of the basic tenets of your approach, and of the consequences of that approach for the psychotherapy of severe personality disorders?

It's difficult to do that because I'm pluralistic by nature, so I borrow from different approaches. As a psychoanalyst I find that one theory rarely has all the answers for the treatment of any one patient. Having said that, I can tell you about some of the prominent organizing ideas that I bring to the treatment of personality disorders. First of all, in the current era we must realize that personality is partially rooted in biology. So it is useful for me to think in terms of the distinction Robert Cloninger's model makes between temperament and character. Especially with the severe Cluster B personality disorders, it is very useful to think in those terms. This means that a personality disorder is made up of perhaps 50 percent biological contributions and 50 percent of internalization of environmental stressors, traumas, objects in the environment, which then become the internal object relations, and this also informs an approach that would involve medication for temperament, and psychotherapy for character. The two work quite nicely together for the treatment of severe personality disorders, especially borderlines.

In speaking about the psychotherapy specifically, I'm guided a lot by the years of research we've done at the Menninger Clinic. What I've learned is that there is an expressive-supportive continuum of interventions. One must be guided by the nature of the patient's psychopathology in such a way as to shift flexibly from an interpretive, expressive approach to a supportive one, when needed. There was a spin-off study of the Menninger psychotherapy research project, which was never published for obvious reasons: it rated the therapists according to skill level. Those with the most flexibility were rated as highest in skill. The ones with the lowest skill ratings were characterized by rigidity. They felt they had a certain theoretical approach and a certain technique that they thought was right, and it was the patient's job to adjust to it. I think the opposite way. One should adjust the treatment to the patient. In our recently completed follow-up study to the original Menninger psychotherapy research project—we call it TRIP, the Treatment Interventions Project—I learned a great deal from listening to audiotaped transcripts of psychoanalytic therapy with borderline patients, learning to monitor the therapist's capacity to shift flexibly according to the patient's difficulty in collaborating with the therapist. If the therapist makes a transference interpretation and the patient's collaboration with the therapist deteriorates, so there is no therapeutic alliance, that makes me rethink the role of transference interpretations. I then shift to a more supportive end of the continuum and try to create more of a sense that I understand the patient, and postpone transference interpretations until the therapeutic alliance is stronger. So flexibility would be another key component of my approach.

The other aspect that is critically important is an emphasis on countertransference. I view psychoanalytic psychotherapy as both a one-person and a two-person psychology. I am looking at the patient's intrapsychic world, but I am also tremendously influenced by that individual and I am influencing the patient by what I think and say and feel. That's one of the reasons I place a great deal of emphasis on projective identification. I think there is a semipermeable membrane that allows things to go back and forth across the dyad. One of the ways that I get to know the patient is by my own reactions to that patient. I think it was Christopher Bollas who said, "To find the patient we look within ourselves."

So I focus a lot on what I'm experiencing with this patient as a way of knowing a little bit about the patient's internal world. Obviously that's also contaminated by who I am and my own subjectivity. Now, over time, I get a sense of what the patient is bringing to the situation and what I'm bringing, because I know myself from one patient to another and I know typical kinds of countertransference difficulties. I guess that another reason I've emphasized countertransference is part of my own background. I've treated, evaluated, and consulted on many therapists who have had severe boundary violations with patients, often sexual involvement, or taking the patient into their home, or making him part of the family. So I've seen some of these disasters and have learned a great deal about how lack of attention to the countertransference produces horrific consequences.

You say a flexible approach from expressive to supportive is needed, and that the better therapists are capable of doing that. We have interviewed quite a few other people who think differently about this. John Clarkin, for instance, says that when therapists who have decided to do expressive therapy are seduced into becoming supportive, the therapy comes to a standstill. Another one is Otto Kernberg, who says the expressive mode is what you have to do, the other thing is just not right, unless the patient is really at a very low level and cannot be helped with the expressive mode. A third one would be Larry Rockland, who says, "You don't even have to be expressive. Supportive therapy cures people anyway," and he refers to the

Menninger study, as described by Wallerstein (1986), Forty-Two Lives in Treatment. You say: "First you are supportive and when the patient can stand it you become expressive."

That would be oversimplifying. I mean that you shift flexibly, depending on where you think the patient is emotionally at the time.

But the question is, can you shift? And do you have to be expressive at all, since supportive therapy seems to be effective enough in its own right?

Well, I find that remarkable, that people would say that you can't shift flexibly. I'm very influenced by Bob Wallerstein, and it's clear that expressive and supportive strategies are synergistic, they are not diametrically opposed in some way. What we found in our TRIP project is that a very frequent development in a session (we are talking about a microcosmic level) was that a series of supportive, empathically validating comments from the therapist would pave the way for a transference interpretation, which could then be heard because the patient would feel himself held in a Winnicottian sense. A surgeon has to have anesthesia to operate. A therapist who wants to make a transference interpretation must create an atmosphere, a climate in which the interpretation can be heard without any damage to the alliance. So I don't agree with someone who would think that a flexible approach is not workable, and Wallerstein's project certainly bears that out. Now, in terms of the question of "Why not just do supportive therapy?" I've read Larry Rockland's book. What he describes as supportive therapy to me has many expressive elements. In fact, it is the most expressive supportive therapy I've ever seen!

So the difference really isn't that big.

No. What I think is that he's describing a kind of flexible, expressive-supportive or supportive-expressive approach.

Actually, when you watch Kernberg and Rockland interviewing the same patient, the differences are very minor.

That bears out what I thought.

On the other hand, the difference with Akhtar's approach is enormous.

I'm sure it is. Actually, when we talk about Rockland, Kernberg, and Clarkin, they're all from the same institution.

Yes! If they were that different, they would split.

Right, but back to the question. I would think that by supplementing the supportive approach with expressive interventions like interpretations, you can sometimes help the patient to go in the direction of mastery through insight. There may be durable changes as a result of supportive therapy, as Wallerstein suggests there are, but keep in mind that Wallerstein also pointed out that from psychoanalysis all the way down to supportive therapy, there is always a mixture of expressive and supportive interventions. The expressive component helps the patient develop a little further in terms of promoting a kind of self-analytic process after termination.

Kernberg has said: "A good interpretation can be very supportive."

Sure! I would also like to stress that since Peter Fonagy has come to the Menninger Clinic, I have also been influenced by his view of mentalization and reflective functioning. He has made the point that from studying traumatized borderline patients at the Anna Freud Centre in London he found a consistent concreteness, a lack of reflectiveness—you might call it a lack of interiority, no inner world. And one of the things Peter and I are trying to do a little research on together is the development of a sense of an inner world, where patients have feelings that lead to actions, where they have internal self and object representations, and where other people have an internal world, so that they become more reflective about their own motives and other people's, rather than feeling like a leaf buffeted in the wind. The promoting of this reflectiveness is a very important aspect of the therapy and even when you do supportive work you want to encourage this development.

Perhaps what Clarkin meant when he mentioned the danger of becoming supportive, is that it may be useful and productive if done with skill, but may be damaging if done by less-skilled therapists, because then it may just be complementary behavior.

Certainly.

You mentioned the fact that the 50 percent biological makeup is amenable to medication treatment. Could you say a little more about that?

There is considerable empirical support for the notion that SSRIs are helpful. They appear to affect temperament in such a way that anger, aggressive outbursts, and verbal aggression are reduced, and that's documented in double-blind controlled studies. What I find as a therapist is that it allows the patient more freedom to reflect, because there is less background noise involving anger, dissatisfaction, and dysphoria. Psychotherapy and medication work synergistically because drugs have an impact on the temperament. Antiseizure medications like carbamazepine or valproic acid also might help, and sometimes lithium. These are very valuable adjuncts to psychotherapy. They are not cures. Nor do they change the personality. They often make psychotherapy more productive.

Kernberg has said that medication in these patients very often only works for a time, like six months, and then loses its effectiveness.

It's variable; it doesn't work for every patient. There is the old quotation from Osler, "When a new drug comes on the market, use it quickly, before it loses its effectiveness." What Otto may be referring to is that there may be an important placebo effect. Some patients manically embrace new treatments, as though they've found a magic bullet, and then over time they find they have the same problems with relationships and so on and become disillusioned. Some psychopharmacologists suggest there is a "Prozac poop-out" phenomenon as well, in which the chemical effects appear to diminish. I have a modest view of what medication can do. You get only modest improvement of certain symptoms, but it does facilitate therapy.

We would like you to tell us a little about your personal motives for this flexible approach. You already mentioned the fact that you're pluralistic by nature. Have other factors played a part?

I'm attracted to working with borderline patients because there is a sense of drama associated with them. I grew up in a theatrical family. My parents were drama professors and later on they became professional actors. I think I'm attracted to dramatic patients. I've noticed this about the patients who interest me in general. In terms of the pluralism, I have always been skeptical of fanaticism, of anyone who says "I know The Truth." I grew up in a family without a family religion. My parents were agnostic, and said "We want you to find your own religious interest. We want you to be a free thinker." As I went through my education I looked at many religions and got the impression that most of them have something useful to offer. They all have some truth in them. As I got into the study of psychiatry and psychotherapy I found that many psychoanalytic theories and many nonpsychoanalytic theories, like cognitive theories, have merit. I find myself trying to draw from many theories according to what is the best fit for this patient. As an analyst I worry greatly about certain analysts who insist on one theoretical perspective. Patients pick up on this, and comply with what they think their analyst wants them to talk about. They develop an analyst-shaped narrative, based on the analyst's favorite theory.

*In this you resemble Michael Stone, both in your interest in dra-
matic people, and in the enormous scepticism toward dogma.*

Right.

*Actually, wouldn't you score yourself pretty high on the Sensation
Seeking Scale (SSS)? You do describe yourself as stimulus seeking.*

No! I am what you might call a "chicken"! I would never do anything like downhill skiing, or bungee jumping. I have more of a
vicarious fascination with patients who are sensation seeking.
That's much safer. Like when watching a film, one can have ad-
ventures without being in personal danger.

*What are your opinions about psychotherapy in general and your
place in the field?*

Well, what I find is that I'm one of an increasingly small number of
psychoanalysts in the USA who are still involved in psychiatry. Some
of my colleagues find it quite remarkable that I keep up with the
psychopharmacology literature to some extent and attempt to integrate mind and brain. Many analysts have given up on psychiatry. I represent a bridging between psychiatry and psychoanalysis
and I write in both areas. Another reason why I'm interested in
severe personality disorders is that it's a diagnostic entity that bridges
mind and brain, biology and psychology. It allows an analytic perspective within a psychiatric entity so to speak.

*Could it be that the atmosphere in the Menninger Clinic is an im-
portant influence on you as well? I remember a book by Stephen
Appelbaum,* Out in Inner Space *(1979). He was sent out to investigate if all these newfangled theories of the sixties might not have
some useful aspects. That attitude of open-mindedness, which you
describe for yourself, isn't that a typical attitude at the Menninger?*

Appelbaum was a teacher of mine who influenced me. I would say that it probably is to some extent a Menninger-shaped influence. And undoubtedly one of the reasons for my interest in severe personality disorders is that for many years the borderline patient has been the specialty of the house. Robert Knight got interested in borderline personality disorder in the forties there, and of course so did Otto. And Don Rinsley was another influence. He was at the Topeka VA hospital, but he taught at the Menninger School of Psychiatry. Many of the patients and the mentors that I had around me were focusing on this personality disorder. I think your point is correct, that there was an attitude of open-minded inquiry there.

One of the unique things about the Topeka Institute, compared to other psychoanalytic institutes, is that there is no "party line." There are always many other theories taught and practiced within the hospital. So I did not grow up professionally with a sense that I had better think exactly like some charismatic figure who was looking over my shoulder and telling me what to think.

Freeman told us some pretty awful stories, illustrating how being pushed into a straitjacket has pushed him out of the field of psychoanalysis.

I can understand that.

Who else has influenced you?

Probably the most influential figure has been the San Francisco analyst Thomas Ogden (1989). I first developed a relationship with him by corresponding after reading one of his papers. Then we became personal friends, and I visit him in San Francisco and discuss cases with him. He runs a seminar there that I have presented material to. I consider him the most brilliant theorist in American psychoanalysis. He also represents a kind of amalgam of Kleinian and British middle school thought. So he's an independent thinker who is not easily pigeonholed into a certain theoretical framework, although very broadly speaking he's an object relations theoretician. His detailed understanding of the unconscious, of projective identification, of countertransference has influenced me greatly. I would say other influences were Kernberg (when I arrived in Topeka as a resident, he had just left and the whole philosophy of the place was steeped in Kernbergian thinking). Then there is Salman Akhtar, who also shares a perspective of looking at different theories, needs versus wishes, Kernberg versus Kohut, trying to balance the theoretical approach against the patient's needs. He is one of my peers, not a mentor, but I read his stuff and I benefit from it.

Have there been important changes in the course of time in your way of thinking or your work with these patients?

Yes. I hope that we all grow! I've become much more spontaneous, much less formal, and also much more willing to allow myself to be sucked into enactments, with the idea that the transference–countertransference enactments are a gold mine of information. Obviously I think the enactments should be attenuated. I try to catch myself as they're developing and then try to process them with the patient. One of Freud's greatest papers was a 1914 paper, "Remembering, Repeating, and Working Through," in which he talked about acting out in its original meaning, which is that the patient is enacting an important object relationship right in front of your eyes. I believe that you inevitably will be drawn into this, so that the therapist is enacting something as well. I am much more convinced now that we need to go beyond just listening to the patient's words. We must have a sense of what's being repeated in the behavior of the patient and (for me) in my own behavior. That's why I allow myself to be more spontaneous. I guess, as I feel more secure, I'm less concerned about violating a boundary or making a mistake or technical error. I feel like mistakes are often very useful to discuss with the patient.

You don't have to be a perfect therapist, just a good-enough therapist.

Thats a nice way to put it.

Salman Akhtar said: "It is good to do things that are not within accepted boundaries, as long as you talk about it with colleagues. Don't keep it a secret."

A very good point. I always tell my students, "Anything you might want to keep secret from your supervisor is the very thing you should talk about!"

For that reason Clarkin uses tapes, because as he says "You can't rely on just the reports of therapists about what they are doing."

Exactly.

One change, then, has been that you became freer. Is there another change?

Well, I think the other one would be a growing appreciation of the important role biology plays in personality disorders. I was skeptical early in my career. But I see many aspects of personality that are hard-wired, where you can see that there is a genetically based temperament. I now have more modest assumptions about what I can change with psychotherapy.

Does your approach have any limitations?

The limitations of my approach are that some patients will not stay in psychotherapy and some of them are so concrete and cognitively limited that it's hard for them to participate in the kind of expressive-supportive approach that I've described. They will be difficult patients for almost any psychotherapist.

Perhaps the question should be, "Are there areas of psychopathology where your approach is not as effective as other approaches might be?" Or should we say that if your approach doesn't work, no other approach would?

I suppose that's right.

Could you say something about particular successes or failures that you remember?

I have described a number of successes in my articles and books. I have occasionally had patients who could not meet my minimum requirement of honest self-reporting, and so I had to stop the therapy due to recurrent deceptiveness. However, I am also convinced of what Gunderson calls the "bucket brigade phenomenon"—you know, referring to people fighting a fire, handing a bucket from one person to the other, which illustrates that there's often a cumulative effect on the borderline patient of several therapists, one after another. Any one therapy may terminate prematurely, or "fail," but over time the patient has other therapists who may pursue similar kinds of issues, and ultimately may get better.

Perhaps a person may have to bang her head against the same wall many times before she gives one more therapist a chance the other ones never got. The trouble is that you keep on wondering what happened to that patient you lose. You worry that she may have committed suicide. Clarkin made a comparison between Kernberg and Linehan, and said, "With all their differences, they both in the end are fully convinced that the decision to live or die lies with the patient.

The decision indeed is the patient's. My technical approach, though, is different. I know John Clarkin very well and respect him. We are involved in research together with Otto, but where I would disagree with him or with Otto is that I think it's impossible to be neutral about suicidality. We do this work because we believe that there is some value in life and I would be phony if I tried to convey to a patient that I don't really care if he lived or died. It's much better and more honest to convey to the patient that you as a therapist want him to find a way to live, and that that is preferable to committing suicide.

I don't really think that John Clarkin and Otto Kernberg try to give the impression that they don't care. They would probably say that they need the patient alive if the therapy is to go on.

Probably not, but Otto says very clearly in his writing that he believes in technical neutrality and I find that's impossible with borderline patients. Harold Searles, another occasional mentor of mine, once said that he had no idea what Otto was talking about when he mentioned technical neutrality, because you are on an emotional roller coaster when you work with borderlines.

When you watch Kernberg on video, you see a therapist who is warmer than you might expect from his writings.

I agree. He is not only personally warm, but he's empathically attuned. I have seen tapes of him as well. I don't equate neutrality with lack of warmth, though. I equate it with being nonjudgmental. I think it is very, very difficult to be nonjudgmental about the self-destructive behavior of borderlines.

Have you ever sinned against your own basic approach?

Well, you can only sin if you think your approach is religious dogma. But I do deviate from my approach and have done things that later on I thought were not particularly good choices. But I see that as not outside of the technique, I see it as part of the technique! You cross boundaries here and there in a kind and benign way, and it may or may not work, and then you backpedal and say: "Let's talk about what I did yesterday," and you find out what you can learn from it.

Which two or three books, not written by yourself, would you advise the reader to study?

One would be Thomas Ogden's book *The Primitive Edge of Experience* (1989), another would be Akhtar's *Broken Structures* (1992), another Harold Searles's *My Work with Borderline Patients* (1986).

Are there any aspects of your work that we haven't discussed and that you would like to mention?

Yes. In terms of sins, boundaries, and enactments, I think it's useful to say what I won't do. Okay? I am extremely distressed about the number of serious boundary violations, which not only destroy a patient's treatment and destroy a therapist's career, but give the whole profession a bad name. So one of the things I would not do would be to say to a patient: "I have sexual feelings for you." This is controversial! I have been engaged in an ongoing dialogue with Jody Davies in *Psychoanalytic Dialogues*; she thinks sexual self-disclosure can be useful. That's one place where I draw a pretty firm boundary. Obviously sexual contact is off-limits; I am even wary of hugging patients. This is an area where you can get in a great deal of difficulty. Even if you think it's a benign hug, the impact on the patient may be quite different from what you think the intent of the hug is. Then, in terms of other self-disclosures, I would not say to a patient: "I hate you," or "You bore me to tears," because it is not the obligation of the patient to entertain us. So even if I may be bored, I would look for other ways to express my countertransference, rather than through direct disclosures of that nature. On the other hand, I have often disclosed anger, worry, or exasperation to patients.

Let's say you have an obnoxious patient. One of those narcissists who always play one-upmanship and get under your skin that way. You must discuss it, it's part of the pathology. How do you give that back to the patient?

I would certainly tell a patient: "I'm angry at you, I'm irritated," and I would say, "You try to one-up me to get me irritated at you. What's behind that? Why would that be of such interest to you, to re-create this situation again and again?" By mentioning those areas of self-disclosure, I do not want to imply that other areas of self-disclosure may not be very useful. You know, it can be devastating to a patient to know the therapist hates him. He might never come back. It would be an acting out on my part, saying one part of my feelings and having the part pass for the whole. It's usually much more complicated than that, and I learned from treating hateful patients that in many cases they are attached and connected to you and quite loving in their hate. I have learned that if I can stay in there long enough, I get to know that other part as well. I think that it would not be useful in any kind of therapy to focus on one hurtful aspect of the relationship in an attempt to retaliate against the patient.

The Situations

In the middle of the night, you're called on the phone by a patient who threatens to commit suicide. What would you do in such a situation?

There are many aspects that would go into deciding what I would do. It would depend on the nature of the alliance with the patient, the issue of baseline suicidality, the life-threatening nature of the suicidality, and the frequency with which the patient has called me before. In general I will say to a suicidal borderline patient, "If you feel you are so out of control that you might act on the suicidal wishes, I want you to call me, even if it's in the middle of the night." If they abuse that and call me frequently, I will set limits and say to them in the session: "I cannot work with you if you wake me up frequently at night. I will lie awake worry-ing about you and the next day I will be too tired to think well. So we have to work out a different way of doing this." With a person who did it once in a great while, I would be concerned that this person was very seriously suicidal and get him to a hospital.

Like Stone, who in some cases would even bring them himself?

No. With a suicidal patient I would have an understanding in advance about which hospital he or she was to go to in such a case. So now I would say "Go to the hospital, I will call them and tell them you're coming." So the understanding is that they will only call me if it's so serious that they really do need to go into a hospital. Now, I would not spend a lot of time in the middle of the night trying to talk the patient out of committing suicide. That's a precedent that, if you establish it, could be exploited. And I would certainly, in almost any situation, talk to the patient in the next session about the meaning of that phone call.

Let's say the patient refuses to go to the hospital, because this is re-ally the end of everything.

First of all, at the beginning of therapy with a suicidal borderline patient, I would do something similar to Kernberg's contract set-ting. I would want to know the history of suicidality, and I would anticipate that situation. I would say: "I don't want to be in a situ-ation where you call me and say you are suicidal and refuse to go to a hospital. If you're going to refuse, I cannot work with you. I can't work with someone who is lethal and still refuses help." Of course they can always violate the contract! (smiles)

The essence of a contract is that two people stick to it. So even if the patient breaks the contract, you don't.

Sometimes I may have to, and call the police to bring someone to the hospital. But then the therapy will probably end. Then I will have to go to the hospital and talk about ending the therapy and transferring the patient to another therapist. I will try to be ethical about it and make the transition possible. If the patient is sufficiently remorseful I might consider continuing the therapy, but with great skepticism. So there is some flexibility in handling the contract. But again, I would not be neutral about the suicide. If I really thought the patient was lethal, I would do whatever I could to get him to a hospital and save him. I would not go to the patient's house or apartment though: that's another thing I would not do.

Would you have a session in the middle of the night in such a case? In some cases Akhtar would.

Well, I've talked to people in the night, for a brief period of time. But part of what a therapist must do is to develop a professional life that's comfortable to him and the patient must adjust to that. And it is not comfortable to me to have sessions in the middle of the night.

As Akhtar would say, "It depends on the burden you can carry." And Lorna Smith Benjamin says, "If you can't stand the heat, get out of the kitchen." You have to be able to bear some burden, but everybody has his limits.

Right. And each therapist must set limits for himself. Some don't, and then they make terrible mistakes. One of the things I teach students is an analogy to a lifeguard. In their training they are told, "Make sure that *you* are safe before you try to save a drowning victim, or the drowning victim will drag you down with him." A lot of career-destroying boundary violations could have been prevented if the therapist had thought of that. I must make sure that I am safe before I try to rescue this patient. If you go to a patient's house in the middle of the night, you put yourself in a position to drown.

What would you do if a patient comes to the appointed session obviously inebriated?

That would be very simple. I'd say, "We cannot work in therapy if you are inebriated. We'll stop."

The person may deny it.

If it's clear to me, I would still end the session. In personality disorders it is so important that substance abuse is addressed immediately. You know Stone's data about the lethality associated with untreated alcoholics.

That's why Stone would even say in this case, "Go to AA tomorrow. And until you have done that, I will not continue the treatment."

I've insisted on the same thing.

You meet one of your patients at a cocktail party and he or she wants to use this opportunity to have an ordinary social meeting with you for a change, and starts to chat with you. What would you do?

That has never happened to me! Most patients in social situations stay away. But I can imagine that it might happen. Then I would say I felt that we should discuss this in the office. If it's just a brief period of time of social chit-chat, I would do what Karl Menninger used to say: "If you don't know what to do, act human." I'd go through the ordinary social graces up to a point. But then if it develops into a lengthy chat, I would say: "I think we ought to talk about this in the office."

A patient turns out to be in the neighborhood of your front door every time you come home. Just standing in the street.

This would be something like a stalker. It hasn't happened to me, but I do know people to whom it has happened. I think this is, again, an example of a situation where you have to set limits. I know one therapist who in such a situation invited the patient into her home, introduced him to her husband and children, and asked him to sit down for tea. This then led to increasing sexual overtures by the patient in her office, because he felt that he was given some kind of permission not to adhere to ordinary professional boundaries. I think that the patient needs to have the communication that you have a private life, and that if he violates this you will have to end treatment. So either the patient stops doing that, or I can't treat the patient. It's that straightforward.

You discover that something from your office has been taken away by a patient—"borrowed," stolen, or just picked up on an impulse. You know who did it. What would you do?

If I was fairly certain who did it, I would bring it up in the next session. "I'm wondering why you did this, and I want you to bring it back to me." In other words, I would not see it as something to shy away from. In general, I think that in the psychotherapy of borderline patients you call attention to what's obvious. You don't shy away from saying the obvious for fear of the patient's exploding because you upset him. Many people do not do this in normal life, and that's why there is so much chaos. I would bring it up in a very straightforward way and assume that it will be returned. Now if it turns out that the patient is a psychopath, denies it, and refuses to bring it back, the therapy will have to be ended because this patient isn't going to be amenable to psychotherapy.

Would this inevitably mean the patient is a psychopath?

Well, it would make me wonder. Certainly I would want to explore it further, but if somebody would lie about this . . .

. . . out of shame?

Well, that's why I would want to explore it a little more.

Could you describe the setting in which you see your patients? Is it an office? Part of your own home? Do you sit face-to-face? Are there personal things in the room? Is the atmosphere businesslike or homey? That sort of thing.

First of all, I see my patients in an office on the grounds of the Menninger Clinic. It's the building of the Topeka Insitute for Psychoanalysis, which is actually part of the Menninger Clinic. So it does have an institutional rather than a homey atmosphere. I have purchased a couple of comfortable chairs. Both the patient and I are comfortable. Over the years I've developed a preference of having the chairs set at an angle of forty-five degrees. I find some patients hate the obligatory eye contact associated with chairs facing each other. They feel they have to look at you. In this position each party has the freedom to look straight ahead and thus not into the eyes of the other, or to look slightly to one side, and occasionally look each other in the face. It approximates the freedom of the psychoanalytic situation of the couch, though not quite. I should mention that occasionally I put people with severe personality disorders on the couch. I reported one case in the *International Journal of Psycho-Analysis* in which the patient was analyzed successfully, but it was an exception. The couch is always there, because I treat other patients as well. The patient sits right next to the door, so he doesn't feel trapped. I have had a number of rather severely mistreated borderline patients. They feel trapped if they cannot get out when they want to. I would not treat someone in my office that I thought might assault me.

I have photographs of my wife and children, but they are in a position where the patient can't see them. I used to have them out in the open. Not that that's such a terrible thing to do, because you can analyze the reaction. But again it's a matter of my own privacy. I don't want them to get into my life and talk about the patient's fantasies about my children or my wife or whatever. Then there are some personal objects, like Kachina dolls, which were given to me as gifts. These are dolls made by the Hopi Indians and they are symbolic of various Indian gods. I'm interested in that kind of art. There are some awards on the walls—I was included in a book called *The Best Doctors of America* (Smith 1992). That produces reactions in my patients! I also have a picture of Freud's couch. It's fascinating to me, by the way, how many people don't see! They look, but don't see.

I can understand Freud's couch, but that award—Don't you think that would evoke many transference reactions?

Yes. There are other things like that on my wall as well. You see, I live my life according to what I want to do and the patient has to react to it. I'm proud of receiving awards, and they are often on plaques so that you can put them on the wall. If I wish to do that, the patient has to adjust. I don't want my family's picture on my desk because it leads to an invasion of privacy that I feel uncomfortable with. I create my office primarily for my comfort. Just like people say, "How can you travel? What about your patients?" I like to travel. It enriches me, like coming to Holland for a workshop. I enjoy it and I learn a great deal through it. So my patients will have to adjust to that. I will not organize my life to please my patients. This only leads to resentment.

I have very extensive bookshelves, and that's always very stimulating for discussions. I remember one patient who was very invested in staying ill, and would have liked to defeat me. He looked at a certain book: *The Treatment of Emotional Disorders*, and said, "I like that book, '*The Treasury of Emotional Disorders*'." I pointed out his misreading. That sort of thing may be very useful!

Since people generally know about your status in the field, not having those awards and those books would be out of character and perhaps that would not be a good holding environment as well.

Good point!

8

Otto Kernberg

Biography

Otto Kernberg was born in Vienna, Austria, on September 10, 1928, the only child of a customs official. As a child he learned of psychiatry through his uncle, Manfred Sakel, who discovered insulin-coma therapy for schizophrenia. The family emigrated to Chile in 1933, when it became obvious what the results of the "Anschluss" of Austria with the Third Reich would be. In Chile he met his wife Paulina, to whom he has been married for more than thirty-five years. She is a leading children's psychoanalyst. They have three children: Martin, Karen, and Adine.

Kernberg studied medicine and psychiatry in Santiago, Chile, and became a psychiatrist in 1957. During his residency he started his training as a psychoanalyst. He became a member of the Chilean Psychoanalytical Society in 1960. An outstanding figure during this period was Ignacio Matte Blanco, whose ego-psychological, Kleinian, and phenomenological interests have been important influences on Kernberg.

The Chilean Psychoanalytical Society gradually became more and more Kleinian oriented. This led to Kernberg's progressively independent orientation, and this developed further when he spent some months in the United States on a Rockefeller grant and met John Whithorn, head of psychiatry at the hospital at Johns Hopkins University (interpersonal psychoanalysis) and Lawrence Kubie (American ego psychology). During that period he also visited Chestnut Lodge, the leading center for residential psychotherapy of psychoses.

In 1961 Kernberg accepted the invitation of Robert Wallerstein to join the psychotherapy research project of the Menninger Foundation in Topeka, Kansas. He participated in the study of *Forty-Two Lives in Treatment* (Wallerstein 1986), and discovered that many treatment modalities may be effective with patients, but that supportive and expressive techniques may interfere with each other in the treatment of borderline patients.

Other influences on his professional development were his contacts with Marty Mayman, Herbert Schlesinger, Ernst Ticho, and Herman Van der Waals, as well as John Sutherland, who brought Fairbairn's theories to his attention. Fairbairn's theories and the work of Edith Jacobson were instrumental in his bridging the gap between drive theory and object relations theory.

Kernberg left the Menninger Foundation in 1973 and went to New York, where three years later he became professor of psychiatry at Cornell University Medical College and president and medical director of the New York Hospital-Cornell Medical Center, Westchester Division, in White Plains, New York. His friendships with Edith Jacobson and Margaret Mahler and his contacts with Harold Blum, Donald Kaplan, Robert Michels, Arnold Cooper, Ethel Person, and Ted Shapiro have all been of further influence, even though some of these colleagues were of a completely different theoretical orientation.

Kernberg is a member of the International Psychoanalytical Society (since 1961), and the American Psychoanalytical Society (since 1964), a teaching analyst at Columbia University Center for Psychoanalytic Training and Research (since 1974), vice president of the International Psychoanalytical Society (since 1991), and president of the Society for Psychoanalytic Medicine (since 1991).

This development and these activities have so far led to the publication of seven books by Kernberg, and five others of which he is co-author, a large number of other publications, and many scientific awards. Margaret Mahler is reputed to have said, "I don't know if the man ever sleeps!" This vitality and versatility impress whomever Kernberg meets, no matter what the subject under discussion may be.

The Interview

Doctor Kernberg, you have published a great number of books and papers on the subject of severe personality disorders, and it will be difficult to give a summary of your ideas on the subject. Nevertheless, we would like you to try to give a brief overview.

Well, in its simplest form, I would say that the personality structure of patients with borderline personality organization is characterized by the syndrome of identity diffusion. This means a lack of integration of the concept of self, and of the concept of significant others, and a decomposition, a fragmentation, a coming unglued of the tripartite structure (ego, superego, and id) so the unconcious conflicts are not embedded in that integrated tripartite structure, but in the components of the ego, the superego and the id, namely, internalized object relations that have as their basic units representations of self relating to representations of significant others, under the impact of a dominant affect. These basic units of superego, ego, and id are normally integrated into these higher-level structures, which in these people has not happened.

Because of all this we have those primitive dyads in contrast, imbued with intense primitive affect. As a result the unconscious conflicts between impulse and defense are expressed clinically as unconscious conflicts involving these primitive internalized object relations, and are represented as contradictory object relations, particularly of an idealized and/or persecutory kind.

I assume that these primitive internalized object relations, which are usually manifest in the split of the self and of the significant others, will show in the interaction with the patients, who will rapidly shift from the objective object relation that you set up. You do this by giving the instructions about the therapy, and by making clear that this is going to be a relationship between, on the one side, a patient who is in need of help and has a minimum of trust in the therapist, and on the other side a person who is of good will and who will try to help the patient. This way you set up the conditions for a realistic object relation. This rapidly gets distorted, in the first session, by the emergence of these primitive internalized object relations in the form of the patient activating such a relationship by enacting the role, say, of his self representation, by projecting his object representation onto the therapist and enacting the primitive intense affect in that relationship. Then he will invert the roles, so that the patient who first is representing his own self will, ten minutes later, project his representation of his self onto the therapist while he identifies with the object representation of the significant other. In other words, the same object relationship is enacted with rapid role reversals.

This is the most typical manifestation of the emergence of primitive unconscious conflicts in the form of such primitive object relations, activated in the transference with role reversals, and activated so that idealized kinds of relationships and persecutory relationships are completely split. A typical strategy of the patient who experiences that, thinking that it is the reality of the situation, is an attempt to force the therapist into some kind of idealized relationship as far as the patient is concerned as a defense against a threatening persecutory one. If the therapist maintains the structure, rather than being seduced into an idealized relation with the patient, the patient may shift from the idealized role into the persecutory one, and you have a severe paranoid regression. The activation of these primitive internalized object relations permits the diagnosis and eventually the integration of the mutually split-off parts, the idealized and the persecutory segments. That integration brings about the integration of the ego, and the superego, and the id—the resolution of identity diffusion, and the structural improvement of the patient's functioning, which is the ultimate objective of the treatment.

Now the way to achieve that has various stages, or steps. Step one is to diagnose which kind of crazy relationship replaces the objective one, created by the treatment frame. For example, it's as if a hungry child were begging desperately for an indifferent mother to feed it. So we diagnose a relationship that we define in a metaphorical way. We don't trace it back and say: "Oh, when you were 3 months old . . ." In an ahistorical way we just define that relationship. Step two is to define a self and an object, and step three, to clarify their relation with each other, and their interchange. In doing that the patient gradually learns about himself that he has identified in a deep sense with both self and object.

For example, a patient who was severely traumatized sexually learns that, subconsciously, that traumatic relationship has been internalized as a relationship between a victim and a persecutor, a rapist and a rape victim. And that he activates that relationship, acting as if he were a rape victim, and the therapist a rapist. And ten minutes later it's as if the patient were the rapist and the therapist the victim. The analysis of the alternation of these two enables the patient to accept the identification with both victim and perpetrator and to become less afraid of the total relationship, to have less need to project it. And that in turn permits him gradually to integrate interpretatively the persecutory with the idealized relationship. The patient understands his search for an idealized relationship to protect himself against the persecutory one, and the impossibility of tolerating the persecutory one, because he had not been able to tolerate his identification with victim and perpetrator. Thus there will be less need to project the persecution onto the therapist. It is easier for him to see that the idealized therapist and the persecutory therapist are really one, and that it was his internal splitting that had distorted the situation.

So these steps constitute the basic overall strategy of the treatment. It is a strategy that implies *techniques* and *tactics. Techniques* in terms of interpretation, with its components of clarification and confrontation, linking what happens to an unconscious motivation in the here and now, and then linking it to an unconscious motivation from the past, the there and then. *Tactics* refers to a number of ways of dealing with typical contents that protect the treatment and the treatment frame, and help the therapist to decide what needs to be interpreted, and how and when it needs to be interpreted. These tactics include, first, the *therapist's being attentive* in each session to what the patient is saying, to how he is saying it, and to what the therapist's reaction to it is. In other words, verbal communication, nonverbal communication, and countertransference—what we call channels I, II, and III. The simultaneous attention to these sources of information permits the therapist to decide what is affectively dominant at any particular point, and the dominant affect is at the same time the indicator of the dominant object relation. There is no such thing as pure affect. All affects imply object relations. Thus the therapist decides what is the most important issue at any particular point by what has affective dominance, what Bion calls the "selected fact."

Another implication of this tactical approach is the importance of the *analysis of the countertransference*, because in the countertransference the therapist oscillates between times when he is able to identify with the patient's experience, is empathic with the patient's subjective experience, (which permits him to understand the patient), and times when the therapist identifies with the patient's objects (while the patient acts like his self), or with the patient's self (while the patient acts like his object). At times, the patient treats the therapist sadistically, while the therapist identifies with the paralyzed child, thus identifying with what the patient projects but can't tolerate. So the concordant and the complementary identification in the countertransference permit respectively empathy with what the patient experiences, and empathy with what is projected, which at the same time helps to clarify the dominant object relation in the transference.

The third tactical aspect is *setting of priorities* in terms of urgency of intervention, and general principles about typical sequences in transference development. "Urgency of intervention" refers to the fact that there are certain emergency situations that have to be taken care of first. Borderline patients may experience tremendous self-destructive tendencies. In general these have to do with massive dominance of primitive aggression over sexuality and co-option of sexuality in the service of aggression, so there are severely aggressive and primitive transferences that may take the form of suicidal, parasuicidal, or homicidal tendencies that need to be taken up first (which means, dealt with interpretatively), and this also makes it necessary to structure the treatment (meaning limit setting), to which there are certain technical approaches: interpreting the issue, setting limits—to protect a patient's life, other people's lives, or the therapist's life—and, once limits have been set, interpreting the conflict, and at the end interpreting the reasons for which limits had to be set. All of this implies shifts in the therapist's technical neutrality.

Would you call this aspect of your work supportive?

No, although it has supportive effects. I think one has to differentiate between supportive techniques and supportive effects. The most supportive effect, for instance, may be the effect of a good interpretation. Supportive techniques are techniques that move on one side of the conflict, reinforcing the adaptive side of the patient's conflicts. For example, if a patient is rebellious and smashes windows on the street, you tell the patient, "Look, you can't do that!" We are on the side of the defense against the aggressive impulse, which helps patient to adapt. When a patient has a sexual inhibition, and we tell him "Look, there's nothing wrong or shameful in enjoying sex," we're on the side of the drive and the impulse, because that's adaptive. Supportive techniques imply emotional support, cognitive support, direct advice-giving and recommending or suppressing behavior, and direct intervention in the patient's environment.

All these are then by definition interventions in which the therapist does not remain technically neutral, but tries to influence the patient directly, or uses the patient's influenceability in the direction of adaptation. For me, limit-setting, the structure of the treatment, has as its exclusive goal the protection of the frame of the treatment, of the space in which interpretive analytic work can be carried out. "To do this treament, we need you alive, so you must do certain things so that you don't die." If you call all of this "supportive," you blur the difference between what is indicated to protect the treatment frame from other kinds of countertransference acting out.

Which are meant more to protect the therapist than the treatment frame, you might say?

Yes! Making this differentiation is, of course, controversial. Many people would disagree with me here. But let me continue with the priorities. The second one is threats to the continuation of the treatment. The third one is a patient's dishonesty; the fourth, severe acting out, inside and outside the hours—so there is a list of priorities that imply tactical approaches. And finally there is an overall tendency of transferences to shift from the predominance of paranoid to a predominance of depressive transferences. This may occur in the course of one hour, or throughout many months of therapy. The Kleinians have written mostly about that. What we've done is to expand the saying that patients who have severe antisocial behavior tend to develop psychopathic transferences, in which there is some basic ongoing dishonesty in the relationship. The technical principle is that you have to interpret and resolve psychopathic transferences first, then the paranoid, and finally the depressive ones.

So, I've talked about strategy, techniques, and tactics, which gives you in a nutshell what the treatment consists of. I realize it was a fairly long overview, but my obsessive tendencies do not allow for incompleteness.

Much has been said about the differences between your approach, which is conflict oriented, and that of Kohut, who was deficit oriented. Could you give us your comments on these differences?

We all miss Kohut. Actually though, Kohut never worked with borderlines, he worked with narcissistic personality disorders. Kohut's entire clinical practice came from psychoanalytic cases.

He never worked in the hospital with the sickest patients. That may have something to do with his conclusions.

Would you agree that the one who comes closest is Gerry Adler?

In the field of borderline personality disorders, yes. He is not strictly Kohutian, but he is one of the leading clinicians in this field. My differences with Gerry Adler have to do with our different ways of working with borderlines, which do not really coincide with my differences with Kohut. Adler would agree with the deficit model, that you have to establish positive introjections, and build up good introjections. Adler certainly works with the same kind of patients we do. My disagreement with him is that I don't believe that these patients don't have good introjections. They have intensively idealized and persecutory, mutually split-off segments of their introjections, of their significant object relations. Whenever it seems that they have lost the good introject, the bad introject has taken over. When the therapist goes on vacation, the patient enters into a panic. A Kohutian therapist then may leave the patient with a photograph, a tape or a toy, or his address—something. It seems to me that whenever you analyze these panic situations, they are unconscious fantasies of rageful attack of the therapist on the patient. The absence of the therapist signifies the activation of the presence of the persecutory object.

I don't think there is such a thing as a void in the psychic apparatus. Frustration means the activation of a negative introject. The analysis of these fantasies that the therapist is rageful and hostile permits the consolidation of the relationship and the resolution of the separation anxieties, without any token of attention or guilty interest on the part of the therapist, and makes it possible to maintain a purely analytic approach. On the contrary, very often these "soothing" gestures, on the part of the therapist who feels he is filling up a deficit, reinforce the idealized segment of experience, drive the negative one into repression, and don't really change the structure of the patient.

This brings me back to Kohut, who denies theoretically the internalization of bad introjects. Adler doesn't do that. He accepts the existence of bad introjects. His approach of providing compensation for missing introjects really refers to the early stages of the treatment; later on, he would continue very much along the same approach as I would.

Larry Rockland says, "Adler starts with the supportive mode and then goes on in the exploratory mode."

Exactly. *I* think you can start with the analytic mode from session one and get along much faster. And, in my experience, much more effectively.

Somebody once quoted you as having said, "Kohut spoils his patients."

Did I say that?

Well, they say you did.

I'm not saying he spoiled them, but he tried to reinforce the idealized segment and contributed to a splitting off of the negative aspects. My differences with Kohut have much more to do with the treatment of narcissistic patients than of ordinary borderlines.

To compare you with somebody else than Gerry Adler, the influences of Marsha Linehan and you on each other are very interesting.

I don't know that Marsha has influenced me in any way, to be quite frank. But I have had the impression that in recent years she has taken into consideration the kind of priorities that I mentioned in the beginning of this interview.

Her priorities are the same as yours.

Yes, but I've noticed them in her work only in recent years, while they have been in mine for many, many years. I think she is able to listen and to learn, which I admire. I am also a person who is willing to listen and learn—I mean I'm not implying that I'm not learning—on the contrary. I always insist on mentioning the people I've learned from. But I don't believe that I've taken up anything from her really.

From the whole field of psychotherapeutic patients, you have chosen to work with these severely disturbed patients. And to work with them from the theoretical position that you have chosen. What were your personal motives for these choices?

There is one general motive that predated my work with borderline patients. I was very impressed with psychoanalysis as a theory that explains personality, personality development and psychological disorders, and that can effect major changes of personality. I don't know any other theory or technique that has that capacity and instrumentality. During my own personal analysis I was able to change certain aspects of my habitual behavior, and sometimes in ways that I discovered only after the changes happened, not because I was trying, or doing what I was told to do. I noticed that the spontaneous development as a result of conflict resolution gave me tremendous confidence in analytic work and at the same time great interest in treating persons who were suffering from the limitations of their own character or personality. That seemed to me extremely interesting.

The second factor that influenced me: chance! I was interested in psychotherapy research and didn't know much about it. I came to the Menninger Foundation. Out of the forty-two patients in their research project, about half had severe personality disorders that had particular peculiarities. They had similarities that had not been described in the literature. That patient material alerted me to what I now call borderline personality organization. It seemed to me that "ego weakness" refers to a specific sort of structure, not just weakness of some functions. So it was a combination of luck, plus the fact that I saw these patients, and at the same time a role was played by the fact that I was trained in a

South American institute where the Kleinian theories prevailed, together with ego psychology. This enabled me to apply analytic instruments then not known in the USA (I'm talking about the early 1960s). The Menninger Clinic, where I worked then, was a hotbed of ego psychology (Hartmann, Kris, Loewenstein, Rapaport). This way, I was able to bring in the object relations perspective, which first came from the British authors (Fairbairn on the one hand, under the influence of Sutherland, and Mahler and Jacobson, under the influence of ego psychology, on the other). So I could combine all these approaches. And doing that, it just came naturally to start treating these patients.

Would you say that combining these various schools, or streams of thought, is one of your major contributions to the field of psychotherapy?

Yes. Also, I have been trying to apply psychoanalytic thinking to the treatment of people with very severe personality disorders. I'm not the only one to have done this, but it certainly is one of my major interests. I have also been instrumental in combining different psychoanalytic theories and finding commonalities and developing an integrated frame. These are the two major approaches that define my work.

Let me add that there is something very controversial in the middle of all this. The treatment that I have developed and described, psychoanalytic psychotherapy for borderline personalities, is considered by many psychoanalysts to be a form of psychoanalysis. They say, "This is not psychotherapy, it's psychoanalysis that you're doing." Other analysts say, "No, it is not psychoanalysis, and we would never do this."

I'll explain. For traditional American ego psychology and for Kleinian psychoanalysis, psychoanalysis is very strictly delimited by classical parameters; for example, the idea that technical neutrality can shift flexibly is not psychoanalysis. The British independents, French psychoanalysis (I mean the mainstream, I don't mean Lacan and his followers), and in the

USA the interpersonal and intersubjective approaches to psychoanalysis, tend to be much more flexible in what they call psychoanalysis, including a spectrum of techniques, and including modifications for very sick patients. As long as it's based on free association, the assumption of unconscious conflicts, interpretations, and so on. For me this is not a real problem. It's semantics, even though lots of people take it very seriously. I have been accused by a number of analysts that I call what I do psychoanalytic psychotherapy in order not to create problems for myself in the USA, where the ego psychologists feel so strongly that if I called it psychoanalysis I would be considered a heretic. It is possible that this was an unconscious motivation of mine, but consciously I made that decision because I wanted to differentiate theory, technique, tactics, and strategies very sharply. So I prefer to have a very narrow definition of standard psychoanalysis. I believe that there are other forms of psychoanalytic psychotherapy that are extremely helpful, based upon the same theory that I have helped to develop, that would have different techniques for different situations: for example psychoanalytic group psychotherapy for borderline patients (I do a lot of that nowadays) and couple therapy or family therapy.

People who see you on video for the first time get the impression of a very aggressive approach. Would you say that this is nonsense, or does it have something to do with your personal makeup? I mean, you could have chosen a more friendly-looking approach, like Larry Rockland's, or Gerry Adler's.

I don't think Larry's approach is very different from mine when he's doing psychoanalytic psychotherapy! He's different, much more gentle, when he's working in the supportive mode, which he is so excellent in doing.

He says that your approach is not suitable for the majority of patients—that they will drop out. He says that where you would choose

*the supportive approach, he would think that no therapy at all is
indicated. I may exaggerate a little, but . . .*

That is in part true. I have never heard him say that, but he certainly is willing to work with very damaged patients and do supportive psychotherapy there. But I am also very direct with them.
I am at the moment treating a patient with a chronic double depression (major depression and neurotic depression), who is also
an alcoholic. He doesn't respond to ECT or antidepressive medication because he drinks. He has been able to manipulate his
therapist to ignore his drinking. I'm not going for that, I'm putting in the structure. He hates me for that! He has never had such
a relationship before in his life and he is right to hate me.

*Michael Stone would say: "If you don't go to AA, the treatment stops
right now."*

Sure. I can only treat them if they're on antidepressives, Antabuse,
and AA. Structure, you know! But to come back to your use of
the word aggressive, that doesn't really cover my approach. If you
assume that these patients suffer from severe primitive aggression and that this unavoidably comes up in the treatment, then
you have to stand up to this before it destroys you and the treatment. And you have to be very firm in standing up to it, in the
service of survival, love, and the treatment. If you assume that
even the sexuality that comes up in the treatment is so infiltrated
with aggression that it destroys the life-affirming aspects of sexuality, to make a caricature of it, what I try to is to highlight what
I think is going on.

Of course if I stayed away from these patients and treated only
much healthier ones, I would not have this problem. So the question is not why am I aggressive, but what interests me in treating
these patients? Well, apart from the reasons I gave you before, I
think about 15 percent of the population suffers from these very
severe personality disorders, so I think it's very important to try
to do something about them. It's like a cancer of the personality.

I became a physician because I wanted to help patients and because I wanted to fight death and illness.

Then why not choose the Linehanian approach or any of the other approaches?

I'll come to that. It seemed to me that you have to face the aggression and to interpret it, otherwise you won't be able to help them. Another part of the answer is that there are different types. The same approach that I have can be expressed in a different style. My own personality is direct, with a strong expression of emotion, but I don't hate or attack my patients. If I get enraged at my patient, I shut up. I only intervene from a position of neutrality. Those who have seen me working and have seen my tapes are aware of the fact that harshness or aggression is not really the issue here. Of course many people who see my tapes for the first time have no experience with these severely disturbed people. To them it may seem unnecessarily harsh.

There is a third answer to your question as to why I do not use another approach: because I find psychoanalytic theory provides me with the most satisfactory model of psychopathology. Freud talked about exactly the kind of primitive conflicts around sex and aggression that I see in my patients. It's not that I believe in Freud, it's the other way around: he helps me understand what I see. Max Gitelson used to say, "There are some people who believe in psychoanalysis, except for sex, aggression, and transference." He has a point. I've known analysts like that.

We are now doing research on the outcome of treatments of these people, exactly the same pathology as in Marsha Linehan's population, perhaps a little more antisocial, I don't know. But anyway, the outcome in suicide and parasuicidal gestures is as good as in her research. On top of this we are bringing about important changes in personality. The number of patients is still too small to publish that, but the first signs justify our confidence in our approach. I believe that it is less influenced by ideology than some of those psychotherapies that seem so culturally based, so ideologically based. Like when you treat patients as if they're victims of society and ignore that there are two sides to these problems.

John Clarkin pointed out, referring to you and Marsha Linehan as examples of effective treaters of personality disorders, that both of you have similarities. You both know exactly what you are about, you both stick to your own method, and in the end both of you really believe that the decision to live or die is, and should be, made by the patient. Do you recognize yourself in this description?

Yes. About the last item I want to make a point: I'm very respectful of the self-destructive forces in patients. I'm limited by the extent to which I find enough of an ally in the patient's wish to survive, and there are cases where the destructive wishes are stronger than the wish to help oneself. In those cases the treatment will not help the patient. I'm not out on a rescue operation against and beyond the patient's capacity to work with me.

In the course of the past years, have there been any major changes in your basic assumptions? How have they developed?

Well, what I summarized to you has been developing gradually over the years. My practice and my theories influence each other. I do think that I have become more impressed by the environmental influences on aggression in contrast to inborn ones. Having been influenced by Melanie Klein, I used to think mostly of inborn sources and of course these are important. The biology of aggression confirms that. But severe family pathology, experiencing and witnessing violence and/or sexual exploitation, are important etiological features. Second, I think I work more systematically with my countertransference, particularly when I am in countertransference fixations. Distortions of your internal relationship to your patient, which are there over a period of many months, are very important. I think that I'm more free in doing this kind of work than I used to be. Also I'm more direct with patients, starting from very early stages of the treatment and in each session. It is because so much is decided early that I have become very aware of the dangers of this. I have greater trust that when you are direct and open and invest in the patient, you can help. Of course patients who hate you because you want to help them will try to destroy you even more, so I'm careful of the negative therapeutic reaction in patients who cannot tolerate somebody who wants to help them, and who does not go under.

Finally, I think I know more exactly where to put limits. To quickly realize "to this point I tolerate the situation, not beyond that." So I don't need to let anger accumulate and then react on that. This directness, by the way, causes a difficulty when I teach other therapists because it is at times interpreted by them to be the style in which they should convey the message to their patients. This will not occur when they have a chance to see me work with patients. People whom I supervise but who don't have a chance to see me work may misinterpret my way of telling them things. Perhaps that's one of the reasons some people consider me aggressive.

Would you say that your approach has any limitations? For instance, are there any specific areas where it should be applied in particular, or where it should not be applied?

Well, obviously there are clear contraindications. Antisocial personality problems (following the criteria of Cleckley, Robert Hare, and Michael Stone, not of the *DSM-IV*) are an absolute contraindication for psychoanalytic work. People with malignant narcissism often cannot be helped either. Normal intelligence is needed with these abstract communication theories. Also, there may be enormous secondary gain. When the family structures militate against the treatment you may expect to run into difficulties. Also, even though the patient may seem to be a little monster, I have to be able to imagine, as realistically as I can, a valuable person who is trapped in this prison of his illness. If, however, I think "this poor person has so completely ruined his life that there is nothing better to expect even if he solved all his problems," then I may not be able to help the patient.

He may even be better off remaining the way he is?

That, or I may not be the right person for him. Somebody for whom I feel pity, that's a dangerous trap. A therapist who says: "Poor patient! His family killed, he was in a concentration camp . . ." You can't treat him like anybody else, and that's a disaster. I treat every patient as if he had some healthy part. If I cannot find this tiny morsel of normality, I can't treat. Also, if at the beginning of the treatment, before any kind of relationship has had a chance to evolve, I have intense negative reactions, then I won't treat the patient. It hasn't happened to me in recent years, fortunately.

Do you ever think, "the biological makeup of this person is so bad, there's no chance"?

I am not aware of the *clinical* implications of Cloninger's work. Sure, there are biological factors that reflect thresholds, intensity, rhythm of affects, all determined by neurochemical circuits, but to go on from there, to trace concrete interpersonal behaviors to such general biological factors, is a very problematic assumption. Cloninger has not had much resonance in the psychotherapeutic field. I can live with the idea that a patient who resists everything I try to give him, which in my book is a very narcissistic resistance, is not biologically determined.

Did you ever "sin against" or fundamentally deviate from your own method?

There have been times when I actively acted out my countertransference, particularly when I saw the patient in a live situation where there was very little time and I thought, "If I interpret what the patient is doing, there will not be sufficient time to correct the behavior."

I'll give you an example.

I had a patient from a foreign country with terrible masochistic tendencies. She was trying to take the Examination Certification for Foreign Medical Graduates (ECFMG) exams, to be allowed to practice medicine in the USA. If she were to fail, other members of her family would then ship her away. I thought it would be helpful for her to pass this exam. If I analyzed her crazy way of not getting the right information, she would just fail. So I swallowed and told her, "You study from a ridiculous text. You will fail this way. You need to study the following five texts in the next three weeks." I gave her a list of texts. I wasn't proud of myself, but I would probably do it again. She passed and she would not have otherwise. Being a foreign medical graduate myself, I knew all about that kind of problem. Another time when I acted out my countertransference was when a patient broke my door on entering, without my noticing it, and when she was to leave, the door was stuck. I then got enraged, but nothing bad happened.

Acting out the countertransference is a danger when it means acting out rescuing fantasies, or when you're provoked into some kind of aggressive action. What I do when I get angry is tell the patient: "Sure I'm angry." I don't deny it, but I don't go into a guilt trip either. In general I'm well protected against this, because internally I tolerate my countertransference fantasies. If it comes to patients where chronic aggression builds up, for instance when I have a fantasy about throwing a patient out of the window, I don't have difficulties with that. With sexual fantasies about patients as well, I can enjoy them! I'm not afraid of them and therefore I don't have to act on them. I'm talking about other countertransference problems, like rescuing fantasies: they're a threat to a therapist who wants to help people. My model was Frieda Fromm-Reichmann. She was the sweetest of therapists, and when she really got mad at a patient, like the time when she discovered, on sitting down, that a patient had peed on her chair, that somehow endeared her to me! It made her human.

Do you have any suggestions about books, not written by yourself, that you would recommend people to read?

About the treatment of borderline personality disorders? I would recommend Bion's books *Second Thoughts* (1967) and *Attention and Interpretation* (1970). Herbert Rosenfeld's collected papers on narcissism came together in a book called *Impasse and Interpretation* (1987). Harold Searles's book on *Countertransference and Related Subjects* (1979). Volkan's book *Six Steps in the Treatment of Borderline Patients* (1987), André Green's book *On Private Madness* (1986), a collection of his papers, many of them about borderline patients. The collected papers of Betty Joseph. Enough? Oh, and I should add: *Creativity and Perversion*, by Janine Chasseguet-Smirgel (1985). She's been very interested in the treatment of severe narcissism.

Have there been any aspects of your work we haven't discussed and that you would like to mention?

Well, you know I'm interested in other fields, like love relations, sexuality. I'm very concerned about the sexual difficulties of my patients—it's a very difficult topic, because the ones who are healthier, those who can enjoy sex and who are open to infantile, polymorphous perverse sexual fantasies—homosexual, heterosexual, masochistic, sadistic, fetishistic, exhibitionistic—I have no problem with that. But those with a primary inhibition, who have no capacity for any sexual feelings, for sexual desire, and where there is such a condensation of any capacity of sexuality with severe aggression, those are the difficult cases. There are times when one starts thinking, you can't do anything where there is no libido! They've run out of libido, there is only aggression. They can be treated, but they are really at the limit, and there is very little written about that. In general the sexual life of borderline patients has been neglected and I am very active now in researching this. We have recently developed a scale on love and sexual relations.

The use of hospital- and milieu-treatment too, I'm very interested in nowadays. As you know, there is a crisis in the USA in this field because of the dramatic reduction in care. It's a sad aspect of my expertise that I cannot use it as much as I would want to. Although I am developing it with the staff of the day hospital I'm working with, where we are using group therapy techniques that are very important—although here, too, the theory has not been developed sufficiently. The interesting thing is that you can have a group of borderlines together and they will behave much more normally in the group than they would individually.

The Situations

In the middle of the night, you're called on the phone by a patient who threatens to commit suicide. What would you do in such a situation?

It depends on whether it's a patient of mine or someone else's. One who is in treatment with me? Then if he's severely depressed, if the suicide is part of depression, I hospitalize the patient. If it's characterological and he threatens me with it, as he has done ten or more times before, I remind him of the contract: either he controls it or he goes to a hospital. If this patient has swallowed enough to make dying a possibility, I'll do everything to save his life. If this is the first time, I go in and save his life and tell him: "If you do this once more, the therapy will stop." If it's the second time, I go, save his life and then refer him to somebody else. I have no problem with that.

Now, this patient wants to give you a long spiel about the reasons, like telling you about this terrible happening that caused it—How long would you give him? In the middle of the night, at 3:00 A.M.

I would say: "It's totally irrelevant why you did it." I'm only interested in his breaking the contract and what consequences that will have.

How would you react if a patient comes to the appointed session in a state of obvious inebriation?

I tell the patient he is obviously not in a condition to have a session. That I appreciate his showing that things are not in control, and we'll discuss this the next time. I'll find out if the patient is in his own car and then say, "My secretary will get you a taxi." If the patient insists on going with his own car, I will tell the patient that this is part of his suicidal behavior, which we have a contract about, and warn him of the consequences. It's the same as with a patient who threatens to suicide. It's very clear.

You meet one of your patients at a cocktail party and he or she wants to use this opportunity to have an ordinary social meeting with you for a change, and starts to chat with you. What would you do?

I have no problem with that at all. I will have this chat. If the patient behaves to me in a socially appropriate manner, and chats about the party and the wine, the painting on the wall, no problem at all. If he starts commenting on the beauty of my wife, I will tell him that his behavior is totally inappropriate and we end the conversation, as I would with any stranger who started talking to me like that. And then in the next session he can get enraged at me and we'll discuss it.

   Behind this, of course, there is a theoretical position that I hold very strongly and that puts me into conflict with certain segments of the psychoanalytical community. I differentiate between technical neutrality and anonymity. The first is essential, the second is an ideological distortion of psychoanalysis that happened in the 1940s and '50s under the influence of the power elites of the psychoanalytic institutes. A kind of distortion within both ego psychology and Kleinian analysis, which we are slowly recognizing as an effort to hide the personality of the psychoanalyst, with an unconscious effort to maintain an unanalyzed and unanalyzable idealization of the therapist. This fosters splitting. So I don't mind if my patients observe me in public and know all about me, as long as they behave socially appropriately and in context. At small parties I like to talk about personal issues, so there I try to stay away from patients, but at large social gatherings there is no such risk. I once had a patient who was in a transference psychosis during analysis. I met her at a cocktail party and she behaved perfectly appropriately, but that did not prevent her from being crazy again two sessions later! And it did not prevent me from interpreting that.

A patient turns out to be in the neighborhood of your front door every time you come home. Just standing in the street.

I immediately bring this up in the next session, and tell him that he is invading my life and that that has to stop. I don't tolerate invasion of my space. The boundary of the treatment situation includes the boundary of the private space of the therapist.

You discover that something from your office has been taken away by a patient—"borrowed," stolen, or maybe just picked up on an impulse. You know who did it. What would you do?

That has happened to me. I confront the patient and tell him, "I am convinced that you've stolen this object and I expect you to bring it back the next session. This is a precondition to continuing the treatment. I do not tolerate any loss or damage to my property." If the patient swears that I'm wrong, I will tell him, "I'm still convinced about this, but I will give myself more time to think whether I'm wrong, and in spite of being wrong end the treatment, because obviously I cannot trust you, or because I am right and it is an invasion that I cannot tolerate." So I confront the patient directly with it. This is what I mean by analyzing psychopathic transference.

Our final question: Could you tell us a little about the setting in which you see and treat your patients?

When I do psychoanalytic psychotherapy with patients, I sit face-to-face. I have a desk and we are sitting across an angle. There is a corner of the desk between us. I have lots of books and paintings on the wall, and there are a few art objects. The room has a warm quality to it. I have a picture on my desk. My youngest daughter gave it to me, a picture of herself and her husband—a small picture, I have it on the desk on a corner. Patients can see it. I did not use to do that. I'm somewhat freer with that now.

9

Marsha Linehan

Biography

Marsha Linehan is a professor of psychology and psychiatry and behavioral sciences at the University of Washington, Seattle, and director of the Behavioral Research and Therapy Clinics, a consortium of research projects developing new treatments and evaluating their efficacy for severely disordered and multidiagnostic populations. Her primary research is in the application of cognitive and behavioral models to suicidal behaviors, drug abuse, and borderline personality disorder.

She is also working to develop effective models for transferring efficacious treatments from research to the clinical community. She received her Ph.D. in experimental-personality psychology in 1971 from Loyola University of Chicago. She then completed a clinical internship at the Suicide Prevention and Crisis Clinic in Buffalo, New York, and a postdoctoral fellowship in behavior modification at the State University of New York at Stony Brook. She was on the faculty at the Catholic University, Washington, D.C., before going to the University of Washington. She is currently president-elect of the Association for the Advancement of Behavior Therapy, on the editorial boards of several journals, and has published numerous articles on suicidal behaviors, drug abuse, behavior therapy, and behavioral assessment. A fellow of the American Psychological Association and the American Psychopathology Association, and a diplomate of the American Board of Behavioral Psychology, she has received several awards recognizing her clinical and research contributions, including the Dublin award for lifetime achievement in the field of suicidal behavior, the American Foundation of Suicide Prevention award for Distinguished Research in Suicide, the American Association of Applied and Preventive Psychology award for Distinguished Contributions to the Practice of Psychology, and the Association for the Advancement of Behavior Therapy award for contribution to clinical activities. She has written three books, including two treatment manuals: *Cognitive-Behavioral Treatment for Borderline Personality Disorder* (1993a), and *Skills Training Manual for Treating Borderline Personality Disorder* (1993b). She is also the founder of the Behavioral Technology Transfer group, a company that trains clinical practitioners and research groups in empirically supported treatments. She has also formed the Marie Institute, a nonprofit organization that nurtures and supports therapists working with difficult-to-treat clients.

Marsha was born in Tulsa, Oklahoma, in 1943. Her father was an executive in the oil business and her mother was both a homemaker and a consistent volunteer across many causes and church activities. Both parents were very active in civic affairs as well as the social life in Tulsa. She has one sister and four brothers. One brother is Chief of Urology at the National Cancer Institute; the other three each started their own very successful companies, two of which were also in the oil business. Her sister is in real estate in New York City.

Friends, neighbors, and family form the community of Marsha's life. Her home, within walking distance of the university, is mostly like a boardinghouse, with young people moving in and out and coming back again. Puttering in her house and garden, reading action novels, and fiddling around with new computer programs are the luxuries in her life. She has a getaway cabin on the water at Camino Island, an area north of the city that lives at half the pace of Seattle.

The Interview

Doctor Linehan, we would like to start this interview by asking you to give an outline of the basic tenets of your approach.

Basically, my frame of reference is coming out of empirical and behavioral science. I will discuss the treatments that I'm putting together right now—you know, I am not particularly wedded to them; they will change, but the basics of the treatments I am developing will still be around when this book comes out and five years from now as well. Or maybe even ten years from now. Dialectical behavior therapy, the treatment I am best known for, is an integration of really very standard behavior therapy. There is nothing unique in my treatment, or different, or created by me, in the behavior therapy part. I have just more or less organized a lot of current, empirically validated behavior therapies into one place.

What happened was that I ran into a group of extremely difficult-to-treat people, where in effect either you could not do behavior therapy at all, or if you tried, the client attacked you or withdrew. Or even if *you* tried behavior therapy, the client wouldn't cooperate. Except for managing contingencies (reinforcement, extinction, punishment), which you don't need the client's collaboration for, behavior therapy is a collaborative effort. Everything else, like skills training, cognitive modification, and exposure treatment, requires agreement. So I ended up developing a methodology that got people to engage in doing effective treatment. Really that's all I've done.

What I added to behavior therapy first was an emphasis on radical acceptance to balance the emphasis on change in behavior therapy. Well, I didn't really add an emphasis on acceptance,

I think I just articulated and expanded the emphasis that I saw in the work of all the behavior therapists who taught me. The most important type of acceptance in dialectical behavior therapy (DBT) is validation. There are six levels of validation in our treatment. The first levels are in every treatment that I know of: listening, being interested, actually caring about what's going on with the person, reflecting, summarizing, "putting it together," communicating that you understand what's being said or what's not being said, and nonjudgmental acceptance. At the high level, level six of validation in DBT, is true genuineness. This is not really unique either, but also not really that common. I discovered recently that I must have stolen this, unconsciously so to speak, from Carl Rogers, who I had read in the original many years ago. In rereading him recently, I was stunned at how radical Rogers is. He is the only person I know who is as radical as me! (laughs) And I was thrilled of course to have his support here for being radical. It's radical genuineness. It is not being without *role*, it's being without arbitrary *rule*. It is role-bound, not rule-bound, for you are always in a role as the professional helper. And, although you may ultimately follow rules with particular patients, the rules come out of your interactions with the individual person and what is most therapeutic for this one person, rather than from books written to cover all patients. The distinction here is like the distinction in behavior therapy between natural reinforcers and arbitrary reinforcers. Behaviorists always favor natural over arbitrary reinforcers. I know my point of view is unique because it's one of our most difficult training problems. With those trained in one of the other approaches we have to get them to drop the arbitrary rules they're following. People don't even realize they're following these rules. The only way I've gotten people to see it is to have them role-play a particular problem with the other person being a patient and then role-play the exact same problem with the other person playing the part of a person they love—like a sister or a son or daughter. It's amazing how different most therapists are in these two role-plays. The idea is to act in therapy more like you act with a person you love. Rogers is the only person I know of who is like that. I'm not even sure of present day client-centered therapists.

The next level down (Level 5) is finding the normal in the behavior, to look for the reasonable, the currently valid part of the behavior. What I dislike about many other therapies is that they focus so much on finding or assuming pathology, while I, from my social sciences background, could quote five studies for each kind of behavior others call pathological that demonstrate that normal people do exactly that in the same circumstances.

In a lot of behavior therapy you do not have to do all DBT. Only when the disorder is severe and complex with crises or other problems interfering with therapy will you have to. But the basis for doing the treatment is behavioral: you define problems in behavioral terms, you analyze them ideographically, you are as theory-free as possible about the content or form of a client's behavior, you use scientific principles of behavior, not a theory of how this person is. You do not start with any assumptions about this person but you focus on the antecedents and consequences of the behavior and determine the probability of its occurring again. So you view behavior from the standpoint of time, and not from a construct in depth. You have to remember that behaviorists consider all activities of the person—sensing, information processing, remembering, thinking, assuming, feeling, emoting, physiological responding, biochemical processing, moving and acting—as behavior. Psychodynamic theories have a construct of depth; behaviorists do not use that construct. Depth is a structural construct; time is a process construct. Behaviorists look at behavior from a moment-to-moment, second-to-second approach, neurone firing to neurone firing, occurring both over time and within specific contexts.

And then, dialectics. In DBT, you have to balance *acceptance and change*, you have to act with movement, speed, and flow, you need to balance goals. You are not always suggesting that they change their environment, *or* that they change themselves, *or* that they tolerate the environment, *or* that they just be aware of an uncontrollable aversive environment. You have to balance, and a

DBT therapist always has the task of balancing acceptance with change.

In any problem situation, your options are to either change the situation, or to accept the situation and to modify your behavior so that it does not distress you so much, or to tolerate being distressed by it and be sort of at peace with the fact that you cannot regulate yourself or regulate the situation. Or the fourth alternative is to stay miserable! The therapist has to balance the attention to all these alternatives. A lot of therapists do focus on only one of these paths. A dialectical behavior therapist teaches a client to respond with all three ways of dealing with situations and constantly clarifies that one option is to simply stay miserable. Also in dialectics there is *a sense of participation*. By the way, although I like that word, the rest of my team did not, so we changed it into wholeheartedness. So it is a wholehearted involvement. You do not have to do this all the time, you do have some time to just sit back and reflect, but there ought to be some element of it somewhere in a session.

And then there is an emphasis on *a set of dialectical strategies*. These all have to do with balancing the logical, rational approach with things like metaphor, story, illusion, and extending, which is a strategy for taking the communication, ignoring the major part of it, and exaggerating a minor part of it to throw the client off-balance. These are all paradoxical techniques that move the client out of being stuck.

I could define DBT another way, by describing the five essential components: first, you have to have *capability enhancement*, either skills training, problem solving, or advice giving, or something. Second, you have to deal with *motivation* (the way behaviorists think of motivation, which is that you have to make sure that dysfunctional behavior is not being reinforced and that effective stuff is not being punished; you have to *stop things that inhibit growth-enhancing behavior*, work on faulty cognitions and/or other behaviors or patterns of behavior that interfere with new effective behaviors. Third, you have to deal with *generali-*

zation from the therapy context to the environment, where they live. That's why we do, for example, phone calls, why we sometimes do sessions outside of our office. Fourth, you have to deal both with setting up a treatment environment (not just in your office but all through your treatment system), and you have to do something about an intractable environment and to make sure that this environment does not reinforce the very things that you and the client are trying to change. Fifth, and finally, we have to *support the therapist*, you know, and to in fact do all DBT with the therapist as well, including enhancing capabilities and motivation of the therapists. Without all of these five things you are not really doing DBT. Validation, dialectics, and behavior therapy on the one hand, and the five functions on the other. You can do without a lot of this when the patient has only one disorder, like someone with a panic disorder and not much else. These patients do what you suggest to them.

You know, DBT is not a static thing, it changes as soon as new data come in, like when I go to a meeting and hear new data about exposure. But behavior therapy is not just a set of ideas, it's a set of principles, and that does not change. The same goes for supervision; when I see a trainee reinforcing dysfunctional behaviors, I try to stop him from doing that. With trainees who already know the basic principles of behavior, and particularly behavior therapy, that is not difficult, but with others I may have a hard time doing it. A behavior therapist can do DBT with very little training.

Does that go for the genuineness as well?

Sure. Genuineness came from behavior therapy. Behaviorists never see the patient as being different from anyone else. They see behavior on a continuum. Non-behaviorists are often trained in not being genuine, and trainees with such a background have to unlearn that.

What are the most troublesome things you come across when you work with these difficult patients? Is it the fact that they want something different each time you meet them? Their impulsivity, the contradictions? With all that, validating alone does not seem to be enough.

Oh, but I don't only validate. First of all, I only validate the valid. But research has shown that validation is much more reinforcing than praise or anything else. What I do not validate is therapy-interfering behavior, like acting chaotically in the sessions. If they do that, I point it out to them right away. I would block it essentially. If a client starts changing her mind I would most likely immediately hypothesize that this could easily be escape behavior. The stimulus might be a fear cue, so I would look for the cue. In general, with anything that happens in a session I always go back to the cue. Once we have that, we go forward again and analyze what happens from moment to moment. And then we look for alternative behavior.

Are there any personal reasons why you made the switch from behavior therapy to DBT?

Well, the main reason was that this treatment [behavior therapy in the '70s] did not work. I was trying to find a way that worked by using a trial-and-error approach. The other part of it is that I was born a Catholic and was brought up to believe that out of all suffering comes some sort of good. While I was watching these patients I thought, "This is absolutely not true!" It is true that all people tend to grow, and that in some cases suffering may be necessary for that. But then there seemed to be others whom the fire destroys. I got intrigued personally by the question of what the difference was. Why do some people get destroyed and others benefit from the same thing? I finally concluded, both from watching these patients and also looking at my own life and myself coming through various pains and traumas, that the difference was that the ones who are not destroyed by the fire are the ones who accept what happens. Radically accept it. (This is some-thing I always do: I combine my observations of the patients with my personal experiences and empirical data.) The whole issue has to do with acceptance. This radical sort of allowing what is to be, without denying it or running away from it. So I had to learn about acceptance and about how to teach it!

In another part of my life I had always been a Christian, mainly drawn to a contemplative mode. My first spiritual director was a Franciscan who told me that when I prayed I should never use words. That is probably the most important advice anyone ever gave me in my life. When I started my treatment development research, I was in training to be a spiritual director in an organi-zation in Washington, D.C., which I had joined when I lived there. I became a member of this group for contemplative prayer. In fact the co-director of it is Gerald May, Rollo May's younger brother, who is also a psychiatrist. He and Tilden Edwards, who happens to be a really brilliant Episcopalian spiritual director and leader, founded this organization called Shalem, that trains all over the Washington, D.C. area in spirituality and contemplative prayer. When I joined I hadn't a clue to what I was getting involved in. There were different spiritual paths each week, fifty a year!

I had a major life-transforming spiritual experience at a much earlier age, what you might call an enlightenment experience. I didn't know what happened, because I didn't have a spiritual teacher at the time, but when I had one later on, he explained it to me. This experience completely transformed my life. About a year later I lost the entire experience (I think because I started to invalidate my own experience!), but not the transformation. The transformation stayed, but the experience left. I went through what Christians would call the desert, for about ten, maybe fif-teen years. Always searching, but making the big error of always searching for that same experience again, which of course would never happen. In the meantime I was giving meditation lessons in Seattle, in which we ended by sharing our experiences, and the only thing I could name that went on with me was that I was bored! Every single day! After fifteen years of being bored I be-

gan to think that I was looking in the wrong place. That I should
quit looking for the experience and that I should start a practice
that did not offer so much, so that if I didn't have much I wouldn't
think I was missing something. What actually happened was that
I was at a bookstore, reading spiritual books, and I happened to
open this book and it had the word "nothing" all through it. I
thought: "Nothing! That's what I need! I need a group or spiritual
practice that has nothing in it!" So I went to the chair of my department, on a lark, actually, and asked if teaching all my courses
in one quarter and taking off the next quarter would meet my job
obligations. He asked me what I wanted to do. And, out of my
mouth tumbled "I want to go to a Zen monastery." He then asked,
"Is it related to your work?" And then, in a split second, it all came
together in my mind and I said, "But of course! I have to learn
how to do it (not knowing, of course, what "It" was), so that I can
teach it to my patients." And then he said, "All right," and I slipped
out of his office.

   I have a lot of spiritual friends and I called them all up, all over
the United States, and said, "I want the best spiritual teacher there
is." I figured if I was going to do it, I might as well go all the way.
Two names came up more than once and both turned out to be
Zen. One was a woman and one was a Benedictine monk, who is
a Zen master. I could not decide if I was a woman first or a Catholic
first, so I decided to try both. That's how I got into Zen. I had
absolutely no idea what I was doing and I was scared to death!
Zen practice is like psychotherapy: it's actually a relationship with
a teacher. I discovered that I had found the path of radical acceptance. But then the question was, how to get it from Zen to
psychotherapy, from me to the patients? I went to Shasta Abbey,
a Zen monastery, for three months and I went to the Benedictine
monk (Willigin Jaeger O.S.B., KO-AN Roshi), in Germany for
three months. (I took a leave of absence from my job for that.) I
go back to Germany once or twice a year. It's like going home.

   In the beginning I knew that I had found it, but I couldn't get
it over to anybody. Every time I came back to the States I would

try to get my patients to do what I had been doing, thinking that that would be all there was to it. This, of course, did not work out at all. This was hysterically funny. I mean the patients just sat there and stared at me or left! They were wondering where I had come from. It was just so weird.

When I went back to Germany again, I noticed the way my teacher handled our relationship, and that taught me a lot. A great deal of what you find in my book is really to a large extent modeled after the things my teacher did with me. Then I started stripping Zen words and *zazen* itself out of it and I stripped spiritual words out, and some other things, trying to find the essence of what I thought I was being taught. Out of that came the mindfulness skills. I took them back to my teacher, asking: "Am I on track here?" Both my teacher and another Zen teacher in the U.S. said, "This is OK." So the result now is very much getting something for me, and passing it on.

Then I started to write down what I had learned. And when I had finished, the word borderline had not come up once. Because the whole treatment was written when I had never yet heard of . borderlines, since this happened long ago and my target was parasuicidal behavior. You know, I have a great allegiance to science, and I never looked for treatment modalities outside of science. All these other things just happened.

But why did you pick on parasuicidal behavior?

Because there was no treatment for that.

Why these patients?

People always ask me that. I'm sort of a missionary person, and I wanted to help the most miserable people in the world. And at the time I thought that clearly the most miserable people in the world would be people who wanted to die. I no longer believe that, but at the time I did. But once I got into that, suicide turned out to be the only area in the field that I can read about like night-time reading. I find it so intriguing! I mean, what can be more intriguing than life and death? As a matter of fact, I'm just as interested in why people *don't* kill themselves. This is actually even more interesting, because suicide can make a lot of sense. What never made a lot of sense to me is why some people don't kill themselves! And this is an area where there is almost no research. This was like a challenge. Everyone in the field was a whole lot better than me, so I felt challenged, and then I did something that actually contributed, so I got a lot of reinforcement.

I tried to get out of this suicide research a couple of times! I started out wanting to be a psychiatrist, or if I wasn't smart enough for that a psychologist, or if not clever enough for that a social worker. Ah, the thinking of youth. But I wanted to work in state hospitals because that's where the poor people were. I didn't need to have a lot of money. And I was anti-research at the time. I thought it was cold and inhuman. But when I found out that there was very little effective treatment, I started to feel the need for doing research, because I didn't feel like spending my life doing something that wasn't very effective. That would be demoralizing. So when I found out that psychiatrists are not trained primarily as researchers, whereas psychologists are, I decided to study psychology. But then I realized I was in danger of psychiatrists taking over my patients, because I was dealing with suicidal patients. Whenever I went out of town, I seemed to always find my patients hospitalized when I returned. I couldn't win this battle because the psychiatrists would say that suicidal behavior was a medical problem. So I thought, "I can't work with suicidal patients without going to medical school, or else psychiatrists will take over control of my patients." Then I realized I didn't want to do that, so I turned to other fields of research, where psychiatrists would not take over my patients. But when you're knowledgeable about suicide, you find out that you're a very unique person. So I was constantly asked to consult and teach on suicide. I couldn't really pull out, and I finally said, "Well, all right." So I went back and I have never left.

Looked at superficially, Zen and behavior therapy might be regarded as true opposites. Do these two aspects of your work reflect an ambiguity in you?

No, no! They're the same! Neither one has the construct of self, so they both are pure process theories and approaches. They're both dialectical, both emphasize observing phenomena without adding inferences or interpretations. Behaviorism is very nonjudgmental and so is Zen. I'm a behaviorist because of this: behaviorism does not pathologize normal behavior. Of course there are many differences: the Zen approach emphasizes acceptance of what is; behavior therapy emphasizes changing what is. Zen attends to the mystery that form is emptiness and emptiness is form. Behavior therapy attends to the unraveling of mystery with science. There is a saying in Zen that can be paraphrased as: On the one hand, you have to want enlightenment so badly that it's like a molten ball in your throat that you're trying to cough up and, on the other hand, if even the letter "E" of enlightenment enters your mind, you've lost it. And that is the paradox of Zen that I try to incorporate into DBT.

The subtitle of the Behavioral Technology Training Group, which is "for effective compassion," really reflects you, doesn't it?

Yes. I realize that these things are important to me: effectiveness and compassion. But there is a third one: self-respect. I would not do anything, even if it would be compassionate and effective, if it would violate my own values. But I would never violate the client's values either.

Referring to the compassion, is that where Rogers came in?

Well, you know, I taught personality research and theory to graduate students for twenty-five years. The question there was, how does one explain individual differences along with stability of behavior over time? Because this is basically what the study of personality is all about. You can't really teach about personality without coming across Rogers. I had not read Rogers in the original for a long time. I was putting together a course for graduate students on the technology of change and the technology of acceptance, and when I did that I started reading Rogers again, and I just about fell over! Because he sounded like me, and while I didn't recall having read these ideas before, now I knew I must have and they must have influenced my ideas about the treatment of borderlines. I was so impressed that I sat back in my chair while teaching students and read Rogers's original texts to them. That was one of my greatest teaching experiences: reading Rogers to my students! What also pleased me was that I had found a friend: many people were criticizing me because of my ideas about acceptance and genuineness, and from then on I knew I could pull out Rogers in my defense. Because no one was going to criticize Rogers!

Did you have to fight a lot in order to get recognition?

I didn't fight at all for recognition! Not in the slightest. I've been unbelievably fortunate. I was a little nobody from nowhere, and then I got accepted by Jerry Davison at the State University of New York at Stony Brook for my postdoctoral studies in behavior modification. At that time Stony Brook was the premier program in the country. I've always thought that the only reason they took me was that I'm a woman, because at that time it was important to have women. But I'm sure another reason was that they thought it was pretty unique that someone wanted to do behavior therapy with suicidal individuals. Jerry was president of the Association for the Advancement of Behavior Therapy, which is the group of almost all of the key behavior therapists and researchers in the country. He was really and truly a mentor and he appointed me to the membership chair of the board of directors of the AABT. Overnight I was part of the inner circle of behavior therapists of the country! That way I got introduced to the NIMH (National Institute for Mental Health) people, who were also intrigued by me, possibly because I was the only person in behavior therapy researching suicide. And I wanted to cure these people in twelve weeks. They have told me since that they all used to joke about that, wondering how long it would take me to figure out that I couldn't. But they liked me because I was passionate and energetic, even if I didn't know very much. They later told me that I so clearly wanted to succeed in what I was going to do that they thought if anybody could do this impossible thing it could be me. They did for me what is less often done for young people now, which is tragic. Really, a lot of the credit for my success should go to all those people. They constantly gave me feedback on my mistakes, they nurtured me, made sure I got money, helped me if necessary to rewrite my proposals. So, right from the beginning I've always been recognized.

What would you say your place is at the moment in the field of psychotherapy of severe personality disorders?

Well, I don't really consider myself to be part of that field. I am now, I guess, but it's like joining an old-boys group or something. In the beginning I was fairly unique in this group, but since then so many behaviorists have followed me that this is a thing of the past. In the future, my place in the field will be determined by whether my treatment approach is effective or leads to the development of more effective treatments.

And what will be your place then?

It will be the position of the one who had a major influence on establishing a rigorous empirical scientific approach as the standard of treatment development for these patients. My whole agenda right now is trying to get the field as a whole going in the direction of rigorous experiments and clinical trials. Half of the field is now dominated by opinions; facts and data should take the place of opinions. I am the first person who published a clinical trial of a psychosocial intervention, in a peer-reviewed jour-

nal. At least two clinical trials of psychosocial approaches to borderline personality disorder were conducted before mine, but they
were not published in peer-reviewed journals so they didn't have
a big impact on the field. Since my published study on a randomized trial in 1991, very few others have been published. I find that
stunning! I don't think they're not being done, people must be
trying, but perhaps they don't get the results they want. The work
of Anthony Bateman in England (Bateman and Fonagy 1999) and
the cognitive-behavior therapists now starting to develop treatments for personality disorders is, of course, very exciting.

*We've noticed that you can become enraged when you see psycho-
therapists be too little compassionate and not effective enough. What
makes you so angry then?*

Well, why does someone get mad at people who steal from the
poor? I'm an idealist. I was at all the marches, in the '60s and '70s,
I've done a lot of volunteer work with poor people, the downtrod-
den, the homeless. The fact that made me go for a data-based
approach is that clinical judgment is not to be trusted. Reading a
lot of research literature on the validity of clinical judgment taught
me that. If this goes for everybody, it must go for me too. Believing that something works does not mean it will.

The most compassionate thing you can do for a borderline is
to be effective in treating him. So if I have to be unkind in order
to be effective, I will be unkind. Believe me! If it's ethical and
effective, it's the thing to do. But if you have two equally effective ways, the more compassionate one is the one to choose.

*Could you name two or three professionals who have influenced you
the most?*

Gerald Davison. Marvin Goldfried. They taught me what I know
about behavior therapy. Then there's Walter Mischel. He is a
personality theorist and researcher. I read his work on social learning theory in graduate school and he had a profound influence on

my thinking and way of addressing issues. He said what I thought. Then there was Al Bandura's 1969 book on behavior therapy. That was my bible. I carried it and Mischel's 1968 book on personality and assessment everywhere and had memorized every experiment described in them. When I started my clinical internship I had never had a clinical course. So I used Bandura as my guide. The principles of change were so clearly laid out that it never occurred to me that I might not know what I was doing. And the one who gave me a way to integrate my thinking theoretically is Arthur Staats, a radical behaviorist in Hawaii. And many other behavioral researchers starting from Pavlov!

Have there been any major changes in your basic assumptions?

Well, that depends on what you think my basic assumptions are. I don't think my assumptions have changed. What has changed is my ability to articulate. You know, assumptions by definition can't be proved. The only major belief that's changed does not really have to do with therapy, but with science. I started out believing that people really cannot combine my interest in spiritual things and being a scientist, so I had to split them. I was a scientist when working, a spiritual person when not working. But then, when I was teaching my advanced personality theory course, I discovered that you cannot cut off a part of your mind and that I had to somehow bring these two things together.

Teaching that class has taught me many other things too, by the way. Not just Rogers's book, but many other basic books on the science of personality. All the basic emotion researchers, like Ekman and Izard, had a huge impact on me. The major books and research studies on learning theory also had this impact. So I kept changing how I was approaching things. I came up with the biosocial theory on borderlines because I needed a theory that could support behavior therapy with these people. Their vulnerability and their emotional dysregulation had to be biologically based. So that prompted an interest in biological research and genetics. And that research is now having a great impact on me.

*Which two or three books, not written by yourself, would you advise
the reader to study?*

I have always been a person who goes back and forth between clinical practice and reading about theory and research. One example
is Walter Mischel's *Personality and Assessment* (1968) which was
the first major scientific analysis of psychodynamic theory, I think.
Then there's Bandura, *Principles of Behavior Modification* (1969),
and Staats's book *Behavior and Personality* (1996). Those three books
put into words exactly what I had always been thinking, and that is
just the effect my own book has on other people. They validated
my thinking, and my own work seems to validate the thinking of
other people.

   If I were recommending books now—this is difficult—I would
recommend basic texts on social psychology, cognitive psychology, learning, and physiological psychology. The most useful journal for my work is *The Journal of Personality and Social Psychology*, which is the most rigorous research journal in the area. You
know, social psychology is the scientific study of social influence
and personality psychology is the scientific study of individual
stability over time and individual differences. What could be more
relevant to psychotherapy!

   So, two or three books. Okay, I have to give alternate selec-
tions for each book. For a good review of basic behavior therapy
read Barlow's *Clinical Handbook of Psychological Disorders*, 3rd
edition or Craighead, Craighead, Kazdin, and Mahoney's *Cognitive and Behavioral Interventions*. In my personality course I teach
from the *Handbook of Personality: Theory and Research*, 2nd Edition, edited by Pervin and John. In developing DBT I was heavily
influenced by that course and by all the readings I assigned each
quarter, including *Emotions, Cognition, and Behavior* by Izard,
Kagan, and Zajonc, and *The Nature of Emotion: Fundamental
Questions* by Ekman and Davidson.

Do you think your approach has any limitations?

Well, as the level of disorder of the patient gets less severe, DBT
will look more and more like other treatments. Being a set of prin-

ciples rather than a cookbook, a specific set of techniques, it can be quite easily adapted to the patient, so there need not really be that many limitations. I don't think there's any treatment that's better than DBT, but I don't think it's very good either. I don't think I will be able to make a breakthrough if I don't find out what's still wrong with it. I do think I have made some breakthroughs and if I did, it will be up to younger people to finish the job by figuring out what's wrong with it. Being based on research on learning and biology, it's based on universal principles. What probably will change is that the whole thing will be simplified. People will discover that many details are not really necessary. I would get rid of those myself if I knew what they were!

Is there anything you would like to add to what we've discussed?

Not really. Well, yes, I would like to add one thing: the single worst thing to do is to have your allegiance to one treatment rather than to outcome.

The Situations

In the middle of the night, you're called on the phone by a patient who threatens to commit suicide. What would you do in such a situation?

I would do a risk assessment first. And then I would act accordingly. If there was high risk, I would work on reducing the risk. For instance if they had a gun in their hand, I would ask if it was loaded and get them to unload it. Then I would try to have them get rid of it. Then I would try to find out if there was any support system nearby and get them on the phone. If they had been using drugs I would try to find out what they were and have them get rid of those. If there was any imminent danger of death, I would get a first-aid car out. If they needed a medical checkup I would get them to go to an emergency ward. And I would coach them on how not to get admitted! If they were afraid that they might go and commit suicide, I would help them protect themselves. In other words, there is not just one thing I might do.

What about if all this is just "manipulative behavior"?

I don't know what you mean by that term.

Well, they want to put you under stress, they want to make your life difficult, and so on.

Well, I never yet had a client who did that!

That's difficult to imagine! Many others do!

I know, but it's true. My patients don't do to me what they do to other therapists.

A patient comes to the appointed session in an obvious state of inebriation. What would you do?

My response would depend on the person's history of substance abuse and how the person is acting. I would first want to be sure the inebriation is due to alcohol or illicit drugs rather than to an overdose or some other condition that needs medical attention. Assuming I'm satisfied that the inebriation is due to abuse of alcohol or other drugs, my next response would depend on whether the session was group therapy or individual therapy. In group therapy, the basic rule in my clinic is that no matter what chemicals you've put in your body, if you can look, act, and smell like you're sober and illicit-drug free, you are expected to stay and participate in a manner that does not appear inebriated.

Depending on how inebriated the person is acting, a few minutes might be given to discuss whether he or she can eliminate any evidence and appearance of inebriation. This, of course, would be unlikely in the case proposed (but stranger things have happened). In such a case, the patient would be reminded of the group rules and asked to leave, and of course reminded to call someone for the behavioral practice assignment for the week, to remember to come back sober and watch the tape before the next session, and to be sure and discuss this therapy-interfering behavior with his or her therapist. If the person had driven to the session, a co-leader would go out in the hall, get the patient's car keys, and instruct the patient to call someone (or a taxi) for a ride home. At this point, it would be all about trouble-shooting safety issues and coaching the patient in using skills when inebriated. Generally, our position is that behavioral skills need to be available in all states—sober and inebriated.

If a patient came to an individual session obviously inebriated, I would first assess when and what the patient had taken or drunk before the session. Assuming he or she could talk coherently, I would then briefly discuss the fact that coming to a session inebriated is behavior that interferes with therapy. If I thought no useful work could be done, I would confiscate the patient's keys, end the session, and, as in group therapy, advise the patient on necessary skills for getting home. Depending on whether the patient hated or loved individual sessions, I would either call later and insist on rescheduling the session as soon as possible or ignore the issue until the next session.

In any case, whether the patient showed up inebriated for group or for individual therapy, it would be considered therapy-interfering behavior and would be treated as such by the individual therapist in the next session. Generally, at the time of the session, I would not treat an inebriated patient much differently than I would treat anyone else who came to see me inebriated. The difference would come in the next session, where I would assess whether the inebriated behavior was a sample of the problematic behaviors bringing the patient into therapy, prioritize it within the hierarchy of behavior patterns needing work, and then give it the attention it required within the frame of other priority behavioral problems. For example, if the patient was also bleeding at the wrists or had taken a serious overdose during the preceding week, coming inebriated would be highlighted and perhaps briefly discussed, but the suicidal behaviors would be the priority behavioral target. In the best-case scenario, links would be found between the two behaviors.

You meet one of your patients at a cocktail party and he or she wants to use this opportunity to have an ordinary social meeting with you for a change and starts to chat with you. What would you do?

It would depend on what they wanted to talk about.

Could you fill this in yourself?

If it was something I'd like to talk about, I would talk. If the subject was not to my liking, I would not talk. I would hope they would talk to me in an ordinary way instead of making it into a therapy session. It should not have intimate details. And I would keep the conversation at a nonintrusive level. To some extent it's just a question of good manners.

A patient turns out to be in the neighborhood of your front door every time you come home. Just standing in the street.

My personal limits are that they may not come into my yard. If they want to sit in front of my house for the rest of their life, they are perfectly free to do so. But we would talk about it. I would never *not* talk about it. And if it bugged me, I would discuss that and tell them not to do that. But you know, clients often have a need of some kind of psychological contact with their therapists. To know where they live and things like that. So as long as it doesn't really bug me, why should I want to take that away from them?

And if it did bug you and they kept on doing it?

Then that would be therapy-interfering behavior, because it would transgress the personal limits of the therapist. And like any behavior of that category, it would be a major focus in DBT sessions. In general, our experience is that this kind of behavior may be there in the beginning of therapy, but it stops when you discuss it appropriately. But I once had a client who tried to break in, and I had to call the police!

You discover that something from your office has been taken away by a client—"borrowed," stolen, or just picked up on an impulse. What would you do?

I would ask the patient if he or she took it. I cannot imagine really knowing that somebody did that, unless I really saw it or the person admits it. If it happened in a situation where it could be any of a number of patients, like in my department at the university, and the patient denies taking it, I would be in a difficult spot. It once happened that a lot of things were being stolen in our clinic, and I called the patients together, told them what happened and that I was distressed about it. The problem was that it could either have been one of my students or one of the patients, and I didn't want to imply that it probably was one of the patients. I had no evidence for that! If I had reason to believe it was a client, I would ask him if he did it. If he denied taking it and I thought otherwise, I would note the threat to our relationship that dishonesty and lack of trust by either of us would cause. Then I would let it go.

And if he denied it when you were sure of it?

I don't think I ever would be that sure! But I would confront the patient with the facts and my reasons for believing he did it. And then I would ask his opinion about that. And I would keep on talking about it until the truth came out or I was convinced that I was wrong. I don't consider the fact that I may be convinced initially to be proof that I'm correct. Much as I would like that to be! (laughs)

How do you like to work with your patients? Could you describe the setting in which you see them? Is it purely functional or are there any private things there, if you want to name some examples.

I've done therapy at home, in my study. But I don't now, because everything I do is research at the same time. Now, my office looks a lot like my study actually. It's got dark red walls, comfortable chairs, bookshelves, a desk that I inherited from my mother. This office is my therapy office, but I have another one across the hall. That's where I have my computer and other things for research. It's much more utilitarian than the one where I do therapy, with university furniture and so on. The therapy office has an oriental carpet in it, and of course it has two cameras, one on the patient, one on me. And we have this wonderful new thing, a monitor behind the patient, so that my graduate students, who supervise me, can make notes that I can read while doing therapy! We don't use that often, only when I think my therapy gets stuck, and I ask one of my graduates to supervise me.

My favorite way to do therapy is to sit in a chair that has wheels so I can move very close to a client if that seems useful, and move back when I feel I should. And with a really out-of-control client I can just move my chair in front of the door. I don't block it, but I make it difficult.

This seems to be the opposite of what crisis team people would do.

Right. I would never do this with people I did not yet have a working relationship with. Nor do I really block their way out. But at least they will have to look me in the face when they leave.

Are there many personal things there?

Do I have pictures of my own family? No. I don't have them in my office either. But I have pictures of my students, group pictures. All the furniture is personal. I have antique brass scales that I love. I do have things that mean a lot to me.

10

John Livesley

Biography

John Livesley grew up in postwar England, in a small town situated along the coast just north of Liverpool. This stimulated an early love for nature and the outdoors. An early interest in natural history gave way to an interest first in biology and later in medicine. At the age of about 14, he decided upon a career in medicine, especially medical research. Then he happened on a book that contained an idea that has interested him since and that is now increasingly dominating his research. It was the simple idea of the schema, in a discussion of Bartlett's work. Funnily enough, when he went to university a few years later, the first laboratory exercise was based on Bartlett's work (see Bartlett 1932).

A psychology department offered him a place before a medical school did, and he accepted it. His undergraduate years were intellectually exciting. As the degree course approached the end, he decided not to go into clinical psychology but rather to pursue an academic career. He was successful in obtaining a demonstrator's position in his department, which allowed him to pursue a faculty Ph.D. Dennis Bromley took him under his wing and honed his interest in personality into a more critical conceptual approach. Since the work of a clinical psychologist at that time looked unexciting to him, he then returned to his old ambition of reading medicine.

Medical school was hard work. He was married by this time and had a child. But his wife, Ann, was enormously supportive. She worked part-time and he taught psychology to occupational therapy students on Wednesday afternoons, and evening classes one or two evenings a week. Along with occasional weekend courses, they earned enough to get by. Although he enjoyed medical school and especially internal medicine, there was never any doubt that he would follow through on his plan to go into psychiatry. He was offered a job at the Institute of Psychiatry in Edinburgh, which was a stimulating place in those days. There were outstanding people in most areas of psychiatry, many with international reputations. It offered him the opportunity not only to get a good training in psychiatry but also to train in psychoanalytical psychotherapy at the Scottish Institute of Human Relations.

On completing psychiatry training, John was on the faculty at the University of Edinburgh before moving to Calgary, Alberta, Canada. His position at the University of Calgary provided the space and opportunity to develop a program in personality disorder research and to develop a clinical team devoted to the treatment of these problems. It was an exciting and rewarding opportunity. However, the prairie and foothills landscapes were not congenial to him and Ann. Eventually the lure of the coast and the sea—something that they had both missed—along with greater opportunities to do the things they like, especially gardening in the English tradition, proved too much. In 1987, they moved to Vancouver, British Columbia. After the move, his research began to take a new direction. Nearly a decade of painstaking work in developing concepts and reliable measures formed the foundation for new studies into the structure and etiology of personality and personality disorder. Greater integration seemed possible between his old interests in normal personality and cognitive approaches to personality processes, and Livesley and his research team began to develop more interesting clinical implications. At present he spends a couple of days each week doing clinical work, mostly but not exclusively seeing patients with personality problems—he really does not like the term personality disorder but he cannot think of an alternative. The rest of the time is devoted to research, writing, lecturing, and editing the *Journal of Personality Disorders*. This is a satisfying combination.

It is an enjoyable time to be working in the field of personality and psychopathology, he says. Modest progress is being made that is forcing us to rethink everything that we have assumed to be the case about personality disorder and its treatment, and Livesley feels that perhaps a recognition of the real significance of personality to psychopathology is just beginning to emerge.

The Interview

Doctor Livesley, we would like you to give an outline of the basic tenets of your approach, and of the consequences of these tenets for psychotherapy.

Let me begin by talking about my research on personality disorder and the kinds of problems that interest me. Then we can look at therapy from that perspective. This will be helpful because my primary interest is in the structure and etiology of personality disorder rather than treatment. Although I have had an active clinical practice throughout my career, it is only recently that I have become interested in the implications of nosological and etiological research for treatment. The approach that I adopt is largely driven by empirical findings. My impression is that many of the concepts and theories about personality disorder that inform some traditional modes of psychotherapy do not always fit empirical fact. Moreover, the concept of personality disorder emerging from recent research is beginning to force us to rethink our ideas about its nature and the way it should be treated.

Let me tell you a little about my early work because this provides an important context for the framework that I use in treatment. This work was directed toward describing the basic components of personality disorder. The overall domain of personality disorder is large, diffuse, and complex. A fundamental question is, "How can we divide this domain in a way that makes it manageable?" My initial assumption was that empirical studies would confirm many of the diagnostic entities proposed by what was then the *DSM-III* classification of personality disorder. Indeed, my early work was conceived as an attempt to validate *DSM* diagnoses. However, as I tried to identify the basic traits that delineate personality disorder and investigate the structure underlying these traits, using multivariate statistical techniques, it quickly became apparent that the features of personality disorder are organized in a way that is very different from that suggested by the *DSM*.

The structure we identified was stable across different samples, including clinical and non-clinical samples. It's also similar to that described later by other investigators such as Clark and Harkness. The fact that other investigators using different approaches obtained similar results was satisfying. It suggests that we have succeeded in identifying some of the basic dimensions of personality disorder.

It also became apparent that the trait structure of personality disorder is best represented by a dimensional model. This idea is important clinically. It suggests that an individual's personality is best described as a trait profile—the individual's scores on a series of dimensions—rather than as a discrete category or type. This in turn implies that it is unlikely to be profitable to develop treatments for specific *DSM* diagnoses.

In the late eighties and early nineties, my research took on a new direction. Largely for serendipitous reasons, I became interested in the etiology of the basic dimensions of personality disorder. We developed a moderately sized twin sample (we currently have about a thousand pairs on our register) and began to explore the genetic architecture of personality disorder traits, a topic that remains an active focus of my research. Studies that we began publishing in 1993 consistently showed that all personality disorder traits that we studied had a substantial heritable component. This finding led to substantial changes in my ideas about personality disorder, including treatment.

Like most people who were trained in psychology in the 1960s (behaviorism at that time was maybe not in its heyday, but it certainly was not dead), I was an environmentalist. The assumption was that the contents and structure of the mind were largely environmentally determined. Hence I assumed that there was a psychosocial etiology to most dimensions of personality and that personality disorder was the product of psychosocial adversity. Clinical research on trauma and adversity seemed to support this idea. However, the data on heritability forced me to think of personality disorder as a psychobiological entity, as opposed to a psychosocial entity, and I became interested in exploring the clinical implications of these findings.

Psychiatry often finds itself in endless debates due to a polarization of viewpoints—arguments about biology versus psychology or nature versus nurture. When we look at the recent history of psychiatry, these debates have had a negative effect that has not been fully resolved. Most models of therapy in common use assume a psychosocial etiology to personality disorder. They usually acknowledge the importance of biological factors but they then continue as if the only issue were to resolve or change the consequences of conflict or adversity. The implications of the genetic basis to personality disorder for treatment and models of change are rarely considered. The evidence suggests the need for a new approach to understanding and treating personality disorder, one that integrates biological and psychosocial factors. As we explore the implications of the genetic basis of personality for treatment, the term *biological psychotherapy* is perhaps not as odd or inappropriate as it first appears.

We also need to consider the implications of the genetic architecture of personality for change. Most therapies seem to imply that major changes in personality, including trait structure, are possible. But this is probably not the case. Although the fact that a trait is heritable does not mean that it cannot be changed, the evidence suggests that personality traits are remarkably stable throughout the adult life span. These factors raise the possibility that some features of personality and personality disorder may have limited potential for change, suggesting that an important goal of treatment is to help patients adapt to their basic traits rather than attempt to change them. This idea may seem a little alien to therapists following a purely psychosocial model.

These findings about the trait structure of personality and genetic and environmental etiology also have implications for classification. This in turn has a bearing on the way treatment is conceptualized. Contemporary classification systems make little sense either clinically or empirically. *ICD-10* and *DSM-IV* may once have been convenient heuristics (or fictions) but they are not anymore. We have not been able to identify discrete categories of personality disorder, whether these are described using *DSM* diagnostic constructs or psychological concepts such as Kernberg's borderline personality organization. It is perhaps time that we moved on and developed empirically based models that are more helpful to the clinician in treatment planning. I think there is conclusive evidence that personality disorder traits are best represented by a dimensional system. Although this approach is consistent with empirical findings it raises the further problem of "What is personality disorder? How do we define what it is?" This is not a purely nosological problem: it also has implications for treatment. The issue is: Do we simply regard personality disorder as an extreme score on a particular dimension, as some authorities have suggested? Or do we need some other definition? I do not find the idea that personality disorders are merely extremes of trait dimensions to be conceptually satisfactory. The reason is simple. It's possible to have an extreme score on some traits and yet not be maladapted. Is an extreme score on obsessive-compulsivity inevitably maladaptive? Is an extreme score on neuroticism inevitably maladaptive? Or extraversion? Obviously they are not.

This means that we need criteria, over and above extreme traits scores, to define personality disorders. There are various solutions. Bob Cloninger, for instance, suggests that an extreme score of some traits such as self-directedness, by definition indicates personality disorder. I do not think there is convincing evidence to support this idea. When we look at the clinical literature in search of a definition, we find two characteristics that clinicians appear to consider the hallmarks of personality disorder. One is the idea, best explicated by Rutter, that personality disorder involves chronic maladaptive interpersonal relationships. The other idea is expounded by both Kernberg and Kohut: that personality disorder involves a structural deformity in the self, such as identity diffusion or the failure to develop a cohesive sense of self. If we take these two ideas, we have the beginnings of a definition of personality disorder. Personality disorder involves the failure to develop adaptive self and interpersonal systems or structures. In this sense, the definition adopts a deficit model of psychopathology. This is a rather stringent definition that assumes that personality disorder implies severe pathology. Individuals who do not have one of these basic defects may have personality problems, but they do not have a personality disorder. This is important because current criteria for personality disorder are overly inclusive. Epidemiological studies report the prevalence of personality disorder to be about 9 or 10 percent. This is far too high a figure.

What is more important for our discussion, the definition has interesting implications for understanding treatment. The definition leads to a model in which personality disorder is considered to involve common or core features shared by all cases and all forms of personality disorder, and specific features that are observed in some cases but not in others. Core features consist of self and interpersonal pathology. Although all cases share these problems they may be expressed differently, according to the other personality failures that are present. For example, an inhibited (schizoid) person may express core interpersonal pathology as an inability to relate to others, whereas an emotionally dysregulated (borderline) person may show the same core pathology as a tendency to move in and out of relationships and as a difficulty with tolerating closeness. The key issue is that both lack the ability to form close, intimate attachments. Individual differences or specific features may be described using trait dimensions.

Although this conception of personality disorder appears to

differ from that adopted by the *DSM-IV*, there are similarities. The *DSM-IV* lists general criteria for personality disorder, that is, features shared by all cases. The ten diagnoses listed on Axis II describe the specific features or individual differences in personality disorder. The field has emphasized individual differences because the goal was to achieve a set of distinct categories and minimize the importance of common features. I think this is a mistake.

This model is useful when thinking about treatment. It suggests that a satisfactory approach to treatment should incorporate general strategies for managing and treating core pathology. Specific interventions can then be built onto this framework, as needed, to treat the problems of individual patients. General strategies dictated by core problems will focus on building a collaborative working relationship, maintaining a consistent therapeutic process, validation and empathy, and motivating for change. These strategies form the framework for other interventions designed to treat more specific problems. This analysis suggests the importance of a tailored approach in which interventions drawn from different schools of therapy are tailored to the needs of the individual and delivered in the context of core interventions. Specific interventions are selected either because there is empirical evidence that they are effective, or on the basis of rational considerations, in that they seem to be the most appropriate way to treat a specific symptom or problem. For each patient, an array of interventions are chosen that are the most appropriate way to treat his or her problems. However, it is not sufficient to offer an array of interventions, it is also important that interventions are delivered in an integrated way that promotes the development of more adaptive and cohesive self and interpersonal systems.

Most treatments proposed to treat personality disorder fail to meet the requirement of tailored integrated treatment. Some use a repertoire of interventions that is too restricted to treat all of the problems encountered in personality disorder. Others do not offer the integration required. Few include all the intervention strategies that have been shown to be effective in treating per-

sonality disorder. None of the therapies in common use balance
the requirements of a tailored approach, incorporating multiple
biological and behavioral interventions as required by the multi-
dimensional nature of personality disorder with the need for integration as required to manage and treat core pathology. We have
good interventions, like Marsha Linehan's strategies for treating
parasuicidal behavior and impulsivity, or medications that are
effective in treating similar problems. But we are not quite sure
how to combine these in an integrated way or how we should treat
core pathology. We are also unclear about how we should treat
problems involving the basic trait dimensions of personality.

Which dimensions are you interested in?

They are not very different from the dimensions of the five-factor
approach that suggests that personality can be represented by five
major dimensions: neuroticism (or emotional stability), extroversion, agreeableness, culture (or openness to experience), and
conscientiousness. Let me tell you how we developed these dimensions so that you understand how they relate to other models. We began by content analysis of the clinical literature to identify the terms clinicians use to describe personality disorder. Then
we asked clinicians to rate these terms for prototypicality or importance. These ratings were used to reduce a list of about a thousand terms to a hundred traits. Then we developed self-report
scales to assess those traits. Factor analysis was then used to reduce these one hundred traits to eighteen basic traits. These eighteen traits provide a comprehensive account of the basic structure of personality disorder. They include features such as
anxiousness, affective lability, stimulus seeking, intimacy problems, insecure attachment, submissiveness, callousness, and so
on. All the traits used in the *DSM* to describe personality disorders are incorporated into this list. When the eighteen basic traits
are factored, four broad dimensions are identified. The first is
emotional dysregulation. This is a clinical equivalent to neuroticism as defined by Eysenck and the five-factor approach. It also

resembles borderline personality disorder. As Tom Widiger, John Clarkin, and others have pointed out, patients with borderline personality disorder have extreme scores on neuroticism. Emotional dysregulation is more broadly defined than the *DSM* diagnosis. I believe that the *DSM* concept is artificially circumscribed to make it different from related diagnoses. The second dimension resembles *psychopathy* as described by Cleckley and Hare. It is also similar to both Eysenck's dimension of psychoticism and the negative pole of the agreeableness domain in the five-factor approach. I am currently referring to the third dimension as *inhibitedness*. In diagnostic terms it captures the schizoid dimension. It also shows some similarity to Costa and McCrae's and Eysenck's introversion factors, although it is more specific. I think there are some components of extroversion that do not hold together well, particularly at the genetic level. Finally, there is *compulsivity*, which corresponds to conscientiousness and obsessive compulsive personality disorder. As you can see they are a lot like the big five, only the details are different. They also capture the main forms of personality disorder described by categorical classifications.

The interesting thing about this structure is that it's stable across clinical groups, such as patients with personality disorder, eating disorder, and mood disorder. Our analyses of twin data also suggest that the phenotypic structure closely corresponds to the underlying genetic architecture.

Which personal motives have led to your choice of personality disorder as an area of research?

I decided on a career in biology and medicine at an early age. Then, in my late teens, I read a book on psychology: Hilgard and Atkinson's *Introduction to Psychology*. This was a standard first year university text in the late fifties and early sixties. I found it compulsive reading. When I came to apply for university I couldn't make up my mind whether to apply for psychology or medicine, so I applied to both. In England at that time it was difficult to get into university, and a psychology department offered me a place before I got into medical school, so I took it. My intention was to pursue a career in clinical psychology. Toward the end of my psychology degree I decided against a career in psychology because in those days clinical psychologists spent most of their time assessing rather than treating patients. I decided to go into research. For three years I taught psychology, during which time I completed a Ph.D. My thesis was on the development of children's thinking about personality and behavior. My research investigated the impressions children form of themselves and other people— what sort of concepts they use, what language they use, and how they organize information about other people into a global impression, and how their concepts change with age. The thesis was published as a book in 1973.

Toward the end of this work I decided to return to my original plan of reading medicine. I applied to the dean, who was an unusual person. When he interviewed me, he said: "You have a B.A., you're completing a Ph.D., now you want to do an M.B.,Ch.B." (which is the British equivalent of an M.D.) "and then you want to do psychiatry?" I said "Yes." "That would mean completing a Diploma in Psychological Medicine. Well, you'll have a B.A., Ph.D., M.B.,Ch.B., DPM. That will look good on your tombstone!" (laughs) While waiting to go to medical school, I worked for a year in a child guidance clinic. I gave two W.I.S.C.s (Wechsler Intelligence Scale for Children) a day there, which bored the daylights out of me, but at least it confirmed my decision. After completing medicine, I went to Edinburgh to train in psychiatry. One of the units included in my rotation was an in-patient psychotherapy unit, supervised by Henry Walton, that treated patients who had personality problems. This stimulated my interest in personality disorder. The topic interested me, partly because of my background in psychology, especially my interest in personality theory, and partly because I was interested in psychotherapy. The training program also gave me an opportunity to work with Bob Kendell, who is an internationally recognized authority on classification. This stimulated my interest in nosology, and hence in the classification of personality disorder.

Around this time, Roy MacKenzie visited Edinburgh on sabbatical from Calgary, Canada. I ran an evening psychotherapy group along with another trainee and Roy supervised it. This was my main introduction to group psychotherapy. It was a very stimulating experience. After the group we all retired to a local pub for a fish and chips supper and an evening of intense discussion. When Roy went back to Calgary he suggested that I move there. During this time I was also completing an analytic training in Edinburgh at the Scottish Institute of Human Relations, which offered psychoanalytic training although it was not then officially recognized. I didn't want to emigrate until I finished that training. Eventually I moved to Calgary with the intention of staying for a year or so but I never went back. In Calgary most of my clinical work involved group psychotherapy and I began to concentrate on personality disorder. In the beginning I worked from the psychoanalytic frame of reference, but later on I was influenced by Irvin Yalom. My Edinburgh background meant that I was mainly object relations-oriented. That fitted my interest in personality.

What was the connection between your Ph.D. subject and the major dimensions you studied later on?

There wasn't much. However, my thesis involved the content analysis of children's impressions and I used content analysis of the clinical literature as the starting point for developing a dimensional system. Recently, I've started using methods that I used in my thesis to elicit descriptions of self states when treating patients. When assessing patients I usually ask them to provide free descriptions of themselves and others, which is what I did for my thesis. This creates a satisfying sense of completeness—returning to techniques I used thirty years ago.

What would you say your place in the field of psychotherapy for personality disorder is, in general?

I really don't have a place. I would like to think that I'm making a contribution to understanding the structure and etiology of personality disorder. This is my main interest. As I've tried to show, this work has implications for treatment that I want to explore over the next few years. In the long run I would like to contribute to the development of more effective, evidence-based treatment and to the development of a classification that offers something more than pejorative labels.

Where did this interest in basic science come from?

I think originally from childhood interests in natural history and biology and later from my study of psychology. But it's not only that I'm interested in basic science, I think it's important that we adopt an evidence-based approach and be prepared to follow the evidence wherever it leads. So I'm interested in the problem of how to translate empirical findings into a treatment approach that makes sense. I suggested earlier that some of our current treatment models are not consistent with the picture of personality disorder that is emerging. The current models have elements that will be useful in constructing a more comprehensive approach, but in themselves they're insufficient. I also agree with Lorna Benjamin (1996), who argues that treatment will be most effective when based on an understanding of etiology.

Can you tell us which professionals have influenced you the most?

That's a difficult question to answer! Some of the more influential ones are not well known.

They don't have to be well known.

Well, as a young psychologist I had the opportunity to work with a clinical psychologist, Leonard Lewis, who probably was the best psychotherapist I ever met. He was an ordinary clinician working in a large mental hospital, but he had a genius for rapport. He was a delightfully eccentric person who was passionate about his work. He made me aware of the significance of relationships and the broader aspects of clinical work. He probably influenced me more than anyone else.

At the same time, I was greatly influenced by Dennis Bromley, professor of psychology in Liverpool, who has contributed extensively to the literature on both aging and personality. Dennis supervised my thesis and provided me with research training. He is an excellent analytic and conceptual thinker, and his approach and outlook had an enormous influence. I owe my enthusiasm for empirical research and conceptual analysis to him. Of the people who influenced me in psychiatry, the most important was Jock Sutherland, who supervised me for several years. He was in many ways the elder statesman of British analysis, who had been head of the Tavistock Clinic for twenty years and was a regular visitor to the Menninger Clinic. He seemed to know everybody in psychoanalysis and was enormously respected. I still fondly recall meeting him every Tuesday afternoon for supervision in his elegant book-lined study. He introduced me to the world of analysis from a very different perspective than that which I had encountered previously. Jock also had a very down-to-earth approach to clinical problems and patients. When I was anxious about starting my first analytic case, he said, "You know, you'll get along fine if you just give your patients the respect that you would give to anybody in any encounter." It was pretty good advice.

In those days, Edinburgh was a stimulating place to train in psychiatry. There were many excellent clinicians and clinical investigators from whom I learned much. There were also excellent psychotherapists who had worked with Fairbairn and Guntrip. Their ideas have had a lasting influence.

Were there any books by well-known people that influenced you?

During my undergraduate years I was one of the few people in my class who read both of George Kelly's volumes. I found his ideas exciting. They formed the basis of my approach to personality and they still influence the way I think about the topic. Also Piaget, Gordon Allport, and the Russian psychologist, Luria, had a big impact on me for a variety of reasons. Allport kept personality theory alive in psychology during the age of behaviorism and thus had a tremendous influence on psychology. As I moved into psychiatry, the object relations school caught my attention because of my earlier interest in Kelly's construct theory. I liked Guntrip's work, especially his *Personality Structure and Human Interaction* (1961), and Fairbairn's *Psychoanalytic Studies of the Personality* (1952). Earlier I mentioned Yalom's work on group psychotherapy. More recently, the ideas of Tooby and Cosmides on evolutionary psychology have had a major influence on my work. One volume is *The Adapted Mind*, which they edited along with Barkow (Barkow et al. 1995).

Have there been any major changes in your thinking over the years? You've already told us that you've moved from thinking about the environment as the cause of the way people are, to genetics.

Yes, but we need to reframe a little. It's not that I think the environment is unimportant—in fact just the opposite—rather that environmental explanations of psychopathology are in themselves insufficient. They need to incorporate an understanding of biological factors in the broadest sense of that term. The challenge is to account for the interaction of genetic and environmental factors in the development of personality disorder.

Another major shift is toward a more cognitive approach. By this I don't mean cognitive in the way it's used in Beck's cognitive therapy but rather as a more general conceptualization of personality as an information processing system. That interest was always there—remember I mentioned the way Kelly's personal construct theory influenced me as an undergraduate. However, it has become increasingly important and my ideas have shifted away from an interest in such things as defenses and motivational systems. I no longer find these concepts useful, at least as they are traditionally stated.

Finally, my approach to treatment has become increasingly eclectic and empirically driven. I think we should use whatever works. Hence I'm increasingly intolerant of approaches that reject effective interventions because they don't fit the theory on which the treatment is based.

Are there any limitations to your approach for treating people with personality disorders?

Let me remind you that I don't have an approach. What I think is that a consideration of the nature and causes of personality disorder and evidence on treatment outcome provide the basis for a rational framework for approaching treatment. The limitation of this framework, like that of any approach, is the limitation of our current knowledge. We really know little about personality disorder, its structure, origins, and development. There are many speculative accounts, but empirical facts are scarce. At the same time, curiously, we probably know more than we think we know. If we ignore speculative theory and metapsychological superstructures and concentrate on distilling what we actually know, we can develop an approach that is to some degree evidence based. Unfortunately it is likely to lack the glamour of more speculative approaches that promise to be the solution to treating personality pathology. The limitation of current approaches that concerns me the most is our limited understanding of how to promote personality integration and coherence. This is the central problem in treating personality disorder and unfortunately the study of personality coherence is still in its infancy. Some interesting work is being done but it's not clear yet how this can be translated into therapeutic interventions.

Which two or three books, not written by yourself, would you advise the reader to study?

Rockland's book, *Supportive Therapy for Borderline Patients* (1992). I don't agree with some of the underlying theory, the framework, but I like his approach. I think it's probably one of the better books on the treatment of personality disorder. It's unfortunate that it's not more widely read. Another is a book I only came across recently by Anthony Ryle, who has a long interest in Kelly's personal construct theory. He wrote a volume entitled *Cognitive Analytical Therapy* (1995) and more recently he had another book published called *Cognitive Analytical Therapy and Borderline Personality Disorder* (1997). My ideas are remarkably like his, so I like his views a lot! (laughs).

The Situations

In the middle of the night, you're called on the phone by a patient who threatens to commit suicide. What would you do in such a situation?

Adopt a commonsense approach. I would listen. If it was a patient I was familiar with, who had not done this before, I would get the details—find out what the precipitating factors were, including whether alcohol or drugs are involved, what was the trigger for this particular moment in time, why the person felt unable to cope in any other way, and I would do whatever was necessary to ensure the patient's safety.

Would you do that in the middle of the night by phone?

Why not? What else can you do? I would not want to become engaged in therapy over the telephone, but I would want to get sufficient information to know how to manage the situation. Now if this was the fourth time, or the tenth, it might be different. I would still do whatever was necessary to keep that patient safe. But this may not be the same response as what I would do in the case of a patient I knew less well. I think it's important to have a framework that helps you to respond to these situations but it has to be flexible, and one has to accommodate the various problems one encounters. Psychiatry interventions should not be a procrustean bed.

Do you work with contracts with such patients?

The word contract has legal connotations to it. Sometimes the idea of a contract is used almost like a legal document. "If you do this, this will happen, and if you do that, the consequences will be . . ." sort of idea. I do not find such an approach helpful. However, it is important to have a contract. Essentially, a contract is an understanding of the goals of therapy, how often treatment sessions will occur, the duration of treatment, how therapy is going to be conducted, and the therapist's and the patient's responsibilities or roles in therapy. This agreement should be the result of a collaborative discussion that occurs after assessment. The contract will also include my availability in a crisis and what we will do in such a situation. I always like to discuss that in advance. I let patients know that if necessary, they can call me. But we also discuss what they can do if they cannot reach me.

A patient comes to the appointed session in an obvious state of inebriation. What would you do?

That never happened to me! If it were to occur, I would certainly want to know why it happened. If I knew that the patient was safe, I would suggest that we leave things until the next appointment and would try to terminate the session in a supportive way, while also confronting the problem. By confrontation I merely mean pointing out the consequences of what the patient is doing. It's important that this be done supportively. The desired outcome is to deal with the problem in such a way that therapy is not disrupted, the alliance is enhanced, the frame is maintained, and the patient ultimately learns from the experience. Later the issue would be discussed and explored.

You meet a patient at a cocktail party, and he or she wants to use this opportunity to have a social meeting with you for a change, and starts to chat with you. What would you do?

I don't consider this to be a major problem. Your scenario reminds me of something else Jock Sutherland said when discussing how to manage a difficult situation: "Whatever you do, be gracious." I may not want to be involved in a lengthy social conversation with a patient who was in treatment with me but I would warmly acknowledge that person's presence and talk with him long enough to make a gracious retreat, one that he would be comfortable with.

A patient turns out to be in the neighborhood of your front door every time you come home. Just standing in the street.

That would be more worrisome and I would take it seriously. I would certainly raise it in therapy and actively address it. My reactions would also be influenced by the nature of the person's problems and pathology. If this was a highly dependent borderline patient, I would not be as concerned as I would be if it was a more psychopathic individual or a schizoid person with psychopathy features. I would not want to overreact, but I would not want it to continue.

Marsha would call this "therapy-interfering behavior."

Yes, and I would deal with it as such but I would also be concerned about safety.

You discover that something from your office has been taken away by a patient—"borrowed," stolen, or just picked up on an impulse. You know who did it. What would you do?

I cannot imagine that such a thing would happen. I would probably do nothing.

Let's say it was a piece of personal value to you.

It wouldn't be there! It's not a good idea to have personal things of value in your office. When I think about this more, I would still be inclined to do nothing, and just let the issue emerge during treatment. It would be difficult to do anything else without destroying treatment.

But what does it do to your mind? If you were bothered by it, you would have to do something about it.

That would depend on the level of certainty about it being this individual. But I accept that if such a thing occurred it would cause countertransference problems and I would have to deal with them. Nevertheless it would be difficult to raise and discuss the issue unless it was brought up by the patient either directly or indirectly.

How do you like to work with your patients? Could you describe the setting in which you see them? Is it purely functional, or are there any private things there? Can you name some examples?

I see patients for two full days a week. Some are seen twice a week, some once a week, and a few are seen only once a month or less. Within a few weeks I hope to start a group again that will meet twice a week. The rest of the week I do research and writing. I see my patients in an office about sixteen by ten feet. There's a desk on one side, some bookcases and a couple of chairs for my patients, one that's very soft and comfortable and one that's a little firmer. They can choose whichever chair they want. I have my chair next to my desk. I have my writing pad on the corner of it. It seems to be a comfortable arrangement. I don't have private things in the office other than books, paintings, and a few ornaments.

Do you do a lot of writing during sessions?

I hardly did in the beginning. Now I do. I don't write detailed notes but I jot down ideas that seem important. You see, my ideas about therapy have changed a lot. I think that I'm just beginning to understand personality disorder a little. I do not use an interpretative approach. Instead I try to help patients recognize the broad patterns of their thinking and experience, behavior and relationships, and to understand how these patterns are expressed in everyday life. To achieve change in behavior, I think it's necessary to focus on the molecules of behavior, so I spend a lot of time encouraging patients to recognize the fine details of these broader patterns. This is why I write notes during the session. I note key phrases that I want to reflect back later. I also note the sequences in their actions, the links that connect behaviors. I often diagram these sequences and show them to the patient and invite comment. Sometimes I push my chair, which is on casters, so that they can look at the diagram with me. I find that this is a very effective way of helping them to recognize the patterns in their life. Seeing a diagram of the links between actions and experience often gives patients a little distance that allows them to reflect on their experience. Done judiciously it's also a very effective way to enhance the alliance. Furthermore, it models the kind of interaction and therapeutic relationship that I want to establish with a patient—a collaborative effort to achieve change.

Actually writing a lot will not really bother a patient as long as he knows that you're truly interested in him.

Right. You know, I'm afraid we haven't always been helped by some of the trappings of psychoanalysis. It's made us uptight about anything we do, even ordinary things.

11

James F. Masterson

Biography

James F. Masterson was born in Philadelphia, the third of four children. His father was a trial lawyer and his mother a housewife. His interest in psychiatry developed early, perhaps influenced by the fact that three of the children had rheumatic fever at the same time and were bedridden for months, so that the family doctor played a very prominent role in their lives.

In high school, he was more interested in sports than in anything else. He attended the University of Notre Dame, in premed, but was drafted at 18. After two years in the Army Medical Corps, he returned to Notre Dame for a year and then attended Jefferson Medical School in Philadelphia as a necessary step toward becoming a psychiatrist. He pursued his psychiatric training at Payne Whitney Clinic (Cornell University Medical College, New York Hospital), where he became chief resident. For the rest of his career, he has always had a part-time activity as an administrator, for twenty years at Payne Whitney Clinic in the adolescent services and later at his own Masterson Institute.

Though he and his wife intended to return to Philadelphia after residency, it became clear that Masterson's professional interests were in New York. He started a private practice half-time, held a half-time job at Payne Whitney Clinic, and began five-times-a-week psychoanalysis. By then, three children were added to the roster and the suburbs became home. Despite commuting and long work days, there was always time for treatment, writing, reading, research, lecturing, traveling, family not least, and his enduring avocations of tennis and pro football.

Masterson became deeply involved in the complex, objective, statistical methodology of a research project following up the borderline adolescent. He and his staff focused on defining of variables, matching of controls, and a plethora of statistical tools. At the same time, he was going to psychoanalysis every day, subject to a very different method—the psychoanalytic. This Devil and Daniel Webster debate raged for several years when he finally resolved it: dismissing the statistical researchers and dealing with the material from an analytic perspective. This determined his analytic approach, which directed the rest of his professional life. Beyond that, the analysis freed up his creativity to apply that approach. This shift was further reinforced by his linking Mahler's child observation research with his work with the borderline adolescent and also influenced his decision to work with adults. After twelve years, the borderline adolescent research project finished and he turned to the borderline dynamic in adults, and then other personality disorders in adults. He left the world of adolescence, never to return. His course was set: psychoanalytic approach to personality disorders in adults.

During the next twenty years, Masterson wrote ten books, edited five others, and published one hundred papers. He left Cornell and set up his own training programs in New York and San Francisco: The Masterson Institute for Psychoanalytic Psychotherapy, which is discussed in this chapter.

It is with some resentment that body and mind have been forced to submit to the demands of time and to lighten the tasks Masterson so willingly placed upon himself. This has been a gradual and successful transition, however, which still leaves him free to do what he loves: treatment and teaching. It is with great satisfaction, as well as a sense of wonder, that he sees other therapists, many of whom he has trained, carry on the commitment to the highest levels of patient care and to teaching others what they themselves have learned.

The Interview

Doctor Masterson, to start this interview we would like you to give an outline of the major tenets of your approach, and of the consequences of those tenets for psychotherapy.

It's called the developmental self and object relations approach and combines the traditions of ego-psychology, object relations theory and child observation research. The theory is that the central psychopathology of the personality disorders is a developmental arrest of the self, along with the ego and object relations, probably occurring in the early development, roughly between ages 2 and 3 during the separation-individuation stage. The etiology of this developmental arrest consists of three inputs, the therapist having to decide which is the most important in each individual case. The three are nature, nurture, and fate. Nature refers to genetics. We don't all have an equal genetic capacity to have an autonomous self. Nurture refers to the mother's difficulty providing regulation of affect and support for the emerging self during this crucial stage, and fate refers to prolonged separation experiences between 2 and 3 before the self is separated. The child experiences the mother's libidinal unavailability as a loss of self, develops an abandonment depression and the developmental arrest ensues as the child defends against this depression. These defenses then determine the varying diagnostic categories: borderline, narcissistic, schizoid, and so on.

In 1975 I presented a paper on this theory, and recent neurobiological studies (Schore 1994) have demonstrated that not only is the mother vital psychologically as I described, but she is also vital neurobiologically for the maturation and functioning of the prefrontal orbital cortex of the brain, which is the center for the emotional regulation of the self and emotional relationships with others.

The pathological results of this interaction are internalized to form the intrapsychic structure of the patient. This consists of an object relations unit, ego defects, and primitive mechanisms of defense. The object relations unit, all of which can be described in clinical terms, consists of two part-units: on the one hand a defensive part-unit, which consists of an object representation and a self representation, linked by the affect, that generally characterized the defensive relationship with the mother, and the other part-unit, the pathologic unit, with an object representation that does not support self-activation and autonomy, the self representation being inadequate, empty, and so on. The affect that links these two is abandonment depression. This intrapsychic structure expresses itself in a key theme that I call *the disorder of the self triad*: self activation leads to anxiety and depression, which lead to defense.

The contents of the intrapsychic structure differ with each personality disorder. For example, the intrapsychic structure of the narcissistic personality disorder is called the grandiose self omnipotent object representation defensive part-unit and the underlying pathologic part-unit is called the harsh attacking unit. In the schizoid personality disorder the defensive unit is called the master–slave unit and the pathologic unit the sadistic object self-in-exile unit.

The consequences for psychotherapy can be briefly described as follows: A key concept is that the personality disordered patient at the outset of treatment relates by transference acting out, not transference. The patient is unable to differentiate between his defensive projections and the reality of the therapist, a function that is a crucial feature of transference. The therapist tracks the triad and helps the patient to overcome his defenses and convert transference acting out to therapeutic alliance and transference by specific techniques to deal with the transference acting-out: confrontation with the borderline personality disorder, and interpretation with the narcissistic schizoid personality disorders. Integration of these techniques overcomes the defenses and es-

tablishes a therapeutic alliance and transference as the abandonment depression emerges to be worked through. Working through
of the abandonment depression frees the self to emerge and grow.
 The treatment approach depends on the therapeutic objective.
One objective is ego repair, helping the patient to strengthen his
defenses. A more fundamental psychoanalytic objective is helping the patient to overcome his defenses against the abandonment
depression, exposing the abandonment depression and allowing
the real self to emerge, bringing with it memories, dreams, fantasies, and transference. These become the grist for working through
the depression, which has been the anchor on the developmentally arrested self, and as this pathologic mourning process is
worked through, this anchor on the self is relieved and the self
begins to emerge and grow.

*Does this mean that in the beginning of therapy with these people,
you would be more supportive to prevent people from dropping out?*

No. Maintaining therapeutic neutrality is vital. This is based on
the assumption that the patient has enough ego-strength to contain his pathologic affect so that it can be worked through. The
low-level–functioning patient who has a weak ego that cannot
contain pathologic affect is not a candidate for psychoanalytic
psychotherapy to begin with, and therefore it is not so important
to maintain therapeutic neutrality. But in psychoanalytic psychotherapy every digression from therapeutic neutrality leads to more
resistance. Therapeutic neutrality is one of the most difficult
things for therapists to maintain. After all, we all can be vulner-
able to countertransference.
 Let me elaborate this issue of neutrality. Some analysts have
what I call a categorical approach to the diagnosis of borderline
personality disorder. This means that to them all borderline patients are lower-level patients. They assume these patients cannot tolerate or contain pathological affect, and they cannot tolerate being alone, so that they must alter therapeutic neutrality in
order to keep the patient in treatment and help him with this

problem. This point of view is consistent with lower-level, poorly functioning patients, but for someone who functions on a higher level and can tolerate pathological affects this would be counterproductive. Without the therapeutic neutrality the abandonment depression can not be exposed and worked through.

Which motives have led to this specific choice you made in the field of psychotherapy?

I went to medical school to become a psychiatrist. As a resident in psychiatric training I had two ideas in mind: one, to become a psychotherapist and two, to have my own personal analysis. After I finished my training I went into analysis and I became interested in what was then called the "theory of adolescent turmoil." The idea was that the problems of adolescents had to do with adolescent rebellion and they would grow out of them. I could find no research to support this view. I then did a series of follow-up studies on adolescents who in retrospect turned out to be borderline. I found that five years later more than 50 percent of them had not grown out of their problems but were severely impaired by them. This was outpatient work. I then changed to an inpatient service to find out what caused these character problems and what could be done about them.

When we controlled their acting-out behavior they would get depressed. Initially we thought this was the result of emancipation issues. However, just serendipitously, I went to a meeting where Margaret Mahler (1975) was presenting her child observation studies of separation and individuation. She presented films of children crying when the mother left the room. I thought this is what the adolescents are talking about. They're talking about separation, not emancipation. This opened up my perspective on the problem and changed it into a developmental one linked to separation-individuation theory.

Then I got interested in how the mother-child interaction becomes internalized. I met Donald Rinsley (1976), who was interested in the same thing, and this led us both to object relations theory. The theory changed from developmental to developmental object relations. The fact that I was at the time in my own psychoanalysis must have had a lot to do with this change. However, in my mind what I was doing was just following the clinical leads that the research provided.

What about the connection between your own psychoanalysis and your developing interest in this field?

I pondered this question myself at the time, but I don't think I can point to a one-to-one connection. The analysis removed many blocks and gave me access to my creativity, which, in concert with the clinical work, turned more and more to a psychoanalytic approach to myself and to the work.

Were there others, beside Donald Rinsley, who had an important influence on you in the development of these theories?

Unfortunately I did not have a specific mentor and was influenced by a host of others: as child researchers: R. A. Spitz, T. Benedek, and S. Fraiberg. The child observation researchers who influenced me were: M. Mahler, D. Stern, J. Bowlby, Ainsworth, and Main. Object relation theorists worth mentioning are: M. Klein, W. Fairbairn, H. Guntrip, D. Winnicott, E. Jacobson, O. Kernberg, H. Kohut. The analysts finally who influenced me were: J. Frosch, P. Blos, E. Geleerd, P. Greenacre, R. Ekstein, R. Wallerstein, and H. Deutsch.

Could you tell us a little more about the development of your theory? Any major changes, for instance?

After working out the developmental object relations theory, we finished the follow-up study of the treated borderline adolescents. The big improvement we found five years later was self activation. At that time, except among the self psychologists, there was not much talk about the self. I went back to observing the manifestations of the self in my patients. I saw that the key psychodynamics issue was the self along with the ego and object relations and this led to the idea of the triad of the self: self-activation leads to anxiety and depression, which lead to defense. This theme integrates all the other clinical observations and gives the therapist specific guidelines for intervention.

What would be a broader definition of self-activation? It has to do with autonomy, basically, doesn't it?

Yes it does. It begins with intrapsychic thoughts and feelings, which lead to actions, all of which revolve around the patient being able to identify what he feels and then articulating it in action and supporting himself when under attack. I have a lot of fancy definitions I could use, like self activation is what can be used to promote adaptive behavior or to maintain self-esteem. It also provides a pathway for creativity. In order to deal with the issue you raised, in some of my books I underline that part of the clinical material that I saw as being the patients' self-activation.

Is your concept of self-activation more or less comparable to what Bob Cloninger calls self-directedness?

It might be. But to continue: we worked a lot on posttraumatic stress disorder and multiple personality disorder. This has therapeutic considerations that are different from the usual work with personality disorders.

With patients with a personality disorder and posttraumatic stress disorder it is necessary to focus initially on strong reassurances that the interview is a safe place to deal with the painful affect and to establish a therapeutic alliance. This contrasts markedly from work with plain personality disorders. Once safety is established the traumatic affect will start to emerge. At this point the therapist must titrate the nature of the work between focusing on the emerging traumatic affect and shoring up the patient's character defenses that inevitably are brought into play.

Our most recent development is the study of the powerful effects of unconscious projective identification: unconscious communication between therapist and patient through the prefrontal orbital cortex of the right brain. I used to think of projective
identification as a pathologic defense. Until recently I had a hard
time conceiving it as a normal form of communication. It's quite
clear from the neuropsychological research as well as from my
own work with patients that you see it in healthy people as well
as in patients. This goes for almost every defense mechanism.

*Are there any limitations to your approach as compared to other
approaches? For instance, Patricia Taglione, in a recent presentation at the American Psychological Association (1999) compared
your approach to Marsha Linehan's, where she says that your approach, as well as Otto Kernberg's, might be more useful with higher-
level borderlines, while Marsha's approach might be more suitable
for the lower-level borderlines.*

I think that's probably correct. What Taglione (Taglione and
Brown 1994) points out is that the patients' pathology is being
used against them, with this reward–withdrawal approach. I think
that for a lower-level borderline who cannot do any analytic work,
our approach is probably not any better or worse than anyone
else's. You have to become a counselor. Linehan (1993) worked
with lower-level suicidal patients who are not candidates for psychoanalytic treatment. She basically performed a counseling role
to help them to be more adaptive. This approach can be appropriate for lower-level patients but the problem is that it is being
widely used with higher-level patients where it is inappropriate, as
it deprives them of the advantages of a psychoanalytic treatment.

*There is a study going on where Marsha's approach is compared with
Otto Kernberg's. They have a grant for doing that.*

Well, let's hope that clarifies the different indications and objec-
tives of these approaches. About the limits of my approach, they

are the limits of any psychoanalytic treatment. Patients have to have the time and the money to come three times a week, there has to be some kind of stability in their lives, and they have to have this capacity to contain and reflect. And of course these techniques are for personality disorders and not for patients who are psychoneurotic or schizophrenic.

Is it reasonable to suggest that one of those people who can hardly be treated at all, once they have been made more amenable to treatment through Marsha's approach, might then become possible indication for your treatment?

If they have developed enough ego-strength to contain painful affect, that's a possibility.

Apart from the general limitations that you mentioned for any kind of psychoanalytic work, are there any other limitations to your approach?

Well, it's easier for me to describe this treatment theoretically than to do it because of the problems in maintaining therapeutic neutrality and controlling countertransference.

Could you mention any specific successes or any specific failures, or cases where you clearly "sinned" against your own basic approach?

The Masterson Institute for Psychoanalytic Psychotherapy has trained about one hundred therapists. And one of the hallmarks of these people is the sense of competence that they report about their work. One of the demonstrations of it is that, in this managed care environment in the United States, which has such a heavy emphasis in the psychotherapy field, they are able to maintain a private practice without using managed care. I think this is because they know what they are doing. I have received so many comments from people who have been trained at our Institute, where they tell me that this training has not only enhanced the quality of their patients' lives, but of their own lives as well, and those of their families.

To give you one wonderful example, there was a young man I treated who had a borderline personality, but he had some paranoid features as well. He was diagnosed as paranoid schizophrenic. His parents were told to put him in a state hospital. He was in our inpatient service for about fourteen months and after that I treated him on an outpatient basis for about two years more. He is now a successful radiologist, married with a family.

Another patient, a young girl who was a severe anorexic and a borderline with all that goes with it, is now a lawyer, married, also with a family.

A more telling example might be a single man, in his thirties who had been a musician. He ran into some disappointment with his mentor, gave up music, and became a stockbroker and was miserable and only middling successful. He also had serious trouble with his love life. He was blocked in his individuation and his object relations. I saw him in intensive psychoanalytic psychotherapy for about four years. He is married now, has two children, has his own very successful business, and also has a very active life with his music.

Another man came to me after his internist gave him sixteen electrocardiograms for "heart pain." He came to me before I became aware of all these separation-individuation issues and I just thought he had a neurosis. In treatment he got a little better and he left. Eight years later, when I had become acquainted with the theory about personality disorders, he walked back into my office! He had had two divorces and his current partner was pressing him for marriage. "But," he said, "I can't afford to pay alimony to three of them so I'd better get back to treatment with you." He did, and I dealt with the personality disorder this time, which made a huge difference in the outcome. He later on left this woman and had a new relationship with someone who was far more appropriate.

These are some examples of the kinds of success that we've had.

*Do you ever really terminate a therapy, or are they ongoing relation-
ships with contacts that may at times have almost no frequency at
all?*

Oh, no, I terminate. I think termination is a very important part
of the treatment! I don't think that patients really fully internalize the changes until they stop. I haven't seen the patients I just
described to you in years. With some people it might not be a good
idea to terminate, but in most it is the right thing to do.

I had one patient who suffered from what you might call therapy
addiction. She really had achieved her objective in therapy, and
her sessions were more or less filled with complaints about how
much trouble it was to come for treatment. I brought it up in the
sessions: "It seems to me that you are about ready to leave treatment." And she said: "If you hadn't mentioned it, I would never
have done it myself." So she stopped and the last time I heard
about her she was doing fine. In my view termination is really a
test of the validity of the treatment, because treatment is about
enabling the patient to develop an autonomous self.

*Which two or three books, not written by yourself, would you advise
the reader to study?*

Well, apart from Mahler's work there has been Stern's work (1985)
and Bowlby's work (1969) and I think they add dimensions to it,
although I don't think they change it all that much. So I would recommend Mahler's (1975) *Psychological Birth of the Human Infant*,
and I think Kernberg's (1975) *Borderline Conditions and Pathological
Narcissism*. As a third, in today's environment, which is moving and
changing so fast, I would recommend Alan Schore's (1994) *Affect
Regulation and the Origin of the Self*. What he does is present a
neurobiological basis for the emotional development of the self.

*Are there any aspects of your work that we have not yet discussed
and that you would like to say more about?*

I would like to say a little more about the teaching in which I'm so involved. We have an Institute in New York and another one in California. They are three-year part-time postgraduate programs and we find that it takes these students eighteen months before they really begin to integrate things. Then, in the second half of the program they move very rapidly. There are all kinds of psychoanalytic training institutes in this country, of decidedly varying quality. The teaching reinvigorates interest in the work, and for me it has been a marvelous combination.

Is it possible to name some of the factors that predict if people will be effective as therapists for patients with severe personality disorders?

That's a good question! It would help if they have an autonomous self. If they don't, it would help if they are aware of their various defenses. But I must say that if we made having an autonomous self a criterion, it would mean eliminating an awful lot of people who may, once they become aware of and able to manage their own defenses, become very competent therapists. The whole business about maintaining therapeutic neutrality is to hold on to reality while trying to immerse yourself with these emotional issues.

When we visited your training center and attended one of the supervision sessions it struck us that it was so well structured. For instance, when the supervisor asked his pupil, "What are your goals with this patient, and where is she at this moment?" the therapist really could give clear answers to those questions.

Some people would say this is a handicap because it may close off opportunities and avenues. But I don't think so. I've been at this for almost thirty years, and it seems to work in exactly the way that I described, in all areas with all people. It gives the therapist a wonderful tool for evaluating where the patient is, at any moment in time.

Anything else you want to mention?

Yes. I just published a new book entitled, *Personality Disorders: A New Look at the Developmental Self and Object Relations Approach.* One of the things I did in this book was to distinguish between what it's like to work with a psychoneurotic compared to working with a personality disordered patient. There has not been much published on this in our area. The following considerations help to differentiate a psychoneurotic from a personality disorder. The patient with a psychoneurosis has successfully developed past the separation-individuation phase and therefore has an intrapsychic structure that consists of a whole self and a whole object relations unit with good and bad affects united in one representation. The splitting defense is gone and its place is taken by repression, a much stronger defense. Since the patient has a whole self he starts treatment with the capacity for a therapeutic alliance so that transference acting-out plays a small role. The content is oedipal conflict, not abandonment depression, and the therapeutic technique is interpretation of unconscious, not defenses. You can, of course, have an added complication like the patient in my book who had a narcissistic defense against a psychoneurosis and the narcissistic defense had to be worked through before getting to the neurosis.

I think John Gunderson did some major work on putting together a list of the essentials of working with personality disorders, but he did not give that much attention to this difference you mention.

In my view the importance of the issue is this. I can't tell you how many patients I've seen who had had a generally high-level personality disorder and they had been in analysis for five or ten years. Their analysts think they're neurotic, work on their oedipal conflicts, and never get to the core of the problem. So being able to differentiate this upper level is very important.

The Situations

What would you do if a patient calls you on the phone in the middle of the night and threatens to commit suicide?

I guess this would depend on my evaluation of the patient. Sometimes we see manipulation, and sometimes there is a genuine suicidal intent. In the case of manipulation, depending on the diagnosis, I would either interpret it or confront it, and say: "I'll talk to you about this tomorrow." If I thought it was genuine, I would try to let the patient ventilate, in order to get a better feel for it, and I would certainly recommend that he go to the local hospital emergency service, and if necessary call the police to follow up.

Would you have a face-to-face session in the middle of the night if you thought this might be useful?

Well, I live up in Westchester, so in our setting this would be hard to do. I suppose that if I lived in New York I might consider it. At least if it was somebody who was in treatment with me.

What would you do if a patient comes to a session obviously inebriated?

That's an easy one. I would tell him to go home. Psychotherapy and alcohol compete with each other for the management of the patient's emotions. While he is using alcohol to manage those emotions, there is no room for psychotherapy.

You meet one of your patients at a cocktail party, and he or she wants to use the opportunity to have an ordinary social meeting with you for a change, and starts to chat with you. What would you do?

If this was a patient I had in analytic therapy, I think I would bring up with the patient that this was not in his or her best interest, or in the interest of the treatment. I would suggest we discuss it in the next session and would then try to stop it.

How would you stop it?

I would take the patient aside and explain.

A patient turns out to be in the neighborhood of your front door every time you come home. Just standing in the street. What would you do?

I would confront him. I would ask him why he was there, what was going on, and then I would say that this behavior was a self-destructive way of expressing his feelings and that they should be dealt with in the sessions. I would say: "Tomorrow, when I see you, we can discuss this."

What if the patient would not leave?

First I would try to make him leave. Then I would say, "Look, I'm sorry, but if you're not going to leave I'll have to call the police." One of the underlying theories for this is that this is acting out, and if you don't correct the acting out, all the affect that's being drained by it doesn't get into the treatment.

What would you do when you discover that something from your office has been taken away by a patient—"borrowed," stolen, or maybe just picked up on an impulse?

Again it would depend a great deal on the type of patient. If it was somebody I had in analytic treatment and he had proven that he was a responsible person, I wouldn't worry about it too much and I would bring it up in the next session. If this was somebody who had a big acting-out problem, I would be inclined to call him up right away.

Would you want to get it back?

Certainly, if it was something of value to me. I also think that if it was something of value it would be important to him to return it.

You would insist on it?

Yes. If it was something of value. There are patients who steal magazines from the waiting room. This seems to be an accepted form of acting out.

Could you describe the setting in which you see your patients? Do you see them at home or only in the Institute? Do you sit face-to-face?

I have a set of offices on the first floor in an apartment building. It's not that personal, but it's comfortable. I might even say it's elegant. I have two couches, a whole wall lined with books, and my own desk with a chair in front of it and on the side. To the right of that are the couches. So when patients come in, they can choose either chair to sit in. With more than half of my patients I work face-to-face. With the other half I may start that way, but when there's a psychotherapeutic alliance and they're working through, they're on the couch. I do have a lot of art works on the wall, which I like, and I also have some sculptures on the tables, but I don't have any personal photographs or anything like that.

Would you object to that, or is it more a matter of preferring art objects?

That's a tough question. I think we have to be careful, it being such an intense personal situation. You have two people sitting in a room, talking about the most intimate part of one's life, so the pressure on everyone to personalize it is enormous. So I think with the kinds of patients we're treating, the more they're able to do that the more they defend. For example I don't think I would put photographs of my wife and children on my desk. Maybe that alone would not be too bad, but I think, for example, of people who see patients in their home. If they're not careful about it and make it clear that this is an office, not a home, they risk the possibility of a lot of trouble. It's almost like asking the patient to enter into a personal relationship.

Recently, in our area, there have been two serious incidents where a therapist had a sexual relationship with a patient. Both of these patients had been sexually traumatized in their past. Now you say, and I agree, that this therapeutic situation is such an intense personal relationship. Is there any safeguard you build in when you work with severely sexually traumatized female patients?

We all know that some female patients can be grossly seductive and others are unconsciously seductive. What I try to do is to get across that they have a right to behave that way. But they also have a right to have it analyzed rather than acted on. The safeguards are in the therapist's valuation of therapeutic neutrality.

Do you think therapists who make this kind of mistake should be supervised or should get some kind of intervention?

I hate to believe that there are so many therapists who get sexually involved. I know it happens. In fact there are a number of good papers on this subject, on working with therapists who got sexually involved with patients. I think it would be very hard to do supervision with these therapists. Again, the idea that the whole profession has got to be policed this way is kind of mind-boggling. Is that the kind of thing you meant?

*No, but there are therapists who say that when you treat those pa-
tients, you should have a tape recorder running all the time. Otherwise you might be in trouble later on, being accused of things you
cannot disprove.*

Oh, I see. You're right, you may not have done anything and they
accuse you. I guess that if you knew it was that kind of patient
the idea of having a tape recorder is not bad. But of course there
are times when you don't know this is that kind of patient, and
you find out when it's too late. But to tape record every patient
who has been sexually abused seems like too much to me.

*I have another question about your office. Do your patients often
shift from sitting in a chair to lying down? And is this fixed for every
patient or is it up to them what they do?*

It's kind of up to them. There's not much shifting from couch to
chair, but the other way around occurs more often. Once they
get on the couch, I think they begin to see the benefit of it for
themselves.

For example, I had one patient who was going from couch to
chair and I had the hardest time figuring out what was going on.
And then, when I was talking to Schore about this, it became clear
to me. He has this whole theoretical perspective about the mother
being the self-regulator of the affect in the child, while personality disordered patients are not self-regulators. They use the object to regulate the self. So the question arises then: "Is the therapist a regulator of affect? Or is the most important element
insight?" What I finally figured out was that this patient would
be self-regulating her affect lying on the couch. She didn't need
me in that sense. But when she would run into some difficult
material and regress, instead of self-regulating she would regulate herself by sitting up and regulate through me, by seeing my
face. But this kind of shifting back and forth is rare.

12

Lawrence Rockland

Biography

Lawrence H. Rockland, was born in New York City, the oldest child of a high school teacher father and a nurse mother. His parents had two more children; his brother is chairman of the American Studies Department at Rutgers University and author of nearly a dozen books, and his sister is a psychiatric social worker in Washington, D.C., and a proud multi-grandmother.

After attending the usual public schools, Dr. Rockland graduated from the Bronx High School of Science, Union College, and Albany Medical College. He did his psychiatric training at the National Institute of Mental Health. The NIMH experience was an important formative one for him and he seriously considered staying on as a research psychiatrist. However, he chose instead to pursue psychoanalytic training at the Washington Psychiatric Institute, graduated in 1967, and returned to the New York area.

He joined the Einstein faculty and practiced half-time until he moved to the Westchester Division of the New York Hospital-Cornell Medical Center in 1976. He will soon be completing twenty-five years in that department. He continued giving about a third of his time to private practice, joined Dr. Kernberg's research team, and became heavily involved in the treatment of borderline patients.

Dr. Rockland and his wife, Charlotte, celebrated their forty-third wedding anniversary this year; they have known each other since she was 16 years old. They have three children: Nancy, a psychiatric social worker and writer of children's songs; Tom, a family doctor; and Peter, a resident in obstetrics and gynecology. Their children have blessed them with five grandchildren so far, with several more planned.

Dr. Rockland's major interests outside of psychiatry are his family, physical exercise—particularly hiking and mountain climbing—and music. His family hiked and climbed since he was small; if he can't do that he goes to a local gym. Being the eldest child, he was "blessed" with classical piano lessons from his father, starting at age 4. Fortunately, he overcame that and became a professional jazz piano player in college and early medical school. He relaxes at the piano to this day, and has plans to study composing and conducting classical music, activities that he hopes do not remain fantasies only.

As he views himself today, at 68, he plans to cut down on his professional activities and to devote more time to his family and to his other interests. To the extent to which he accomplishes that, he will consider his future years successful.

The Interview

Doctor Rockland, to start this interview, can you give us a brief outline of the basic tenets of your approach?

I have written about supportive therapy of patients who would be classified as borderlines. This is not the only treatment I do, but it's the focus of this interview. Supportive treatment as I see it is based on psychodynamic theory. I think that way because it's the way I've been trained and it's familiar to me. Supportive therapy goes on less intensely and is less ambitious, but it is, I believe, more practical for most borderline patients (in the broadest sense of the word, "lower level personality disorders" so to speak) than exploratory treatment.

You say, "because of the way I've been trained and it's familiar to me." Do you mean to say that you can imagine supportive therapy to be based on other approaches?

Sure. For example, Henry Pinsker, who was at Beth Israel Hospital, in Manhattan, has an essentially atheoretical approach. He sees supportive therapy as a series of interventions and techniques that can be grafted onto any treatment. Another thing I've been thinking about recently is the comparison between Marsha Linehan's Dialectical Behavior Treatment (DBT) and supportive treatment. People who have seen my tapes have said, "Your therapy looks like DBT!" How much it looks like the same thing, I don't know. It's certainly based on a very different theoretical system. I don't think DBT looks exactly like psychodynamic supportive therapy, but I do think that if you look at it from a dynamic standpoint, it's fair to say that DBT is a supportive therapy. You could call any cognitive-behavioral approach supportive, with a different theoretical base for something that has more or less similarity to dynamic supportive therapy. DBT, by the way, is becoming very popular at the Westchester Division, primarily, I guess, because it's the only treatment that has good outcome data. We all are prisoners to the training we've had and this is what I was trained in and so, on my own, I would never have thought of these other therapies.

Do I hear you imply that you have more affinity to Marsha's approach than to the approach of Henry Pinsker, with him having only a set of techniques instead of a frame of reference as a basis?

Henry Pinsker and I know each other, and I've participated in some of his workshops, but it's hard for me to conceptualize therapy without a theoretical frame. For example, I think a lot about supporting or undermining defenses; I can't think of how you would do that without conceptualizing defenses. So I don't see things the same way that he does. As to Marsha Linehan, at this point I feel I don't know enough about her methodology.

Although we're training the residents in DBT, we still look at it primarily as a psychologist-run treatment. And I certainly don't feel at all savvy about it. That's why I would be interested in having a DBT therapist and a supportive (maybe expressive?) therapist, treat the same kinds of patients. Bruce Sloane did a comparison between psychodynamic therapy and cognitive-behavioral treatment and asked the patients at the end, "Were you in this treatment or that?" They could not distinguish the two treatments consistently. There's a difference between a theoretical system and what one actually does in the office. Even with the same systems, the therapist's style, personality, focus of comments, and so on, are different.

How did your shift from exploration to supportive therapy develop?

I came to the Westchester Division at the beginning of 1976 and Otto Kernberg came in October, about nine months later. I had read his material prior to that, so I was very excited to join his research group. At the beginning I did my best to learn his structural interview and to do the expressive treatment that he did. I did a fair amount of it and I supervised a lot of it. But I felt more and more that it was not appropriate for the majority of patients, just as I think that only a small minority of patients in general are suitable for psychoanalysis. I saw the patients drop out of treatment at an alarming rate and I began to think, "This isn't the way most of these patients are geared."

Later, several of us were asked to prepare a course in supportive therapy for fourth-year residents. We did whatever reading we could in the field to prepare ourselves, for example David Werman's book (1988). Then three of us began to write a book on supportive therapy and after awhile the other two dropped out for reasons of their own. And because we had a contract, and it was promised, and I felt obligated, I kept on writing. I was also having the feeling from clinical experience and supervising that it would probably be a preferable treatment for these patients. All these things together led me to first write the book on supportive therapy (Rockland 1989), and then the one on supportive therapy for borderline patients (Rockland 1992).

In my private practice (we all do fifteen hours or so of private practice), for practical reasons I do as much psychoanalysis as I can. By "practical" I mean that with a full-time job, training, supervising, and such things, it's easier to combine it with a part-time psychoanalytical practice. So most of my actual experience in the treatment of borderline patients has come in the clinical treatment of these people and supervising their treatments. Although I generally carry one such patient in my private practice, too many would be disruptive—the emergencies that come up, and so on. It would overload my schedule terribly.

In summary, I didn't set out to do supportive therapy, nor did I set out to write a book about it. Doctor Kernberg was very encouraging of me, and I'm very indebted to him. It was he who got me interested in borderline patients. I myself, through my experience and supervision, felt that his treament was, to my mind, not the best treatment for most of these patients. I feel more comfortable with Gerry Adler, because he begins supportively with most patients, and gradually becomes more exploratory. I think that approach is more practical. Many patients would fit that paradigm, although with others you have to be supportive all the time. And of course there are some with whom you can be exploratory from the beginning.

Did you develop your method of supportive therapy on your own, or were there teachers who influenced you?

I started by reading the literature. For example, Merton Gill wrote a seminal paper on supportive therapy. Actually, when we started on our course, we said, "Gee, there's almost nothing in the literature about it! Let's write a textbook." By now there are others. For instance the papers Frans De Jonghe wrote in the *Journal of the American Psychoanalytic Association* are excellent, and develop some of the theory in a better way than I have. Pinsker and others at Beth Israel have written too, as have Werman, Kernberg, and, prominently, Paul Dewald. But I can't say that I had a mentor. I never "learned" supportive therapy. You certainly don't learn it in a psychoanalytical institute. It really came out of a need in the department and the developing interest on my part.

I feel that the psychotherapy field in general is excessively based on the model of psychoanalysis: "This is the way you should do treatment." I use the metaphor to residents that it's like training a surgeon to do very complicated third ventricular ureteral shunts, and not how to do appendectomies or cholecystectomies, what most surgeons will do most of the time. There is also a very subtle devaluation of supportive treatment. "You just clap somebody on the back, give him a drug, say 'Buck up! It will all get better soon . . .'" That's a kind of simplistic model, and the treatment is assigned to the junior trainees in the clinic.

Do you think your work has been of influence in setting this right?

From what I understand, my first book, *Supportive Psychotherapy* (1989) is being used in many training programs—psychology, social work, and psychiatric. I hear from many people "I've read your book." That's a pleasant surprise; I never set out to be well-known. I even get positive feedback from psychoanalysts. The book is sold by the New York Psychoanalytic Institute. I actually expected the second book (on borderlines) to get more response, because of the combination of the treatment and the type of patients. It has done well, and I've received many compliments about it, but I don't think it has done as well as the first book.

Perhaps because book number one was a truly new thing and book number two was part of a flood of books on the same subject?

Well, most of the borderline books tend to be about expressive approaches. A frequent comment I've received about the second book is, "You didn't really write anything I didn't already know, but thank you for legitimizing what I've been doing, felt guilty about, and didn't feel I could talk to colleagues about."

There obviously was a real need for such a book. But do you have any explanation of why from then on supportive therapy got very little attention? After all, after your book only very few people wrote about it— while at the same time almost everybody practices supportive therapy.

I can't give you a simple explanation. I've felt that the next logical thing would be collecting data, and comparing it with, for instance, DBT and Otto's treatment. As a member of Otto's research group, I suggested we do such a comparison. John Gunderson, who was present as a consultant, said: "Our 1984 treatment of schizophrenia study put the next to last nail in the coffin of psychoanalysis. If you do this, and supportive treatment is as effective while less intensive than expressive therapy, or even better, that would be the last nail."

You mean it would not have been politically correct?

He was talking politically, of course. I think psychoanalysis is having enough problems of its own without demonstrating that from an outcome or cost-effectiveness basis it doesn't pull its own weight. There is so much trouble even having a psychoanalytic practice, you know. The Westchester Psychoanalytical Society, which used to be a very active group, has stopped meeting due to demoralization and discouragement. It's very sad. That's not true of the New York Psychoanalytic or Columbia Societies, though.

You must realize also that it's very difficult to do research on the relative effectiveness of psychotherapies. You have to make sure that the product is being delivered, that it's being delivered with skill, that there is a system for identifying therapists who slip below the competence line, and then to improve their skills. And there's not much money available for that kind of study. Furthermore, the differences in effectiveness tend to be slight; it's still mainly a matter of the common factors deciding the issue, not really the technical differences. And a big part is played by patient differences, which we are not sensitive enough to be able to quantify meaningfully.

Wallerstein's follow-up of the Menninger study (*Forty Two Lives in Treatment* [1986]) has found that all the treatments became more supportive over time; "structural change" as a result of expressive treatment and psychoanalysis on the one hand, and supportive treatment on the other, could not be differentiated. The expressive treatments accomplished less than anticipated and the supportive treatments more. That book was a blockbuster! Everybody knows the book, but most don't take the results to heart. There were, of course, many methodological limitations, but still . . .

Will you share some of your thoughts about psychotherapy in general? We have already discussed some of this, but there may be more you want to say about it, and about your personal development. We would like to know, for instance, who you think has influenced you the most.

Well, Otto Kernberg especially. Having been in close association with him for so long has been extremely important for me. I already mentioned Gill and Wallerstein. The only other people that quickly jump to mind are the follow-up studies of Michael Stone (1990) and Tom McGlashan (1983) of Chestnut Lodge; and Allen Frances and I think very much alike.

We already covered much of your personal development. Is there anything to add to that?

Well, there was a study group, led by Charles Brenner, with Abend, Porder, and Willick as members of that group; they were his "young Turks" so to speak. They wrote a book (1983), admittedly on only four patients, about the questionable usefulness of the concepts of splitting and projective identification as well as many other issues. Their publication has influenced me as well.

Does your approach have any limitations?

Here I am strongly in agreement with Frances, Clarkin, and Perry, who wrote *Differential Therapeutics in Psychiatry* (1984). It has a chapter on "*No Treatment as the Treatment of Choice.*" Many thera-pists feel that if they are there and the patient is there, there should be a treatment. We should ask ourselves not only "Which treat-ment?" but also "Should there be any treatment at all?" There seem to be patients who get worse every time they're in treatment. Now I don't know if that's a "negative therapeutic reaction," or "severe masochism," or an attempt to defeat the therapist or whatever, but certainly a change in approach is worth thinking about.

I don't see supportive therapy as a panacea. It's a treatment, probably appropriate at least initially for about 75 percent of bor-derline patients. *DSM* borderline personality disorder includes a wide variety of patients, many different types of patients, and differing severities of illness. There could not possibly be one "THE psychotherapy." Anything from psychoanalysis to support-ive therapy could be useful. Otto and I would disagree on the percentages! He would consider the patients for supportive therapy to be pretty close to what I would consider the group for "No Treatment," like intractable lying, withholding information from the therapist, very intense destructive or self-destructive psychotic transferences in the past. I may be exaggerating a little, but that's how it seems to me.

Where do you draw the line between "therapy yes" and "therapy no"?

I don't know any psychotherapy that's been impressively successful with severely antisocial people. I think that unless you have them in a structured situation where they cannot continue the acting out, you're probably wasting your time. And then you have the patients who are severely substance abusing. If you cannot get them into a program to control this, that's it.

There once was a patient who said "I cannot get into treatment with you until I know as much about you as you know about me. Otherwise I feel put down and inferior. So tell me, what are your problems?" That's not the kind of patient who can be treated, at least at that time; later she did enter treatment. You can also ex-pect problems if patients are unwilling or unable to come on some

kind of regular schedule, or won't agree to certain kinds of reasonable protections built into the treatment. For instance, with
anorectic patients you might say, "If you fall to 75 percent of your
body weight, you can't be in outpatient treatment." If they will
not follow that rule, there's no basis for an outpatient treatment.
Very unrealistic goals may also be a reason for not starting treatment at all. Then there are people who replace life with therapy—
therapy addicts.

*Can you remember any case where you failed and where you think
some other method might have succeeded?*

> There was a borderline patient who suicided. The horrible
> thing was that she suicided by accident. Suicide should gen-
> erally be seen as a failure. You know, people drop out of sup-
> portive therapy as well, and that too should be considered
> to be some kind of failure. But this patient was very bright,
> she had a very supportive family, and I thought the treat-
> ment was going okay. She made an impulsive suicidal ges-
> ture, taking everything she had been prescribed, and in the
> process added a handful of aspirin. She immediately told her
> mother, who was in the house, who rushed her to the local
> hospital. They lavaged her stomach, nobody took it seriously,
> and half an hour later the girl was dead. She died of acido-
> sis from the aspirin, which she did not throw up because of
> the Mellaril she had taken.

Would anybody else have been more successful?

I don't think so. Most people would have hesitated to take an
expressive stance. I was doing what I thought was right for her,
wondering every now and then whether she should be hospitalized. The tragedy was she did not want to die.

*John Clarkin told us that as long as you stick to your own method,
and do not allow your patient to seduce or blackmail you into be-*

coming supportive when you're doing an expressive therapy, the therapy will go on well, but when you do become supportive in an expressive therapy, you will discover that the therapy comes to a standstill. What are your opinions about that?

(laughs) I noticed that a lot. Usually that would happen when the patient in some way became frightening, usually suicidal. This was a problem primarily when the therapists were relatively inexperienced.

John Clarkin was talking about experienced therapists as well!

Senior people! That's a project they're doing right now. I've seen some of those tapes and some of the patients too, because I'm the medicator for them. I don't know how I became that, but this way I've seen some of those tapes and the treatments don't look like the manual to me. If those therapies don't go well, it may be not as a result of them becoming more supportive, but as a result of not following the manual. With every kind of patient you will come across situations where you have to be supportive or else the patient will drop out of treatment.

There are therapists who work either in an exploratory or a supportive way, and there are therapists who work in an exploratory way, but include supportive elements when they consider this appropriate. What is your opinion about that?

We all do that! For instance when a patient is experiencing a transference psychosis you say, "Listen, I'm not your father, and I'm not trying to kill you!"—that is, you stress reality issues.

Then why does Clarkin say, "Do not switch to supportive elements!"?

I think Clarkin is talking about patients who frighten the therapist by threatening to commit suicide. And apparently that goes for experienced people too. That's something you have to interpret and confront. Ted Jacobs argues that in order to keep a psychoanalysis viable, or any exploratory approach for that matter, and not just with borderlines but with any kind of patient, you have to be supportive sometimes, or the patient will leave therapy.

Do you have any suggestions about books, not written by yourself, which you would recommend to people?

Otto Kernberg is the outstanding writer, however difficult he is to understand. Wallerstein's *Forty-Two Lives in Treatment* (1986) will, in time, become a classic. Michael Stone's (1990) book on the follow-up of borderline personality disorders and schizophrenics is very important. Merton Gill (1964), like Wallerstein, has influenced me greatly. DBT (Marsha Linehan) is getting so much attention nowadays that I think everybody should have at least some understanding of it. Personally I'm always more taken with data than theory, so Stone and McGlashan, who have data, are very important. One of the key things in McGlashan's writing is that he stresses the importance of work for borderlines; most of the patients I see at Westchester are on welfare and say that they can't get a job that pays as well as disability payments. Welfare may gratify them in the short run, but they're badly hurt by the system in the long run.

In all psychotherapies we have to worry about countertransference acting out. That's something I'm very concerned with. Supportive therapy especially contains a strong temptation to tell people how to live. And with borderline patients that danger is even worse.

Are there any aspects of your work that we haven't discussed but that need some further comments? Some recent developments for instance?

Well, I've reached 68 and am now working part-time on an inpatient unit; formerly I was director of the outpatient clinic. I'm having a lot of trouble finding time to attend the research meetings.

Finally, I'm learning that getting older is no fun; about the best you can say for it is that it beats the alternative. Thank you.

The Situations

In the middle of the night, you're called on the phone by a patient who threatens to commit suicide. What would you do in such a situation?

That's a complicated question because many factors are deliberately left out of it. What is the patient's history of calling? And of suicide attempts? If she cried "Wolf!" many times before, you don't take it as seriously. Also, has this been taken care of in the initial contract? That's as important in supportive treatments as in expressive treatments, although I think it has to be done more bilaterally than is described in expressive therapy. Not "When this happens, that will be done, take it or leave it!" But "Look, if this happens, what do you think would be the best thing for us to do about it?" In the case of suicide threats, I've been struck by the fact that Otto's trainees tend to tell a patient, "Look, if you threaten to commit suicide, you have to go to an emergency room." These students have seen a video recording, where Otto did that with a patient who had thirty-five suicide attempts in the past, which ruined multiple previous treatments; then you have to take that stand. That tape is so impressive that it kind of sticks to people, even though it's only appropriate for some patients.

You also have to know if there's a social support system. Is the patient alone in the apartment or not? After ascertaining exactly what the situation is, I would decide what to do and I'd be more flexible about it than many people. I might even say, "Look, can you hold on for three hours? I'll see you at six o'clock in the morning." Anything else may be in order, from a referral to the next session to acute hospitalization. When there's a contract in place, I would want to know why that contract is being threatened or broken.

How long would you give that patient in the middle of the night?

I don't want to gratify her unduly, but I have to make a clinical decision, which I cannot do without knowing these things. If that takes twenty minutes, it takes twenty minutes.

How would you react if a patient comes to the appointed session in a state of obvious inebriation?

I would discuss briefly with the patient how this has come about, why he or she is doing it. And unless I have the feeling there is still a fair amount of ego functioning, I would tell the patient: "Look, it makes no sense to have this session. I'll see you next week, and if you have feelings about that, I'll talk about them with you next week."

You meet one of your patients at a cocktail party and he or she wants to use this opportunity to have an ordinary social meeting with you for a change, and starts to chat with you. What would you do?

I would say very briefly, "Look, this is complicating the treatment. This is not a good idea. Don't take it personally, but the treatment goes on in the office. So I'll now move to another end of the party and if you have feelings about that, we'll talk about it next time." Supportive therapy is not being like a bartender or a taxi driver. At the other extreme, a colleague of mine met his analyst at a concert and went over to him during the intermission and extended his hand. The analyst ignored it and just walked away. Next day during the session he asked his analyst, "Didn't you see me?" And the reply was, "Sure, but I get enough of you four or five times a week, I don't want to do that also on Saturday night!"

This is countertransference acting out.

Sure.

A patient turns out to be in the neighborhood of your front door every time you come home. Just standing in the street.

These are all examples of acting out on the part of the patient. I would say, "Why are you here all the time? This is making me uncomfortable. I'm happy to talk about whatever there is to talk about, but not here. You're intruding into my life." And eventually after trying to set limits and getting him to understand the underlying wishes and affects, if he still goes on I would end the treatment. "I can't treat you under these circumstances."

You discover that something from your office has been taken away by a patient—"borrowed," stolen, or maybe just picked up on an impulse. You know who did it. What would you do?

Let's assume you're really sure that it was this patient. Again, it's an acting out. I would discuss all the motives, and assume that sooner or later this object will be returned. With most patients I would not see the treatment continuing with an overt theft from the office. The bottom line is, don't allow a major transference–countertransference issue to undermine the treatment.

Can you tell us something about how you like to work with your patients? Do you have a desk between you, or do you sit more or less opposite from one another, or maybe more side-to-side? Do you have easy chairs or fairly comfortable ones? Are there many personal objects in your room or office? That sort of thing.

My office is about twenty-one by fifteen feet or thereabouts. It's also the office for my job, so there's a computer in it. There is artwork on the walls. One patient recently said, "You are a very boring guy because you haven't changed those pictures in about five years!" They are not personal, although there is one that has some figures, one of which is my brother, but the patients don't know that. There's a couch, a couple of chairs, a desk, a lot of bookcases, and a couple of diplomas. Eighty to 90 percent of my patients are on the couch. When we do sit, it's at an angle. That way we can look at each other when we want to, but we don't have to.

13

Michael Stone

Biography

Michael Stone was born in 1933 in Syracuse, New York, and grew up in an upper-middle-class Jewish family where great emphasis was placed on learning, and where it was expected that he would enter medicine as a first choice, and the law if the first choice were not realizable. He spent the first sixteen years of his life in Syracuse, and then went to Cornell University, at Ithaca, New York, where he concentrated in ancient languages (Latin, Greek, Sanskrit, Hebrew, Anglo-Saxon) although also taking all the required "pre-med" courses in chemistry and zoology. His interest in medicine, and in the brain in particular, was spurred by an illness of his mother's—tic douloureux—that had been misdiagnosed as a "brain tumor" before she visited specialists in New York City.

At 20 Dr. Stone entered Cornell Medical School in New York City. Having fallen in love with the metropolis at an early age, primarily because of its cultural opportunities, he has remained there for the past forty-seven years.

His original intention was to become a psychoanalyst but psychiatry was so poorly taught at Cornell in the 1950s, that he briefly settled for his second choice: hematology. After four years of internal medicine, he switched to his first choice, and took a psychiatric residency at Columbia University (at the department still known as the New York State Psychiatric Institute). His psychoanalytic training was also at Columbia, and was completed in 1971.

In the meantime, Dr. Stone married a fellow psychiatric resident, Dr. Clarice Kestenbaum, who also graduated from Columbia Psychoanalytic Institute. Both took posts at the New York State Psychiatric Institute, and also maintained a half-time private practice. Their two sons, David and John, were born in 1966 and 1970 respectively.

His first marriage having ended in divorce, Dr. Stone was remarried in 1984 to Beth Eichstaedt, a teacher and also cantor in a large church. Her unusual degree of spirituality stimulated his interest in this important attribute notoriously missing in many personality-disordered patients, especially those with depression and suicidal proclivities—the kinds of patients in whom he had become more and more interested.

In 1976–1977 Dr. Stone moved to the New York Hospital's Westchester Division to become chief of a "borderline" unit, at about the same time Dr. Otto Kernberg became medical director there. While there, Dr. Stone was impressed by the high proportion of female borderline patients who had been sexually molested by an older male relative during childhood. He was among the first to draw attention to the "incest factor" in the etiology of many borderline patients, just as he had been among the first to point up the high proportion of borderline patients at the Psychiatric Institute who had close relatives with manic-depressive illness in one form or another. Dr. Stone's first book, *The Borderline Syndromes* (1980), was an integrative effort, synthesizing all the then existing theories of borderline personality.

In the late '80s, Dr. Stone began to trace the 550 former inpatients at The New York State Psychiatric Institute who had been hospitalized there between 1963 and 1976. He was able to trace 520 of them (at intervals of ten to twenty-five years after admission) (Stone 1990). Another book (1994) dwelt on all types of personality disorder, including psychopathy and other extreme forms found in violent criminals. This in turn served as the springboard for his interest in forensic psychiatry, and in 1996 he took a post at the Mid-Hudson Psychiatric Center for the treatment and research of mentally ill offenders. For his history of psychiatry (1997) Dr.

Stone made use of his extensive collection of antiquarian psychiatry books, which include a number of incunabula from the 1400s.

Since 1977 Dr. Stone has lectured on borderline personality, schizophrenia, and other personality disorders, and more recently on forensic topics, including the subject of serial killers. He has at this point published eight books and 150 papers, and has both published and lectured in Japanese, a language he became fascinated by during his first visit to Japan in 1990. He is currently a consultant to Dr. Kernberg's new Personality Disorder Institute, which has invited collaboration from many psychiatric centers in Europe and South America.

Apart from being an enthusiastic book collector, Dr. Stone enjoys music and the study of foreign languages.

The Interview

Doctor Stone, we would like to ask you a number of questions about your work—the theory, and the practical consequences. The first question should of course be, Will you give us a brief outline of the basic tenets of your frame of reference, of your approach, and of the consequences these have for psychotherapy as you practice it?

Well, to put it very briefly, it boils down to: $a + b + c + d = e$. Or, to put it a little less briefly, analytic therapy plus behavioral therapy plus cognitive therapy plus drug therapy equals the kind of eclectic therapy that is needed for the treatment of severe personality disorders. Not just for borderlines, by the way—for severely disordered patients in general.

My first training was psychoanalytical. Harold Searles, my main supervisor, developed a style that incorporates all the major approaches, and this is what I do as well. What exactly I use depends upon my understanding of the patient's problems, his cognitive style, whether he can work with the symbolism of dreams, whether he works well, and whether he is interested in discovering and in working through the underlying psychopathology. If, on the other hand, the patient is mainly surface-oriented, I feel that a more cognitive approach is called for. I did that at an early stage, when I didn't even know yet that what I was doing was called cognitive therapy. And then, if a patient of mine was in a crisis, I would try to use some behavioral or very supportive maneuver to shock him out of a suicidal wish. And then again, a patient might be going through a depressive phase and I would use medication. Patients with a borderline personality disorder need a more flexible and diverse approach than healthier patients. The *DSM* definition of borderline doesn't describe a true personality disorder at all: it's a mixture of symptoms, not purely a description of traits. Dissociation, identity disturbance, the cutting of wrists—all these are symptoms, not traits. This strong symptom component requires flexibility in the person who wants to treat these patients.

For other personality disorders, for instance severe obsessive-compulsive disturbances, you also need a flexible shift. A truly psychoanalytical or cognitive-behavioral approach may not be sufficient, although less severely disturbed obsessive-compulsive patients often make very good clients for psychoanalytic therapy. Actually, the severity of the disturbance is crucial in deciding one's approach, not just the diagnosis. For instance, some truly hysterical people may be harder to treat than some severely obsessive-compulsives, who may be more amenable to treatment because of their neurosis—being punctually on time, always wanting to do the right thing, and so on. Other obsessive-compulsives have no feeling for underlying pathology. There you have to use a more cognitive mode.

This eclecticism is not new. As early as 1910 Maeder in Germany, and Burich in Sweden worked with paranoid patients, and they adapted their approach. They found that you can't be as quiet, sitting back and puffing on your pipe, as when you treat an ordinary neurotic. In the twenties there were all kinds of articles stating that you need to be active when you work with what they then called schizophrenic patients and other kinds of sick patients. Sullivan was finding in his own language the need to deal with his own feelings, because these patients tend to stir up much more intensely powerful emotions than the classical psychoanalytic patients do. So they drag us into being more alive, more aware of our own feelings, and into recognizing the occasions when they project their own powerful feelings into us, which makes us feel uncomfortable until we can take a step back and understand what's happening.

Are you saying that this insight in transference and countertransference issues is needed to work with these patients, whether your major approach is psychoanalytic or not?

Yes.

Speaking of the emotions elicited by patients, which emotions are the most difficult ones for you to handle?

When I become the most loud and pugnacious, is when a patient comes in and blandly says, "I am going to kill myself." That gets to me. Those are desperate moments in the life of a therapist because you now are in effect being saddled with a life-or-death responsibility for another human being. You have so many minutes in a session to try and deal with this—see to it that she's not going to do it, or else get her to be hospitalized. I don't always trust a patient in that state to be healthy enough to take herself to a hospital, so on six or seven occasions over the past thirty years I have personally driven patients in my car to a hospital that I'm connected with, brought them into the emergency room, and had them settled in a safe place. One of them at the time greeted me with the comment, "Who told you to save my fucking life?" But nevertheless, she is alive. I'm happy for that. Many others have come back later and said they were grateful afterward, when they came to their senses.

Is it an advantage then, to be able to switch from method to method? Or is there an internal struggle, like: "Michael, you are now doing something that is therapeutically not correct"?

I'm comfortable with it; if this is what the patient needs at that moment, I'll throw my early training out of the window, to save the patient. But I'm nervous, have butterflies in my stomach at such a moment, out of anxiety as to what it's going to be like, and which steps will be necessary.

All this gives the impression that you prefer the analytic approach unless you feel obliged by the limitations of the patients to use another approach?

Yes. That was the early part of my training, and it's the way my own mind works. If I had been Philadelphia-born, I might have been trained by Wolpe, Beck, or Freeman. Then I would perhaps have preferred another approach, unless forced by countertransference problems and so on to use a more analytic approach. Cognitive therapists like Marsha Linehan nowadays *are* using more and more analytic concepts because of what happens between the therapists and their patients when they do cognitive therapy.

We can pull our patients in our direction, but they also pull us, by their possibilities and limitations. The several approaches all have their own good points and their own shortcomings, but they're actually on the same level. I prefer to work analytically because I am not as skilled and disciplined in the cognitive-behavioral approach as a result of my primary training. Behavioral methods are very good in cases of inappropriate behavior, impulse conditions, handwashing compulsions, and conditions of that kind. Behavioral therapists have very clever ways to cope with that that I do not feel come naturally to me. I consult them because it was not in my training. To put it in a nutshell, the treatment has to fit the patient, but it has to fit the therapist as well.

Is there nevertheless one approach that you find less useful in your own practice, compared to the others you mentioned?

Yes. Classical analytical therapy can not really be used as stringently as a more eclectic approach because patients who are "good" for classical analysis tend to be referred to other centers, since I have earned some reputation of being able to cope with the sicker ones. I'm even then alive to countertransference issues: I try to pick up projective identifications, I like using dreams, things of that nature. But classical analysis? I rarely have the opportunity for it, these days.

Nevertheless I like to get to the level underneath the complaints or problems the patient presents. For instance, if somebody presents with marital problems, wanting me to help him through a divorce, I prefer to work with his relationship to his wife, finding out why he picked that abusive partner in the first place and why he makes such masochistic choices, because otherwise he will set himself up for similar misery in the future.

With cognitive therapy this could also be achieved, but I feel that it would be more difficult then.

Do you consider the cognitive approach a little inferior to the analytic approach?

Yes, in this instance it would have less chance of succeeding. If you try to convince patients that their basic assumptions are wrong, this might lead to a more seductive approach. You could end up doing the same thing over and over again, for instance, trying to make it clear to a female patient that she is more attractive than she thinks, while internal dynamic forces tell her that this is not so.

We would like you to tell us a little about your personal development. For instance, which personal motives have led to this specific choice in the field of psychiatry? Will you share some of your private thoughts about psychotherapy and related subjects, and about your place in the field? Which two or three professionals have influenced you the most?

I got interested in psychiatry because of my situation at home, where my mother had been very depressed after the death of her father and had seen a psychiatrist in the city of Syracuse, New York, which is where I come from. That stimulated a great rescue fantasy to help mother. I then became interested in medicine, the brain, psychiatry. I was 13, 14 then, and I made up my mind at that time to become an analyst, even though I hardly knew what that was. I had read a lot of the Freud papers from the public library; that was enough to make me enthusiastic.

I then went to medical school and, still having the same aspirations, took psychiatric training. The place where I worked at Columbia University was a long-term unit that was very analytically oriented. That was in the heyday of Kolb and Polatin (Kolb et al. 1964), the men who coined the term "the pseudo-neurotic schizophrenia," which turned out to be a kind of borderline patient. Of the people who taught me, one in particular was very influential—Harold Searles. He used to fly up from Washington every month to supervise the psychiatric residents. When I finished my training I flew to Washington to meet him, so I had a long exposure to his Sullivanian, active approach in working with these sicker hospitalized patients. That got me into the personality disorder area.

Why pick these very difficult patients? You could have a great time with the easier ones!

(laughs) You sleep more soundly at night when you work with more healthy patients, but there must be something in my makeup, which has to do with my early experiences, family or whatever it is, that makes me feel more stimulated by these patients. They're more challenging, and because of their suicidality there is more to rescue. Healthy hysterics, or healthy anybodies do not need as much rescuing. So I retained that interest. And then in the same unit, when my boss left, Doctor Kernberg came, in approximately 1974. He took over with his way of doing things, which was also very stimulating. He told me about object relations theory, and taught me his way of working with borderlines and very narcissistic patients, which broadened my horizon. I have stayed on that track ever since. Then I got interested in the extremes of personality when I was invited to do forensic work. Somebody who committed a very serious crime would be labeled as having a personality disorder, and I was invited to pass judgment on whether this person really had one or not. That attracted me to studying the outer edges of personality disorders, and now in my work in a forensic setting with antisocial and psychopathic people my rescue fantasies are again evoked, but this time vis-à-vis society. I now want to protect society against psychopathic people. So I suppose I have a strong need to fix things.

You love a challenge in general, and this is just one way of expressing this trait?

Yes! (grins)

You score high on novelty seeking.

True, I am not the pipe-smoking, contemplative kind of person who treats eight patients a week for years on end. I'm more scrappy, I like to get in there and fix things.

You're a remarkable person, with your extensive knowledge of languages, your very broad interests in all kinds of things. How would you describe yourself? As very different from normal people?

Yes.

In what way?

I suppose I'm sort of a Renaissance person, to the extent of having a very wide range of interests—probably partly because of being an only child. The world did not automatically get divided up between siblings, as when one of your brothers would be supposed to be good at math, another would become the expert in football. There are very few things, other than botany and geology, that I'm not interested in.

In an earlier part of this interview we discussed certain changes over time in your methods and approach. For instance, you've become less fixed in one approach; you've become more flexible. Could you give us some more information on that?

There have been more changes. For instance during my residency, in the years 1963 to 1966, my colleagues and I were very cross with one of our trainers, Dr. Kolb, who was an analyst but who stressed the idea of AA contacts for alcoholic people. To us alcoholism was "oral pathology," not something to deal with the way AA does. He knew that oral interpretations and a dollar and a half would get you a subway ticket downtown—in other words, would be of no use at all. Maybe with the higher-level alcoholics Antabuse might be of help, but for most of them that wouldn't be enough. Later I learned that the old man was right!

Another thing I've become aware of is the power of genetics. Even then Franz Kalmann, a prominent geneticist, was working two floors above us, but he didn't talk to us and we didn't talk to him. A few years after I finished my training it became very clear that there were things you just could not explain only on the basis of what mother or father did. When one has his own children one begins to see this more clearly. One of my sons would play in a certain way, another in a very different way. One was rather hyperactive, the other one was very calm. These tendencies asserted themselves long before my wife and I had the opportunity to foist our pathology onto them. It was innate. Over the past twenty years there has been an accumulation of evidence that genetic factors play an important role, on the order of 50 percent, except for narcissistic personality disorder. All this has moved me away from putting all the burden of causative factors on family influences, like ideas about "schizophrenogenic mothers" and all that.

What has been most helpful in the course of this development—for becoming, to your standards, a good therapist for these very difficult patients? For instance, what has made it possible for you to be more flexible in the course of time?

Being exposed to teachers from different schools. In my early days, I was not much exposed to the behavioral people. There was a behaviorist, the psychologist Howard Hunt, who was very good, just as we were about to leave our training. But also the fact that the classical analysts who were my trainers had important differences between them, for instance Searles, who was very interpersonal and in a sense more object relations oriented, although he did not use that language, and then of course Kernberg, who did. This causes a built-in flexibility. All these influencial teachers, bright, highly respected, who were still so different!

There were more people, even in the psychopharmacological field, like David Dunner, and others who I became friendly with like Paul Soloff in Pittsburgh. These made me very sympathetic to the biological aspects, the need for medication, which again was contrary to my original teaching when I was a psychiatric resident. Then there was a tendency to avoid medication because it would "introduce impurities in the psychoanalytic process." This goes for ideal analyzable patients, but with the sicker patient who is desperately depressed or anxious or has some other need for medication, you just have to introduce it in your work with her.

So exposure to these prominent people over time has helped me develop this flexible approach.

Everybody is exposed to different influences, but not everyone picks up those messages. You did, so what makes you different in that respect? Others might have become more strict or rigid in such a situation. You opened up.

That's not easy to explain. There's something in my nature that's open to new ideas. The super-factor of openness, for any genetic or other reason. I very much enjoy learning about different cultures. I studied Latin, Greek, Sanskrit, Russian, Hebrew, and German when I was in college, and whenever I go to a country I try very eagerly to learn something about the country. I have history books from all over the world. That may be a parallel phenomenon, the eagerness to absorb, to get under the skin of people of very different circumstances.

And you are not very frightened of what might happen if things go wrong. You have a high tolerance for anxiety.

(nods) Yes, I'm a risk taker. Searles taught me early on with respect to suicide. As he put it, suicide is something a patient does in his own time. If they commit suicide, no matter how hard we've tried to help them—poof . . . You feel bad for so and so many days, but life goes on. They're dead forever, your life goes on. In the same way you try to get this across to family members, who are affected by the possible demise of a patient. They should not blame themselves internally.

I remember a patient who was treated by a fellow resident, and committed suicide. She had run away and hidden under a false name, in another state, to test her therapist. If he could find her, that would have proven that he was as godlike as her former therapist, John Rosen, had said he was. Of course, she could not be found and in the end she came back to the hospital and committed suicide there. This resident was devastated as a result. All Searles had to say to put things in the right perspective was, "Well, small loss" meaning, "You and I have done what we could, but this patient just could not be rescued. That is not your fault." This attitude helps us to prevent these very difficult patients from twisting our arm all the time, to manipulating us. We are not as susceptible to being manipulated by them.

Fortunately I have not had a suicide, possibly because of this attitude. I am not timid.

That could also be a result of your willingness to bring them to a hospital personally, if you think this is necessary. This brings us to another question we wanted to ask you: Has there ever been a patient with whom you failed?

I remember a patient I worked with for eight years, and still it was a total bust.

He was in his mid-thirties, and had a personality with borderline traits, and avoidant, obsessive-compulsive, passive-aggressive, and dependent ones as well—everything in Cluster C.

He came from a well-to-do family, was the third of three children, one of those who are much younger than the siblings and therefore get the special message that they're supposed to stay at home and keep the parents company till they die. Since he was designated to be the companion of the aging parents, it was not right for him to be independent and to leave home. So he also was socially phobic: if he did well, others would be murderously envious; if he did not, they would make fun of him. So he had to balance between being not good and not bad. He was also witheringly contemptuous of me and psychoanalysis and psychiatry in general. Massive resistances. Only after a year and a half did he really become a patient. Because of the severity of his social phobia I sent him to a very prominent psychopharmacologist, because I had run out of things I could think of to do. Parnate did absolutely nothing. I had him on the couch for a number of years, then I had him sit up again, as in the beginning. I used pressure, encouraged him to enter the phobic area. He would fall in love, for instance, but only with wildly inappropriate girls. For instance, being Jewish, he would fall in love with a Muslim girl. He would bring in dreams from time to time, but I would practically have to light a fire under him to get him to associate to them. The interpretations, the behavioral push, the medication, in short: the whole a + b + c + d led to zero in this case.

Can you think of any approach that might have helped him better?

I did refer him to a very prominent cognitive therapist, who did not succeed with him either. As far as I can tell, he was one of those unfortunate people who are committed to not accomplishing anything. And he had used up so many of the important years for acquiring skills. He had not worked at his intellectual and social level, so if he were to meet a girl, he would feel inadequate as to his social status and earning power.

Couldn't you have said after three months, "Look, forget it!"?

Not after three months. He had to get through that initial period to the point where he had at least become a somewhat motivated patient. I have had successes with patients who started as slowly as this one did. Now, I would have speeded up the process and referred him much sooner than I did, which was after about five years, to people using other approaches.

As you're a person who likes a challenge, and who tries to rescue people, one of your pitfalls might be that you work too long with patients. Can you imagine that some other therapists might have become bored much earlier?

Well, there were many fascinating things about this fellow. He was a fetishist. He liked the smell from his anus [continues with a great many other details about this therapy].

This is one of those times where all you need is a very brief question, a small stimulus, and a world opens. Isn't that exactly what happens in your therapies? Any stimulus from your patient is enough for you to continue being interested in him?

(nods and grins) However, with psychopathic people I get tired very quickly. I cannot work with people who are malicious liars, or who manipulate the people around them and destroy their lives. But this doesn't happen often; in all my years as a therapist I may have rejected a total of three people.

Would you say that, indeed, your approach has limitations, but that these concern patients who could not be helped by people using other approaches either, since all these other approaches already have a place in yours?

(smiles) I suppose so!

Can you give us an example of a treatment that you really enjoy remembering?

I remember a girl from the South, from a well-to-do family. She had for a long time been rebelling against her mother: she was an alcoholic in her teens, sleeping around, getting pregnant, everything to shame her family, making suicide gestures, being very self-destructive, picking up men in bars, being very promiscuous.

She did have a good job as a jewelry expert. I got her past the point of that self-destructiveness. She then took up with an older man whom she knew before, and who had been married to a very vindictive woman who did not allow him to see his own two children from that marriage. He therefore did not want to have children again. So in order to make him happy and to get him to marry her, she had her tubes tied, although she desperately wanted to have children of her own. She regretted that decision after a year, and by that

time he had gotten over his fear of being hurt again, she being
so different from his first wife. She had her tubes untied,
she got pregnant, and now she has a nice boy of 7 and that
family is truly a happy one. She now lives in California, but
whenever she's in New York City she comes and visits me
and I see the three of them. This therapy took three years.
We still communicate regularly with annual Christmas
cards.

*In this group of questions there is one that I hesitate to ask because
I think I already know the answer. Is it true that there is no situation in which you deviate from your approach because deviations are
a basic component of your approach? Might one even say that a true
deviation from your approach would be to be rigid?*

(smiles) That's right.

*Next question: Which two or three books, not written by yourself,
would you advise the reader of this book to read?*

The first people who come to mind would be my own teachers:
Searles for instance, and Kernberg. Searles's book is not as deeply
theoretical as the ones by Kernberg, but it is full of wonderful and
poignant examples of the ways in which he presents deeply re-
pressed and unusual dynamics. It stimulates that kind of thinking in readers who are open-minded. It's called *My Work with
Borderline Patients* (1986). Kernberg's books, the one on *Borderline Conditions and Pathological Narcissism* (1975), or one of the
later ones on aggression, are more interesting from a theoretical standpoint; they're not as clinically enthralling as Searles's
writings.

    In the area of personality disorders, Glen Gabbard has added
a nice book, *Psychodynamic Psychiatry in Clinical Practice* (1994),
and Mardi Horowitz and his group in California published a book,
Personality Styles and Brief Psychotherapy (Horowitz et al. 1984),
with the usual array of the disorders, and then discussing the way

they can be treated with brief therapy. Now, I don't believe in brief therapy with these patients, but nevertheless there are many good clinical gems in that book. From the standpoint of cognitive-behavioral therapy, the book by Beck and Freeman, *Cognitive Therapy of Personality Disorders* (1990), gives a nice display of the basic assumptions of the different personality disorders and how you might be able to use different methods to treat these patients. I take exception to the enthusiasm they have in working with even the antisocial patients because once you get beyond the most minor kinds of antisocial behavior and to true psychopathy and callousness, then nothing works. I think they have some points to make with respect to the milder variety.

Nobody can convert a true psychopath into a moral person who is capable of feeling genuine remorse. You can maybe teach him to play the odds in line with what's more favorable to society.

Our final question now: Are there any aspects of your work we haven't yet discussed, and about which you'd like to say a little more?

Well, something about my most recent change. Out of my interest in the extremes of personality disorders, and my work in forensic psychiatry, I have become a staff psychiatrist in a state forensic hospital four days a week, in addition to participating on Thursdays in Doctor Kernberg's Personality Disorders Institute. This happened a few years ago, and I now have a chance to work closely with the kinds of patients I always had opinions about, but no personal experience with before. So I am now becoming more genuine in my opinions on these people. It is, of course, too early to say if this will change my opinions.

Studying these people, we can learn a lot about prevention. Many of them come from incredibly destructive backgrounds, and quite a few of them have experimented with psychotomimetic drugs, like crack, cocaine, and amphetamines. Both these factors should be addressed. Anything that can be done to reduce the danger to the next generation, with respect to the punitiveness and the abusiveness in the home, may help to reduce this factor in society. The other thing is to educate people from school age on about the severe dangers of drug abuse.

The Situations

In the middle of the night, you're called on the phone by a patient who threatens to commit suicide. What would you do in such a situation?

This depends on my previous experience with that patient, and the degree you judge the suicidality to be, in comparison with other people you have known. How well you know the patient. How manipulative you sense the patient to be, versus truly in despair. If you sense that the patient is truly in despair, and the manipulative factor is small—or, as Linehan would put it, if the operant (the manipulative) factor is little, and the respondent (the despair) factor is large—and the patient would probably be more ready to be rescued, I would say, "Can you control this until next morning? Or do you feel you cannot? In which case would you be willing to go to a hospital?" My next move would depend on what the patient's response to this would be. Curiously, in my thirty years of practice, I have not once been called in the middle of the night.

If it's more manipulative, I would tend to confront the person with what I would feel was the manipulative nature of that call. I might say, "Look, your calling me at two in the morning with this message would mean that you like to be absolutely sure that I have the most rotten possible night." (laughs) For example, I once had a patient who called me on New Year's Eve, at 7:30, just when my wife and I were on the point of leaving for the theater. Here we were in our formal wear, and I said, "That's an interesting choice. I am now going to call the police and ask them to bash down your door so they can rescue you." She was very angry with me! I told her I thought her real reason for calling me was that she felt lonely on New Year's Eve, and wanted my evening to be miserable too. I went to the precinct on my way to the theater and the police did go and batter down her door.

Why did you call the police?

I was mad and I wanted to teach her a lesson. I wanted to trump her card, as they say. But she was unstable enough, so I also wanted to be on the safe side, since people do commit manipulative suicides.

How would you react if a patient comes to the appointed session in a state of obvious inebriation?

That happened once or twice. I then said, "I cannot work with you when you're inebriated. You must enroll in AA as soon as possible, this very day. You must be sober for therapy, and only AA can accomplish that. If you give a damn about yourself, you do this. If you don't, we part company." I have called AA in front of such patients, given them the address of the chapter, and said, "This is the place where you have to go."

Suppose they say, "Look, this is only once, why go to AA for just one slip?"

There is no such thing. If this happens, it's likely to be a serious problem, and I would say there is no such thing as only once. And besides, you can destroy your whole life in one day.

You meet one of your patients at a cocktail party and he or she wants to use this opportunity to have an ordinary social meeting with you for a change, and starts to chat with you. What would you do?

If it's an analytic patient I might be cordial for a minute or two, then I would say, "You know, I don't think this is the kind of place where we should have this kind of interchange," and I would tend to make some kind remark and then excuse myself. Once or twice I have met more fragile patients, who were in supportive therapy. I have one patient who is in supportive therapy, and with whom I share a mutual friend. I feel perfectly comfortable in talking with that person, who is interesting in his own right, and because he is not trying to manipulate me in a long conversation. If he were to buttonhole me, I would do the same thing as with every manipulative patient.

A patient turns out to be in the neighborhood of your front door every time you come home. Just standing in the street.

That happened once in my life when I was in the process of courting my first wife. We were both residents in the same hospital, and this patient was a very paranoid schizophrenic woman. She rented an apartment on the other side of the street where we lived. When I found out about it, I said, "This is inappropriate behavior. Either we talk about this, to help you understand what are some of the forces behind it, or else we stop the therapy, because I cannot work in a situation where my life is made uncomfortable by you."

You discover that something from your office has been taken away by a patient—"borrowed," stolen, or just picked up on an impulse. What would you do?

Well, if it's an old magazine or something like that, I might ask the patient to tell me about the fantasies she had in connection with taking it. A minor thing in value may have major meanings to a patient. But if it were to be an object of value, it would be theft. I would say, "Look, we have two jobs here. One is to try to understand the motivating forces that led you to do this. The other is trying to find out what this says about your character that has more serious implications about the possibility of continuing therapy."

I once had a schizophrenic patient who, every time she paid me, would go to a department store and steal something of the same value as my bill, to sort of break even. I told her that this could not continue, that she had to return the goods. She did not, so I dropped her from treatment. She was one of the maybe three patients I dropped from treatment.

How do you like to work with your patients? Is there a desk between you, or do you sit more or less opposite from each other, or maybe more side-to-side? Do you have easy chairs or fairly comfortable ones? Are there many personal objects in your room or office? That sort of thing.

In recent years I use my apartment. There is a wealth of personal objects there, including a Bechstein piano. Some patients think it's a very lavish office; others know I live there. There are many art objects, paintings, furniture, and other things. I like this, it saves me rent money, and if the patient cancels, I can do what I want in the time that's now free. Also, many patients feel comfortable in this sort of room, much better than if they were to be in a bare office. Having seen Freud's office, I became interested in oriental rugs, on the walls and on the floors of that room.

Do you think that, working with these very disturbed patients, it is actually an advantage to be so clearly you? This is not like being a living Rorschach.

I think so. However, some of them are completely oblivious to what surrounds them. That will then be something to talk about. Others love or hate a painting and we can discuss that. Everything can be grist for the mill.

14

Jeffrey Young

Biography

Jeffrey E. Young is founder and director of the Cognitive Therapy Centers of New York and Connecticut. He is a licensed psychologist, on the faculty in the Department of Psychiatry at Columbia University College of Physicians and Surgeons, in New York City.

Dr. Young received his undergraduate training at Yale University and his graduate degree at the University of Pennsylvania. He then completed a postdoctoral fellowship at the Center for Cognitive Therapy at the University of Pennsylvania with Dr. Aaron Beck, and went on to serve there as Director of Research and Training.

Dr. Young is the founder of Schema-Focused Therapy, an integrative approach for personality disorders and for other treatment-resistant patients. He has published widely in the fields of both cognitive and schema-focused therapies, including two major books: *Cognitive Therapy for Personality Disorders: A Schema-Focused Approach* (1994) for mental health professionals, and *Reinventing Your Life* (1994), a popular self-help book for the general public. He has also developed several assessment scales related to his schema-focused approach, as well as instruments for measuring therapist competence.

Dr. Young developed most of the original cognitive therapy training procedures and materials that have been widely utilized over the past twenty years in teaching the approach. He has trained thousands of mental-health professionals at workshops throughout the world.

Dr. Young is also co-author of a psychotherapy outcome study evaluating the effectiveness of cognitive therapy in comparison to antidepressant medication. He has served as a consultant on several cognitive and schema-focused therapy research grants, including the large-scale NIMH Collaborative Study of Depression, and on the editorial boards of journals including *Cognitive Therapy and Research* and *Cognitive and Behavioral Practice*.

The Interview

Doctor Young, we would like you to start this interview by outlining the basic tenets of your approach and of the consequences these have for psychotherapy.

The core of schema-focused theory is that a child has certain basic needs: the need to be accepted, to be loved, to be able to express itself, to be independent, to have fun, to be nurtured, to be held and so on. What happened in people's childhood when there were problems is that the parents frustrated those needs in some way. They were too critical, too controlling, not loving enough, they were not there enough. All parents may be that way sometimes, but when they do this sort of thing on a day-to-day basis, year after year, children develop early maladaptive *schemas*, which are conceptions of themselves and of their world, that block them from getting these needs met in their later life.

I developed this theory over fifteen years, including a list of eighteen schemas, which are like life themes or core conflicts, and which are essential to personality disorders. With all the patients who have come to our center, we can conceptualize their problems in the framework of these eighteen schemas. They involve themes like abandonment, emotional deprivation, mistrust,

subjugation, entitlement, enmeshment, and unrelenting standards, and we think that we can understand almost all of our
characterologically disturbed patients through some combination
of these schemas. A schema is a set of beliefs, along with all the
emotions that go with those beliefs; it also includes all the early
memories.

This creates a sensitivity. For example, patients with a mistrust–
abuse schema will view the world as if in some way people are
out to hurt them. They begin to anticipate this and may even see
people as doing it when they are not. They become hypervigilant
to being hurt. People develop this schema because as children
they were mistreated, maybe not intentionally, but in some way
the parents, or other people, abused them, or lied to them. It was
at that time not a delusion or a distortion.

*In what way does this differ from, for instance, the ideas of Aaron
Beck, Arthur Freeman, and others like them?*

Well, first of all they define a schema as a belief; they stress the
cognitive part much more than the other parts, while I believe a
schema is much more than just a set of beliefs. In fact I think it's
primarily a set of emotions and memories that later get cognitions
attached to them. These schemas are usually developed in a period when a child doesn't even have language, so it's mostly
preverbal. Another difference is that they use the word 'schema'
to refer to a less deep construct. For example, they would say a
schema might be "I have to follow the rules of my religion." To
me that would not be a core schema. It's a deep belief, but it's
not quite emotional enough, not quite powerful enough.

*What if you change this into "If I don't follow the rules of my reli-
gion, I'm an utterly worthless person"?*

That would put it in the same conditional way Beck, Freeman,
and others do: "If I don't do this, this will happen." A schema is
usually an unconditional thing: "I'm bad, no matter what I do." A

schema feels like there is no way you can get out of the problem. It's a given about yourself and/or other people.

In transactional analysis (TA), they differentiate between the drivers, which are conditional, and the injunctions, which are more or less what you're describing—total convictions. Do you recognize this similarity?

I don't know that part of TA but it does indeed sound similar. I don't know how broadly they interpret it, though, and whether it is a view of themselves, or of the world.

What has been growing increasingly important in our model is the interaction and elaboration of the concept of *coping styles*, which overlaps with the concept of defense mechanisms. I realize more and more that we should differentiate between the schemas that rule a person's mental life and the coping styles that decide how he or she deals with them behaviorally. For instance, the schema might be, "You can't trust anybody." The coping style might be: "Punch others before they punch you." Or, avoid people. Or, ask people questions all the time because you don't trust them. It's whatever you do in response to your schema. We have developed a preliminary list of coping styles that helps patients to recognize the ways they behave in reaction to their schemas.

I developed the concept of schema *mode* to describe the state a person is in from moment to moment, encompassing the schemas and the various coping styles. Each mode contains within it a specific schema or coping style. Coping styles and schemas are like traits: they are there over a long period of time. Modes may vary from moment to moment. This differentiation between the coping styles and schemas on the one hand, and modes on the other hand, explains why a borderline patient, who has the same schemas and coping styles over a long period of time, still flips all the time between various behaviors, because the modes vary all the time.

These ideas can be found in many other theories, like TA, or Adlerian therapy, but the difference is in the way the ideas are put into practice; Schema-Focused Therapy is an integrative approach, incorporating behavior therapy, cognitive therapy, Gestalt and experiential therapy, and object relations approaches. This implies, for instance, that one may, within the limits of therapy, become like a parent in order to do reparenting work, such as holding a patient who needs it at the time. This is a systematic way of integrating various theories into one workable model. It may be obvious that this model is quite open to other ways of thinking, not in a loosely eclectic way, but in a very systematic way, and using the therapeutic relationship throughout the entire therapy.

What strikes me is that your approach stresses the possibility for real change, while others, such as Cloninger or Livesley, claim that these possibilities are quite limited and that in many cases people have to be helped to learn to live with their limitations.

Yes. Even Marsha Linehan, who does such excellent work with borderlines, really in many cases teaches people ways to tolerate difficult affects, and to manage and regulate them. Instead, in Schema-Focused Therapy we do try to actually change the underlying structure of the personality. We do not just try to change or improve a certain coping style, but to change the schema that lies behind it.

How long does a therapy like that take?

That's a complicated question. Because "limited reparenting" is an important aspect of the treatment, many people remain in therapy even if they no longer have a diagnosable disorder. The actual therapy can be brief, in which case we limit ourselves to relapse prevention and to teaching them the basic model and offering them some techniques they can use, and then it takes fifteen or twenty sessions. For fundamental change, a longer time is needed, because this means that basically the underlying schema will have to be overcome. That may take a year or two.

For borderlines it may take much longer than that—two, three, four years. But long before the end they have already begun to feel better, so where do you decide the therapy ends? And as I already said, many people stay in therapy for a much longer time than that, on a much less frequent basis, even indefinitely, because of the reparenting function of the therapy. After all, a spouse or a friend can rarely substitute for a healthy parent-figure.

It's a little like the question: "When does one stop being the child of one's parents?"

That's right. Just like in that kind of relationship, even if we don't meet again, the therapy never actually stops. We will always remain in these roles: "I will keep on being available, you can always call again, we can always resume the therapy if you feel you need it." I present it as, "We don't need regular sessions anymore, but should any problem come up, call me." I have many, many patients from ten years ago, who call every now and then. And often two or three years later they call me with a different problem.

Is there anything you might like to add, or have we discussed all the important aspects?

Perhaps one thing more: I want to stress that I do feel a strong personal attachment to these patients. I do feel like a parent to them; I feel very, very caring toward them. This was one factor in my changing from cognitive toward Schema-Focused Therapy. Both in cognitive therapy and in behavior therapy or REBT (I worked with Ellis for a while), I found that this implied sticking to a theoretical model much more than I thought was appropriate. Instead of moving from technique to technique I wanted to be able to allow myself to feel with patients, being open about myself, letting them talk about things that were not exactly on target. I wanted a real relationship to develop between us. I believe this changes the essence of the therapy in a very important way. I do want to emphasize that the therapy also involves a lot of cognitive work and imagery work. It's not just the therapy relationship.

I've heard from people who have seen you work that they feel you're a very warm person.

I hope that's right, and actually I believe that much of my earlier training took the warmth away from me with patients. Happily that part of me has reemerged!

Which personal motives have led to this way of looking at children, childhood, and development?

Well, when I started working with personality-disordered patients using cognitive therapy, I found it wasn't working very well. I realized the reason was that they had beliefs that just were not amenable to that kind of therapy. A great deal of my theory comes from problem solving in the therapies I did, and coming across the difficulties there. You see, to a certain extent, patients are a problem to solve. They're having difficulties and I want to help them get better, and if I try this and it doesn't work, I feel the need to find another way to understand this or work with it to get them better. I then just keep trying many, many different therapeutic strategies till I find one that works. Once I've defined a problem I want to solve, I'm really dogged, I don't let go of it until it's solved. This is intuitive.

What got you into wanting to work with these difficult patients in the first place?

There were certain things in my childhood that led me to this field and eventually to work in this subarea. In terms of my family background, my parents were both Jewish. My father owned a family business, while my mother stayed at home with the family. I have a brother two years younger than I am, and a sister four years younger. My grandmother lived downstairs from us. The family atmosphere was calm and normal, at least on the surface. My parents had a very happy marriage, and the home was very stable.

However, apart from my relationship with my father, I wouldn't say we were a close family. We expressed very few emotions with each other, so there was a certain flatness. One thing that was very important was my own loneliness as a child, feeling I didn't get enough affection in certain ways, and feeling different from other people. I had friends, I wasn't excluded, but I didn't feel like one of the kids around me. That has always led to my feeling a tremendous amount of sympathy for other people who have been hurt this way. Many people with severe personality disorders, when you get to the core of it, feel isolated and lonely. That's one of their core issues. So there's an affinity that I feel. Even though I don't have many of their maladaptive coping styles, underneath I think I have some very similar schemas.

Another factor was the love and idealization that I got from my father and his side of my family. I was sort of an idealized child, I was perfect in their eyes. On that side of my family everyone loved me, and my father was very nurturing. From that, I have a very trusting feeling that makes me want to help other people, not just because I identify with them, but also because I see myself as someone who could really help people because I was looked to as someone who helped my family. If my grandmother had a problem, she would talk to me, my nieces would . . . Even when I was 5 years old, after having dinner at a restaurant my father would hand me the check and say, "Can you see if this is correct?"—so I was taken care of by him and got the message that I could be a caretaker myself. There really is no gap between what I did in my childhood and what I'm doing now in that sense.

Were there any other important influences in the development of your approach?

I think some of my own experiences as a therapy patient were very important. I was raised to be very rational and logical. My experi-

ence with my first therapist, who was a very warm, self-disclos-
ing person, definitely influenced my own view of therapy. We
became good friends after the therapy, which I never regretted
or found inappropriate. Another therapy experience with a Gestalt therapist had a tremendous impact. It opened me up to the
importance of feelings . . . and of using techniques like imagery
that bypass "rational" thinking.

*But what made you choose cognitive therapy? It might just as well
have been behavior therapy or psychoanalysis, isn't that true?*

I have a very practical side that likes to solve problems. I read
psychoanalysis when I was an undergraduate and I felt it was too
abstract, not phenomenological enough. When you read Freud,
it's as if the theory and the interpretations were already there, they
were not coming from the individual patients. It was like the analysts formulated their ideas and then presented them to the patient. And I always thought, "Where do they get these far-fetched
explanations for things that could be understood much more simply? Why not just explain this person's problem in terms of his
not getting enough love and now needing it?" Some of their explanations just didn't connect for me. Also, the analytic style
seemed too passive. I like to be very active and problem-solving;
just sitting back and listening felt frustrating to me. On the other
hand, some of the themes I came across, like those of Karen
Horney and others, I could certainly identify with.

Then as an undergraduate I went to a course by Arnold Lazarus,
who was one of the early behaviorists and who was a very charismatic speaker. He played tapes of patients and he was very phenomenological. He would go very actively into the things the patients felt and what they thought while feeling them. I don't think
the theory of behaviorism appealed to me as much as the very
active nature of Lazarus, and his very interactional way of working, and the fact that the theory about each patient seemed to
come from the patient and not from the therapist's mind. All
through the developing of my model I've been attuned to what

my patients told me; each of the eighteen schemas I identified came about directly from listening to patients.

Isn't that the way Freud built his own theoretical model?

Sure. But the ones who came after him took his model, which was based upon what his patients told him, in his time, and made that their model. But his observations don't fit many patients today. We need new frameworks, new ways of understanding certain patients, but many analysts were locked into what they had been taught, at least until object relations and some of the other recent psychoanalytic models.

In your view, the basis of everything is those needs that were not met in early life. Now Masterson, for instance, views the basis for borderline pathology as abandonment depression, while Kernberg would say that the basis is aggression. Do you feel connected to one of these stands?

I think they, and many other psychotherapy theoreticians, just take one element and make that the focus of their theory. I believe that borderlines cannot be understood primarily in terms of aggression. They actually have several components and you need to take all of them into account. My goal was to have a theory that was broad enough to encompass the whole range of personality disorders that I saw. And there was not any one element that was central to all of them. Of course, there will be many particular patients with whom abandonment depression or aggression is the basic theme, I have no problem with that.

In fact, I think abandonment depression is an important part of the problems of most borderline patients. But there is much more to it than just that. Other important issues are their tendency to be self-punitive, their inability to express their feelings because of the lack of validation of their feelings when they were children. And don't forget the abuse most of them experienced!

Which two or three professionals have influenced you the most in this development?

Clearly the number one person would be Aaron Beck, both professionally and personally. First of all, he is very phenomenological. Beck listens to depressed patients and tries to get into their thinking. That's also the way he actually works with patients. I've watched him do it. I would listen and watch how he would keep tuning into the patient. Never with a rigid theory in the back of his mind but open to whatever the patient told him, until he would completely understand the patient's perspective. Unfortunately, later on, other people took the model and systematized it into a rather rigid, rapid treatment, which in some ways lost what Beck actually did in therapy. He does basically what someone like George Kelly does, which is really trying to understand the unique phenomenological stance of that one patient. It now has become a system of techniques, where you give patients a sheet and they write down what they think and feel in a mechanical kind of way. That's not what I learned from Beck, which was a really intense focus on understanding patients, and then a really strategic ability, almost like a lawyer or a tactician or something, to be able to find a way to show them a different way of looking at themselves.

For instance, we were sitting in a train once, on the way to an NIMH conference, and we were discussing the question of my leaving his institute and going to teach at a university, or staying with him. He wanted me to stay, and the way he got me to stay was to ask me what I really wanted, and if I thought that I would really get that at a university, with people doing this to me, or that to me. He would ask me, "What do you really want?" This is a typical example of the Socratic dialogue, where, through very skillful questioning, he got me exactly where he wanted me to go and where I felt I would be happiest. That's a very important skill.

In cognitive therapy, Albert Ellis is a very well-known figure. He is, himself, a brilliant technician, I'm told. But most people who do REBT just take his tricks and his techniques without having his brilliance. Would you say that's comparable to what you just said about Beck?

Actually I have a somewhat different view of Ellis. Having met with him and having had discussions with him, I don't think people have distorted his approach that much at all. He is brilliant, but within a very limited model that he does not veer from very much. Other people haven't distorted his model, they just are not as brilliant in using it. His model, in my opinion, is very rigid, while Beck's model is very flexible. To have the preconception that everyone has just three basic problems, you will have to fit people into that theory, and he does that with only a minimal attempt to actually get inside the person. This is one reason why, in my opinion, REBT is still a fringe therapy, while Beck's approach has become so much more widely accepted and mainstream.

Have there been others beside Beck who have influenced you?

In terms of other people, I already mentioned Arnold Lazarus, who was important because he was the first one who got me interested in cognitive-behavioral therapy. Wolpe played an important role, in a limited way. I no longer use his technique of systematic desensitization, but the basic framework of being very active and setting up sessions of instruction and using strategies was very important for me. But these influences were not personal, the way Beck was a very important personal influence.

What's happening now is a little like what happened with Freud and his disciples: there are now the issues of breaking away. My developing my own model has created an ambivalence in me, and it caused a schism between me and some other cognitive therapists. It feels as if, by breaking away from a model, I'm also losing an entire community of people. This separation has had a great influence on me.

Did the loneliness come back?

A very good point. Now I have the feeling that I'm respected by other cognitive therapists, but I'm no longer fully accepted as one of them. Doctor Beck and I developed the scale that helps you assess who is a good cognitive therapist, but I now no longer believe in much of that scale! The scale assesses what makes a good cognitive therapist, but not necessarily what makes a good therapist. So I guess, in a sense, some of my loneliness has returned, in my professional life.

That takes care of a question we have asked the others as well as in passing you have given us your ideas about psychotherapy in general and about your place in the field. Or is there anything to add to that?

Well, I think I occupy a kind of in-between place, in that I'm no longer in the mainstream of cognitive therapy, although people associate me with it. Because mine is an integrative approach, it's really different from cognitive therapy. As it's still developing, it's too early to say where it stands. I think there are two advantages to this approach: one is that it uses simple language that can be communicated to the patient and other professionals much more easily than psychoanalytic language, and two, it's phenomenologically more accurate. It's what the patient actually feels, not what the therapist speculates is behind these feelings.

Does your approach have limitations? Are there specific areas in which it should be used and others where it should not be used?

Remember I told you that I'm a problem-solver. So whenever it looks like there's a limitation to my approach, I see that as a challenge to work on my model, to evolve it in such a way that the limitation is taken care of. Schema-Focused Therapy is not at all like it was ten years ago; it evolves all the time. Therapists at my center are always complaining, "What are you going to add now? What are we going to have to learn next?" (grins)

In general, I'd say that if any long-term characterological problem can be treated with psychotherapy, it can probably be treated
with Schema-Focused Therapy. There are limitations in the sense
that there are many groups of patients that we haven't treated yet.
In the groups that we have worked with, and for which the model
was developed, it works very well. And they're a varied lot: depressive patients, chronic anxiety, higher-functioning personality disorders, borderlines, narcissists. But we haven't worked with
other personality disorders yet, and it may not be useful there.
Like schizotypal, schizoid, or antisocial personalities. They may
turn out to be problematic, but those people do not come to our
center, so we haven't tried it yet. I am confident that when we
do, I will find solutions to most obstacles we come up against and
I'll expand the model. The system wasn't developed to work with
families, so that might be a limitation; and of course there are
people who won't even come to therapy, so we can't do anything
with them. I don't want to sound arrogant; I'm just stressing the
flexibility and constantly evolving nature of the therapy.

*Michael Stone says that people who have no functioning superego
are totally unamenable to therapy, any kind of therapy. Would you
agree with that?*

Well, there are people who write to me about their using my model
in criminal settings. They've developed manuals, and use it in
groups. They say that people are responsive to it. But does it actually make them not-antisocial, or give them a conscience? I like
to hope it will, but I have no way to know that. With antisocials
or schizoids there could be something biological, or damage that
was so early in life and so deep that none of these strategies would
be of any help. I did do an interview once in Canada with a patient in a setting for the criminally insane, who they said was
impossible, and that went extremely well. I broke through with
her, which they had not been able to do in two years, in one session, through this process of empathizing, understanding, getting
into her world—but in my mind that woman clearly had a con-

science, so this does not prove or disprove what Stone says about the most difficult antisocial patients.

Putting the constantly shifting feelings, emotions, and behaviors (modes) of a patient into terms like the Abandoned Child, Angry Child, Punitive Parent, and Detached Protector, makes these modes much more amenable to therapy. I should say, though, that I'm easily conned by such people. One of my own flaws is that I'm very trusting, and I might get the impression that this type of patient is getting better when he is not. That may be a limitation not of my model, but of me!

Which two or three books, not written by yourself, would you advise the reader to study?

Well, most of what I've learned has not come from reading books, but from watching people, doing therapy, and reading biographies. I never have relied very much on other people's psychological writings to guide me. I'm more often disillusioned by the professional books I read than influenced by them, because they just don't capture the essentials of the problems of our patients. I can recommend some books though. Beck's early book (1979) on cognitive therapy of emotional disorders clearly is one. Another one would be Bowlby's books (1969, 1973, 1980) on separation and loss, about understanding children and their attachments to their parents and what happens when those attachments are broken. Along with that, books by other writers who describe attachment theory, object relations theory, who describe childhood experiences of having parents who don't deal with them effectively in different stages of their development are very helpful.

What you leave out is Cognitive Therapy of Personality Disorders *(1990) by Beck and Freeman.*

Right. I find that book to be a good example of the failure of many cognitive therapists who followed Beck. Although Beck oversaw the editing of that book, it was mostly written by people who were following Beck's early model, which was not developed for personality disorders. In fact the opposite! It was developed as a movement against Freud, because his ideas were not very useful in the treatment of affective disorders. Freud's ideas are *most* helpful in the treatment and understanding of personality disorders. Treating a symptom is fundamentally different from treating characterologic disturbances; most of the chapters in that book do not reflect that difference. Because of its rather strict adherence to traditional cognitive-behavioral therapy, I think the book is much too limited.

I also don't hear you mention Alfred Adler, while many of your ideas about narcissistic personality disorder could have come straight from Adler's books. Have you been influenced by him at all?

I had only read limited samples of Adler's work prior to developing Schema-Focused Therapy, so I don't think it had much of an impact. No, I would not say I've been influenced by him, but there is definitely overlap in terms of theory.

The Situations

In the middle of the night you're called by a patient who threatens to commit suicide. What would you do?

I would start by saying, "I appreciate your reaching out to me," to make sure that they don't feel guilty about it. Because I do want them to call me when they're suicidal. The next step would be trying to find out what's going on. I spend quite a lot of time in doing that. I look for triggers, try to find out if there is anger or

, sadness underneath it, try to get a real sense of why they think that suicide is the only option now. Then I try to intensely connect personally to them, to self-disclose and let them know how this upsets me, which I really do feel, but I make it a very personal thing. I want to be more than just a psychologist giving advice, but to be a personally involved human being. The next step would be to give them as many reasons for hope as I can give them, while making it clear that I do understand their problem. Often such people really think there's no way out, so I try to show them that there are other paths. And I make clear to them that I do want to work with them throughout this process.

I would mention any other people, besides myself, who could be hurt by this suicidal act, but naturally I make it clear that this is not the most important issue. This will perhaps induce feelings of guilt, but it's useful to stress that they do have responsibilities toward other people: their children, their parents. I ask them to agree not to do it now, and at least wait until tomorrow when we can meet and discuss it, and to call me if they're thinking of it again. During such a crisis I basically talk with them each day until the suicidality has passed. And I try to get the other people around them involved as much as possible. For instance I try to get the person to stay overnight with someone who knows that he's suicidal, and who will watch over him. And if I still don't feel secure about it, I would hospitalize him.

While you say that if you give them the attention they need in such a situation the suicidality will eventually disappear, others, like learning theoreticians, would say that you reinforce their manipulative behavior by doing so.

I have never yet had a situation where patients called me on a repetitive basis after I asked them not to, so I don't believe that their behavior is truly manipulative. Of course there are people who find this kind of call to be the only way they can justify frequent contact with their therapist, and in such a situation, if they're suicidal on a day-to-day basis, their situation is too severe to treat on an outpatient basis. "If you're really as severe as you're saying, it's not appropriate for me to do outpatient therapy with you right now. We can resume after you come out of the hospital and no longer need daily therapy."

And if they refuse to go to the hospital?

That's never happened to me. But what I would do, if I felt that they would truly make an attempt, is to call the police and use coercive measures. In less serious cases, I might suggest that we find ways to give them more frequent therapy time. "It's obvious that you need more contact with me, or you would not be calling so often." So I would try to fit this into my daily schedule on a regular basis, to get it out of my nightly schedule on an unexpected basis.

"Manipulative" behavior is very often caused by their healthy needs not being met in other ways. Those needs are only excessive from the therapist's point of view. Whether we feel they are manipulative or not, we must realize that they're genuinely desperate.

How would you react if a patient comes to the appointed session in an obvious state of inebriation?

This has also never happened to me. I've had some people come in who had had some drinks and were perhaps a little bit high, but not to such an extent that they were not able to focus. As long as they can give coherent answers and can concentrate on what I'm saying, I keep on talking and focus on the need to do something to find help for this drinking problem. If they were so drunk as to be unable to concentrate on the session, I'd stop the session and explain that it's useless to continue. "Call me when you're sober again." I might make going to AA sessions a condition for continuing therapy. In any case, the drinking and the need to get help for it would remain the focus until it was solved.

You meet one of your patients at a cocktail party and he or she wants to use this opportunity to have an ordinary social meeting with you for a change, and starts to chat with you. What would you do?

If the patient initiates it, I would have no problem with the conversation. Actually, since our therapeutic relationship is a very genuine, real connection, it would be inappropriate *not* to allow such contact. If the conversation was friendly and social, I would have no trouble with it, but I'd keep it brief. The questions they ask should not be invasive, and by keeping it brief I prevent the situation from developing in such a way that I would have to start acting unnaturally. I don't want them to start seeing us as friends instead of people who have a therapeutic relationship. Of course I wouldn't do any kind of therapy in that setting, like listening to their problems, but it would be very offensive to the patient to treat him as if he didn't exist!

A patient turns out to be in the neighborhood of your front door every time you come home. Just standing in the street.

I've had a variation of that. I had two borderlines I was treating who met in the hospital. They would park their car across the street from my apartment in New York. Just waiting there and watching. What I would do in such a case (and what I did do), is to discuss it in the next session so I would understand the reasons. As with everything, I first want to know the background, because that defines my reaction. If for instance they did this because they missed me, I would give them more attention. If it's because they want to know more about my personal life, I would set limits on that. But I wouldn't do it in a punishing way. I would explain that it felt like they were taking my privacy away, and I would try to explore other ways to keep the connection between the sessions. But I would tell them that I could not continue working with them if this went on.

Would you act differently in various cases, like in different diagnostic categories, such as paranoid psychosis or psychopathy?

Certainly. In such cases there obviously would be more danger. But I don't see such patients in my practice, because they haven't come to me for treatment.

You discover that something from your office has been taken away by a patient—"borrowed," stolen, or maybe just picked up on an impulse. What would you do?

When I saw the patient at the next session, I would be very direct about it. However, again, I would first want to know why he did it. I would consider it to be a very serious thing, not just because it might have hurt me, but also because I would see this as a symptom of something operating on a schema level. Again, if it's a healthy need, expressed in a distorted way, I would try to find other ways of meeting this need.

Many of the others we've spoken to would be very indirect, fearful of hurting the patient's feelings. It strikes me that you're so much more direct.

True. I think that as long as directness doesn't come from anger, you can be very direct. I know that it comes from a warm place in me, not from an angry part, so I trust that when I'm direct, it will not be hurtful. Actually I prefer being talked to in a direct way as well, instead of being approached in a roundabout way. If I were a patient I would want it to happen like that as well.

How do you like to work with your patients? Is there a desk between you, or are you sitting behind a couch, or face-to-face? Are there many personal objects there? Are the chairs very easy to sit in or only fairly comfortable? That sort of thing.

I see my patients at home. Originally I had an office, but it changed over the years. I see them in my living room. It doesn't look at all like an office. It's a big room with lots of windows, there are trees around. The patients are sitting on the sofa, I'm sitting in a lounge chair, face-to-face. It would not in any way seem different from meeting a friend or a guest. It's very much a home situation. I don't have personal objects in the room, but not because I wouldn't. I just don't like a lot of mementos and stuff like that in my room. If I did, I wouldn't hesitate to have them there. I often say to people that whether you hear me talking to a patient or to a friend, you wouldn't really hear much difference, except that with patients it's one-sided. The tone of my voice, the things I say, the context are the same; they even call me by my first name, Jeff. I think they feel me to be more like a parent or close friend, and my "office" reflects this.

Epilogue

DIFFERENCES AND SIMILARITIES

Looking back on what our master clinicians have said, one might well be confused or surprised, because they have presented great differences as well as striking similarities in their work. Let's begin by looking at some of the differences. Of course there is a major dispute over how to describe the condition of borderline personality disorder, as well as how to address the symptoms.

Gerald Adler has referred to the quality of aloneness as being distinctive of the borderline patient. According to Adler, borderline patients lack soothing and holding introjects that can protect them in the face of separation: this is the *deficit model*. Otto Kernberg, on the other hand, is convinced that borderline patients do have good introjects ("I don't think there is such a thing as a void in the psychic apparatus"), but that the bad introjects have taken over. He believes the main focus of the condition is these patients' inability to accept both good and bad as part of the same person, with respect not only to others but also to themselves—this is the *conflict model*. According to James Masterson, self-activation and the fear of abandonment constitute the core conflict. From yet another perspective, Robert Cloninger and John Livesley stress the strong biological and genetic roots of the condition and propose a *vulnerability model* to account for the complex interactions between biology and the environment. And Marsha Linehan ("my frame of reference is coming out of behavioral science") has no theory or depth construct of persons, but looks at behaviors "from moment to moment."

Of course these fundamentally different concepts have led to different treatment approaches. During the interviews, we spoke extensively about the *expressive-supportive continuum*. Kernberg firmly advocates an expressive approach for the majority of borderline patients. It is his belief that "soothing gestures" can actually prevent people from making structural changes, and that they are thus not in the patients' interest. This position is also taken by Masterson, who states that using supportive therapies for higher-level borderline patients is counterproductive and deprives them of the possibility of real change. Livesley, on the other hand, states that "neutrality has done more harm than good." Salman Akhtar, Adler, Lawrence Rockland, and Glen Gabbard speak for the *dynamic frame of reference,* and always offer both *expressive and supportive techniques,* although they may favor a specific sequence or one approach over the other. Adler mentions the work of Elvin Semrad, who felt that therapy is giving with one hand and taking away with the other. Akhtar remarks that "We have to say unacceptable things to patients sometimes, but there are always ways you can make the unacceptable acceptable." Gabbard notes that "A surgeon has to have anesthesia to operate." Kernberg makes a distinction between supportive effects and supportive techniques, with the former as "those that move on one side of the conflict, reinforcing the adaptive side of the conflict." He states that "the most supportive effect may be the effect of a good interpretation." Lawrence Rockland, favoring supportive modes, warns against the misuse of supportive interventions, as, for example, when the therapist gets frightened by a patient threatening to commit suicide. "That is something you have to interpret," he says.

The behavior of therapists who turn to supportive modes in the face of death is very nicely described by John Clarkin: "Some therapists believe in a theory only up to a certain point."

Of course, differences within the same frame of reference are no privilege of the psychodynamic approaches. Within the *cogni-*

tive frame, for instance, it seems that Arthur Freeman is more oriented toward changing what Jeffrey Young calls "the coping style" of his patients, while Young focuses on the *underlying schematic structure* itself. Both thus deal with maladaptive cognitions, but on different emotional levels. Indeed, in talking about his contribution to cognitive therapy, Young even says, "I am no longer one of them," and it is clear that arriving at that point has not been an easy process: "Breaking away not just from a model but from an entire community of people is something that has had a great influence on me."

On the *behavioral* level, Marsha Linehan is not the only one who uses behavioral techniques and principles. Linehan's methodology is also shared by Lorna Smith Benjamin, although Benjamin's approach is founded in *attachment theory,* while Linehan attempts to be "as theory free as possible." By the way, is Lorna Smith Benjamin the ideal therapist that Adler talks about when he refers to "a Marsha Linehan who is dynamically trained"? What do you think about her crisis intervention approach to the borderline patient who has been sexually abused by her father and threatened to cut herself the night before her engagement? "Well, you'd better tell your father. I think he will be more interested than I am." She presents the process of psychopathology as "a gift of love."

The question, of course, is not which approach is superior, but which method is more appropriate for the patient.

Have you been surprised, as we were, by the *existentialistic orientation* of Robert Cloninger? Cloninger is a scientist who is well known for his work on the genetics of personality. He argues that the most severe personality disorders need a predominantly behavioral approach, and sees psychodynamic and interpersonal strategies as more applicable for patients who have more ego strength and who yet suffer from the inability to form relationships and be cooperative. Livesley introduces "biological psychotherapy," and Michael Stone puts it very briefly as "a + b + c + d = e"—that is, "analytic therapy, plus behavioral therapy, plus cognitive therapy, plus drug therapy, equals the kind of eclectic therapy that is needed for the treatment of severe personality disorders." No matter what we do, Rockland warns us again, "In all psychotherapies we have to worry about countertransference acting out. . . . Supportive therapy especially has a tendency to tell people how to live, and with borderline patients that danger is even worse."

During the interviews we found many similarities on various issues and questions that run across all schools.

One major issue is the protection of the therapy and the therapist against the aggressive impulses of the patient. As you have read in the answers to the uniform questions posed in "the situations," all our interviewees use some form of treatment contract to prevent patients from destroying the therapy (and their lives).

They anticipate potential risks, look for alternative actions, and specify the consequences of breaking the contract. The specific ways in which this may be done differ from person to person; some therapists may sound harsh, others more friendly, but inevitably they draw a line between what is and can be accepted and what is not allowed.

Adler gives Linehan credit for being so clear about her limits: "I learned from Marsha that we had better be firm on this." Kernberg, in speaking about the underestimation of the severe aggression of these patients, uses almost the same words when he says, "You have to be very firm in standing up to it, in the service of survival, love, and treatment." Concerning his own style, he adds, "My own personality is direct, with a strong expression of emotion, but I don't hate or attack my patients."

On this topic John Clarkin made an interesting comparison between Linehan and Kernberg: "They are both convinced that they know what they're doing, they both are tenacious—neither one gives up on a patient—they both love the challenge, and the potential for suicide does not frighten them."

Gabbard points out the fact that therapists should not "organize their lives to please their patients, because that will inevitably lead to resentment" and says that "part of what therapists must do is to develop a professional life that is comfortable to themselves, and the patient must adjust to that." Stone even sent the police to a patient who attempted to disrupt his New Year's Eve.

Akhtar presented one of his many apt metaphors: "When your little son or daughter climbs on your lap, too tired to walk, it's all right. However, when the child also pees or shits on your trousers . . . You see? A burden is all right, but there are limits." He stresses that burdens go with the job: "You can't be a psychotherapist if you want to avoid psychological burdens"—but he also tells us to be respectful of individual differences. "Some people can carry one suitcase, others can carry two. If it is burdensome and painful, it has to be stopped."

Livesley reminds us that we have to set limits as soon as possible: "If there's a need for limit setting and you do it immediately, it will usually not be too hard to do. But if you delay and let it go on for a longer time, then you'll find that it may have become impossible to counter, or at least you will need a lot of correcting and limit setting. Problems don't start big." Masterson points out that if the acting-out is not corrected, "all the affect that is being drained by it doesn't get into the treatment."

Beyond these points are the similarities found in the orientation toward normality versus pathology. For example, Linehan argues that normal people can show pathological and strange behavior similar to that seen in people with a severe personality disorder, and so part of her working stance is "finding the normal in the behavior." Akhtar has the same focus, and states that where many people may look at pathological behavior in a way that implies only sickness, "I look at its adaptational value to the patient with a comparable value." This is why Linehan's behavioral and Akhtar's developmental views coincide perfectly.

Jeffrey Young speaks about "healthy needs" of borderline patients, though these are expressed in a maladaptive way. Perhaps this is caused by the fact that these healthy needs have not been met in a more appropriate way. Freeman's pragmatic stance implies the same orientation: "Can we use their characteristics instead of fighting them?" He seems to have done so himself, as well as with his son. Kernberg believes in treating every patient "as if he had some healthy part."

As for their backgrounds, all the therapists here have been fortunate to have been exposed to bright, experienced, and often well-known teachers. This undoubtedly stimulated ever more open-mindedness beyond that already present. Using Cloninger's seven-factor model we can surely detect some novelty seeking. For example, Freeman gets bored by Cluster C patients, and Stone, who is working in forensic psychology and is interested in keeping people safe, experiences challenging opportunities to protect society against psychopathic people. Finally, Akhtar says, "I am not the kind of person who stays with one position in a sustained way."

What else makes people become psychotherapists?

Having a parent who is ill probably facilitates choosing to work in a healing profession. Indeed, both Stone and Akhtar took care of their sick mothers. Akhtar cared for his mother while she was staying in a dark hospital room and notes that his therapy office now is often dark, hence his nickname the "prince of darkness."

In order to become a scientist, one needs "a good relationship with your mother and an engineer as a father" (Clarkin); or, alternatively, an attachment to a father and falling in love with a chemistry professor (Benjamin). To become intensely dedicated to suicidal borderline patients, Linehan believes, "you must be a sort of missionary person. I wanted to help the most miserable people in the world. At the time I thought that clearly the most miserable people in the world were those who wanted to die." Feeling different from other people around you also intensifies the connection between the therapist and his patients (Young).

As the final list of common characteristics, many of our master clinicians have had teachers who taught them a simple but important lesson. We will close with some of these "only human" quotes and hope you have enjoyed reading the book.

- "I've learned the hard way that you can often offend people in really hurtful ways by not being willing to give them the benefit of the doubt." (Gerald Adler)

- "If you don't know what to do, act human." (Glen Gabbard)
- "You can get along very well in your clinical career if you just give your patients the normal respect that you would give to anybody in any encounter." (John Sutherland, as quoted by John Livesley)

References

Adler, G. (1985). *Borderline Psychopathology and Its Treatment.* Northvale, NJ: Jason Aronson.

Akhtar, S. (1992). *Broken Structures: Severe Personality Disorders and Their Treatment.* Northvale, NJ: Jason Aronson.

——— (1995). *Quest for Answers.* Northvale, NJ: Jason Aronson.

——— (1999). *Inner Torment: Living Between Conflict and Fragmentation.* Northvale, NJ: Jason Aronson.

Allport, G. W. (1949). *Personality.* London: Constable.

American Psychiatric Association (1994). *Diagnostic and Statistical Manual of Mental Disorders,* 4th ed. Washington, DC: Author.

Appelbaum, S. (1979). *Out in Inner Space.* Garden City, NY: Anchor Press/Doubleday.

Balint, M. (1968). *The Basic Fault: Therapeutic Aspects of Regression.* New York: Brunner/Mazel.

Bandura, A. (1969). *Principles of Behavior Modification.* New York: Holt, Rinehart & Winston.

Barkow, J. H., Cosmides, L., and Tooby, J., eds. (1995). *The Adapted Mind: Evolutionary Psychology and the Generation of Culture.* New York: Oxford University Press.

Barlow, D. H., ed. (1993). *Clinical Handbook of Psychological Disorders: A Step-by-Step Treatment Manual,* 2nd ed., 3rd ed in press. New York: Guilford.

Bartlett, F. C. (1932). *Remembering.* Cambridge, UK: Cambridge University Press.

Bateman, A., and Fonagy, P. (1999). Effectiveness of partial hospitalization in the treatment of borderline personality disorder: a randomized controlled trial. *American Journal of Psychiatry* 156:1563–1569.

Beck, A. T. (1979). *Cognitive Therapy for Depression.* New York: Guilford.

Beck, A. T., and Freeman, A. (1990). *Cognitive Therapy of Personality Disorders.* New York: Guilford.

Benjamin, L. S. (1996). *Interpersonal Diagnosis and Treatment of Personality Disorder.* New York: Guilford.

Bion, W. R. (1967). *Second Thoughts.* London: Heinemann, 1987.

——— (1970). *Attention and Interpretation: A Scientific Approach to Insight in Psychoanalysis and Groups.* London: Tavistock.

Bowlby, J. (1969). *Attachment and Loss,* vol. I, *Attachment.* New York: Basic Books.

——— (1973). *Attachment and Loss,* vol. II, *Separation, Anxiety and Anger.* New York: Basic Books.

——— (1980). *Attachment and Loss,* vol. III, *Loss, Sadness and Depression.* New York: Basic Books.

Brenner, C., Abend, S., Porder, M., and Willick, M. (1983). *Borderline Patients: Psychoanalytic Perspectives.* New York: International Universities Press.

Casement, P. (1985). *On Learning from the Patient.* London: Tavistock.

Chasseguet-Smirgel, J. (1985). *Creativity and Perversion.* London: Free Association Books.

Clarkin, J. F., and Lenzenweger, M. F., eds. (1996). *Major Theories of Personality Disorder.* New York: Guilford.

Clarkin, J. F., Marzali, E., and Munroe-Blum, H., eds. (1992). *Borderline Personality Disorder.* New York: Guilford.

Clarkin, J. F., Yeomans, F., and Kernberg, O. F. (1998). *Psychotherapy for Borderline Personality.* New York: Wiley.

Cloninger, C. R. (1986). A unified biosocial theory of personality and its role in the development of anxiety states. *Psychiatric Developments* 3:167–226.

———— (1987). A systematic method for clinical description and classification of personality variants. *Archives of General Psychiatry* 44:579–588.

Craighead, L. W ., Craighead, W. E., Kazdin, A. E., and Mahoney, M. J. (1994). *Cognitive and Behavioral Interventions: An Empirical Approach to Mental Health Problems*. Boston: Allyn & Bacon.

Depue, R. A. (1996a). A neurological framework for the structure of personality and emotion: implications for personality disorders. In *Major Theories of Personality Disorder*, ed. J. F. Clarkin and M. F. Lenzenweger, pp. 347–390. New York: Guilford.

———— (1996b). Neurobehavioral systems, personality and psychopathology. In *Major Theories of Personality Disorder*, ed. J. F. Clarkin and M. F. Lenzenweger. New York: Guilford.

Ekman, P., and Davidson, J. R., eds. (1994). *The Nature of Emotion: Fundamental Questions*. New York: Oxford University Press.

Fairbairn, W. R. D. (1952). *Psychoanalytic Studies of the Personality*. London: Routledge & Kegan Paul.

Frances, A., Clarkin, J. F., and Perry, S. (1984). *Differential Therapeutics in Psychiatry: The Art and Science of Treatment Selection*. New York: Brunner/Mazel.

Frankl, V. E. (1959). *Man's Search for Meaning: An Introduction to Logotherapy*. Boston: Beacon, 2000.

Freud, S. (1914). Remembering, repeating and working-through. *Standard Edition* 12:146–156.

———— (1917). Mourning and melancholia. *Standard Edition* 14:237–260.

Fromm-Reichmann, F. (1959). *Psychoanalysis and Psychotherapy: Selected Papers*. Chicago: University of Chicago Press.

Gabbard, G. O. (1994). *Psychodynamic Psychiatry in Clinical Practice: The DSM-IV Edition*. Washington, DC: American Psychiatric Press.

Gabbard, G. O., and Gabbard, K. (1999). *Psychiatry and the Cinema*. Washington, DC: American Psychiatric Association.

Gill, M. M. (1964). Psychoanalysis and exploratory psychotherapy. *Journal of the American Psychoanalytical Association* 2:771–797.

Green, A. (1986). *On Private Madness*. London: Hogarth.

Gunderson, J. G. (1984). *Borderline Personality Disorder*. Washington, DC: American Psychiatric Press.

Guntrip, H. (1961). *Personality Structure and Human Interaction*. New York: International Universities Press.

——— (1968). *Schizoid Phenomena, Object Relations and the Self*. London: Hogarth.

Hilgard, E. R., and Atkinson, R. C. (1967). *Introduction to Psychology*. New York: Harcourt Brace & World.

Horowitz, M. J., Marmar, C., Krupnick, J., et al. (1984). *Personality Styles and Brief Psychotherapy*. New York: Jason Aronson, 1997.

Izard, C. E., Kagan, J., and Zajonc, R. B., eds. (1984). *Emotions, Cognition, and Behavior*. Cambridge, UK: Cambridge University Press.

Kauffman, S. A. (1993). *The Origins of Order, Self-Organization and Selection in Evolution*. New York: Oxford University Press.

Kelly, G. (1969). *Clinical Psychology and Personality: The Collected Papers of George Kelly*. New York: Wiley.

Kernberg, O. F. (1975). *Borderline Conditions and Pathological Narcissism*. New York: Jason Aronson.

——— (1980). *Internal World and External Reality: Object Relations Theory Applied*. New York: Jason Aronson.

——— (1984). *Severe Personality Disorders: Psychotherapeutic Strategies*. New Haven, CT: Yale University Press.

Kernberg, O. F., Selzer, M., Koenigsberg, H. W., et al. (1989). *Psychodynamic Psychotherapy of Borderline Patients*. New York: Basic Books.

Killingmo, B. (1989). Conflict and deficit: implications for technique. *International Journal of Psycho-Analysis* 70:65–79.

Kohut, H. (1971). *The Analysis of the Self*. New York: International Universities Press.

—— (1977). *The Restoration of the Self.* New York: International Universities Press.

—— (1984). *How Does Analysis Cure?* Chicago: University of Chicago Press.

Kolb, L. C., Kallman, F. J., and Polatin, P. (1964). *Schizophrenia.* Boston: Little, Brown.

Kramer, P. D. (1993). *Listening to Prozac.* New York: Viking.

Krishnamurti, J. J. (1973). *The Awakening of Intelligence.* London: Victor Gollancz.

Linehan, M. M. (1993a). *Cognitive-Behavioral Treatment of Borderline Personality Disorder.* New York: Guilford.

—— (1993b). *Skills Training Manual for Treating Borderline Personality Disorder.* New York: Guilford.

Livesley, W. J., ed. (1995). *The DSM-IV Personality Disorders.* New York: Guilford.

Loewald, H. W. (1960). On the therapeutic action of psychoanalysis. *International Journal of Psycho-Analysis* 41:16–33.

Mahler, M. S. (1975). *The Psychological Birth of the Human Infant.* New York: Basic Books.

Masterson, J. F. (2000). *The Personality Disorders: A New Look at the Developmental Self and Object Relations Approach.* Phoenix, AZ: Zeig, Tucker & Co.

McGlashan, T. (1983). The borderline syndrome: Is it a variant of schizophrenia or affective disorder? *Archives of General Psychiatry* 40:1319–1323.

Millon, T. (1981). *Disorders of Personality: DSM-III, Axis II.* New York: Wiley.

Mischel, W. (1968). *Personality and Assessment.* New York: Wiley.

—— (1973). Toward a cognitive social learning reconceptualization of personality. *Psychological Review* 80:252–283.

Ogden, T. (1989). *The Primitive Edge of Experience.* Northvale, NJ: Jason Aronson.

—— (1994). The concept of interpretive action. In *Subjects of Analysis*, pp. 107–135. Northvale, NJ: Jason Aronson.

Pervin, L. A., and John, O. P., eds. (1999). *Handbook of Personality: Theory and Research,* 2nd ed. New York: Guilford.

Rinsley, D. B. (1976). *An object relations view of borderline personality.* Paper presented at the International Meeting on Borderline Disorders, the Menninger Foundation and NIMH, Topeka, KS, March.

Ripley, A. (1992). *Scarlett: The Sequel to Margaret Mitchell's Gone With the Wind.* New York: WarnerBooks.

Rockland, L. H. (1989). *Supportive Psychotherapy: A Psychodynamic Approach.* New York: Basic Books.

———— (1992). *Supportive Therapy for Borderline Patients: A Psychodynamic Approach.* New York: Guilford.

Rogers, C. R. (1951). *Client-Centered Therapy.* Boston: Houghton Mifflin.

Rosenfeld, H. A. (1987). *Impasse and Interpretation.* London: Tavistock.

Ryle, A. (1997). *Cognitive Analytical Therapy and Borderline Personality Disorder.* New York: Wiley.

————, ed. (1995). *Cognitive Analytical Therapy: Developments in Theory and Practice.* New York: Wiley.

Schore, A. N. (1994). *Affect Regulation and the Origin of the Self.* Hillsdale, NJ: Lawrence Erlbaum.

Searles, H. F. (1979). *Countertransference and Related Subjects.* New York: International Universities Press.

———— (1986). *My Work with Borderline Patients.* Northvale, NJ: Jason Aronson.

Semrad, E., ed. (1969). *Teaching Psychotherapy of Psychotic Patients.* New York: Grune & Stratton.

Settlage, C. F. (1989). The interplay of therapeutic and developmental processes in the treatment of children: an application of contemporary object relations theory. *Psychoanalytic Inquiry* 9:375–396.

———— (1993). Therapeutic process and developmental process in the restructuring of object and self constancy. *Journal of the American Psychoanalytic Association* 41:473–492.

———— (1994). On the contribution of separation-individuation theory to psychoanalysis: developmental process, pathogenesis, therapeutic process, and technique. In *Mahler and Kohut: Perspectives on Development, Psychopathology, and Technique*, ed. S. Kramer and S. Akhtar, pp. 19–52. Northvale, NJ: Jason Aronson.

Smith, G. W. (1992). *The Best Doctors in America*. Aiken, SC: Woodward/White.

Staats, A. W. (1996). *Behavior and Personality: Psychological Behaviorism*. New York: Springer.

Stern, D. N. (1985). *The Interpersonal World of the Infant*. New York: Basic Books.

Stone, M. H. (1980). *The Borderline Syndromes*. New York: McGraw-Hill.

——— (1990). *The Fate of Borderline Patients: Successful Outcome and Psychiatric Practice*. New York: Guilford.

——— (1994). *Abnormalities of Personality: Within and Beyond the Realm of Treatment*. New York: Norton.

——— (1997). *Healing the Mind: A History of Psychiatry from Antiquity to the Present*. New York: Norton.

Strenger, C. (1989). The romantic and classic vision in psychoanalysis. *International Journal of Psycho-Analysis* 70: 595–610.

Sullivan, H. S. (1953). *The Interpersonal Theory of Psychiatry*. New York: Norton.

Taglione, P. A., and Brown, L. M. (1999). *Treatment of borderline personality disorder: Masterson approach vs. dialectical behavior therapy*. Paper presented at the American Psychological Association Annual Convention, Boston.

Tahka, V. (1993). *Mind and Its Treatment: A Psychoanalytic Approach*. Madison, CT: International Universities Press.

Volkan, V. D. (1987). *Six Steps in the Treatment of Borderline Patients*. Northvale, NJ: Jason Aronson.

Wallerstein, R. (1986). *Forty-Two Lives in Treatment*. New York: Guilford.

Werman, D. S. (1988). *The Practice of Supportive Psychotherapy*. New York: Brunner/Mazel.

Winnicott, D. W. (1949). Hate in the countertransference. *International Journal of Psycho-Analysis* 30: 69–74.

———— (1960). On the theory of the parent–infant relationship. In *The Maturational Processes and the Facilitating Environment*, pp. 37–55. New York: International Universities Press.

World Health Organization (1984). *International Classification of Diseases.* Europe: Author.

Yeomans, F., Selzer, M. A., and Clarkin, J. F. (1992). *Treating the Borderline Patient: A Contract Based Approach.* New York: Basic Books.

Young, J. E. (1994). *Cognitive Therapy for Personality Disorders: A Schema-Focused Approach.* Sarasota, FL: Professional Resource Press.

Young, J. E., and Klosko, J. S. (1994). *Reinventing Your Life: How to Break Free from Negative Life Patterns.* New York: Plume.

Index

ABOUT THE EDITORS

Henk-Jan Dalewijk, Bert van Luyn and, until his retirement in 1999, Gerben Hellinga, are the organizers of *Psychiatry in Progress*, an internationally recognized program for postgraduate education in psychiatry and psychotherapy. *Psychiatry in Progress* is an educational program of the SYMFORA Group, a cluster of institutes for mental health located in the middle of the Netherlands. These researchers have organized several courses on personality disorders in which the people interviewed in this book—all leading professionals in the field—participated.

Gerben Hellinga, psychiatrist, was the Director of the Psychiatric Resident program, specializing in the psychotherapy of patients with severe personality disorders. Author of a Dutch-language book on personality disorders, he is currently preparing a series of historical novels on the history of the United States.

Bert van Luyn, psychologist-psychotherapist, heads a community mental health program for people with chronic disorders. He is extensively involved in the development and teaching of methods of crisis intervention, with special interest in the management of severe personality disorders.

Henk-Jan Dalewijk, psychiatrist and psychoanalyst, is Executive Medical Director of the SYMFORA Group. For many years, he has been involved in the treatment of personality disorders in various settings. He is also actively involved in organizing symposia, congresses, and workshops both nationally and internationally.